Protecting Your Business on the Internet

KATHLEEN SINDELL

John Wiley & Sons, Inc.

Published by John Wiley & Sons, Inc., New York
Published simultaneously in Canada.

ISBN 0-471-07962-6

Printed in the United States of America.

10 9 8 7 6 5 4 3 2 1

To my husband, Ivan Sindell,
for his profound advice.

Acknowledgments

My thanks to Matt Holt, senior acquisitions editor, for recruiting me into the fold of John Wiley and Sons, Inc. Thanks to my literary agent, Doris S. Michaels, and her staff for their encouragement. My appreciation to Tamara Hummell, editorial assistant, for her guidance in submitting the manuscript. Thanks also to Nadia Chekiri and Amanda DeWees for their fine editing. My appreciation to everyone who worked behind the scenes, especially the people listed on the credit page. Thank you for making this book happen.

I am deeply grateful to Don Dietrich, of the Dietrich Lockard Group, for reading the manuscript and for his incisive technical comments. My thanks to Reuven Goren, who assisted in researching the glossary and verified web sites for the resource center. And a special thank you to my brother-in-law, Gerald Sindell, for his astute counsel on everything related to the business of publishing.

And, finally, my thanks to all the folks who find new ways to protect web-based enterprises and their willingness to share that information with others. They have made the Internet a much safer place for consumers and businesses.

Contents

p 48   Other useful sites

Contents

P 48   Other useful sites

Introduction

Welcome to *Safety Net: Protecting Your Business on the Internet* and the exciting world of managing the security decisions of your web-based business. Without a doubt, e-business is big business. Industry experts predict that U.S. business-to-business (B2B) online transactions will reach $1.3 trillion in the year 2003. This means that about one out of every four B2B transaction will be online. However, every day online businesses are threatened by fraud, sabotage, espionage, piracy, identity theft, and other forms of electronic warfare. A 2001 CSI/FBI survey of 538 organizations indicated that 69 percent of respondents had experienced computer breaches within the last year. Of those, 33 percent reported 1 to 5 incidents, and 36 percent reported 6 to over 60 incidents. Financial losses due to these security breaches are costly in terms of hard costs (monetary and productivity losses) and public relations (customer and reputation losses). The Yankee Group, an Internet research organization located in Boston, Massachusetts, estimates that denial of service attacks (a type of hacker attack that stops customers from interacting with your online business) can cost U.S. companies $1.2 billion. The FBI estimates that computer crime cost U.S. companies around $10 billion in 2001.

Securing your web-based business is a critical new area of management. *Safety Net* shows managers the different types of attacks online businesses can experience and provides practical information for a clearer understanding of prevention, detection, and recovery countermeasures. Additionally, *Safety Net* provides managers with easy-to-follow directions with which to determine exactly how vulnerable the current system is and to create an effective security policy that meets the unique requirements of the online business. Whereas most information security manuals are for technical people, everything described in *Safety Net* is in plain English, but technically accurate.

■ WHO ARE YOU?

This book is written for today's decision makers, who must be able to develop appropriate security policies and effectively communicate with their management, information technology and marketing staff, software product developers, system integrators, and product users in order to avoid problems and take advantage of business opportunities. Today there are about 72.4 million web servers connected to the Internet, with about 25 million servers dedicated to commercial web sites. The Internet has matured beyond the early adopter stage, and large corporations are now online and doing business. The surviving dot.com companies have matured into serious businesses that need steady management. This phenomenon highlights the need for *Safety Net,* a book that provides practical solutions to the most pressing concerns of managers as well as offering concise explanations that can assist them in the analysis and evaluation of the security risks and opportunities of an online business.

■ ABOUT THIS BOOK

All online transactions are based on trust. This fact makes security the prime enabler of e-business. In brick-and-mortar stores, customers can inspect the merchandise and make judgments about the store. On the Internet, which does not provide physical cues, it is more difficult for consumers to assess the safety of an online business. Therefore, to succeed in this marketplace, managers must become fully aware of the wide variety of Internet security threats, take advantage of the technology that overcomes those threats, and constantly win the confidence and trust of customers.

In the early days of the Internet gold rush, many online businesses transmitted credit card data without any type of encryption, posing a security risk for customers. Some companies used firewalls for their entire operations and did not establish internal firewalls between applications, posing a security risk for the online business. A few companies simply deferred all security decisions to the merchants who hosted their web sites. Today it is essential to assure the personal privacy of customers in the networked environment. Companies can acquire a competitive advantage by ensuring that each customer feels that that his or her consumer rights and privacy are protected online. However, your web-based business may be fair game to anyone who is "bright, persistent, online, and so inclined." As more and more people shop online, security threats will increase. Managers must be prepared to battle online fraud, ensure privacy for their customers and partners, fend off cyber-terrorism, and not only protect the company's data and systems but also guard the company against charges of negligence. *Safety Net* shows managers how to make security risk assessments and create an effective security policy that meets the needs of their online businesses, accommodates the organization's peculiarities, and can be safely administered.

Protection for your online business is no longer a luxury or last-minute afterthought added to a system before it is rolled out the door. Whether it is a matter of protecting your customers' credit card data and personal information or your business processes and intellectual property, without effective security you cannot compete. *Safety Net* presents expert advice for managers on such matters as these:

➤ Becoming familiar with the top security issues for online businesses. Gaining an understanding of common Internet security mistakes and recognizing why security is important for web-based businesses.

➤ Assessing the security level of your web-based business. Identifying threats and potential business losses. Determining and documenting what assets need protection.

➤ Determining the impact of security on your bottom line. Deciding how much security is too much and determining how much risk your online business can take.

➤ Protecting your system from intruders. Safeguarding data transmitted on the Internet. Understanding intrusion detection systems and what kind of intrusion detection software is best for your type of enterprise.

➤ Understanding the security risks to your web server. Gaining a clear understanding of the common vulnerabilities of web servers and the anatomy of a typical intrusion.

➤ Guarding your wireless operations. Recognizing the impact of wireless commerce on your web-based business.

➤ Reducing the likelihood of denial of service attacks. Gaining an understanding of the different types of denial of service attacks and calculating the severity of an attack.

➤ Understanding insider threats. Discovering how social engineering can lead to data losses and how insiders may represent internal threats.

➤ Handling public relations after a cyber-attack. Preparing and planning for crisis communications. Looking into the guidelines for making a press release.

➤ Protecting your web-based business from invisible crimes and frauds. Taking stock of your intellectual assets and digital rights management.

➤ Determining what you can expect from a firewall. Creating a network connection policy. Understanding the various attributes of different firewalls.

➤ Safeguarding customer privacy and personal information. Learning how some customers react to the use of cookies. Finding out how some cookies can be pirated.

➤ Protecting your web-based business with antivirus technology. Uncovering the different types of viruses. Recognizing virus hoaxes and developing a user antivirus policy.

➤ Developing an effective security policy. Learning how a good security policy supports your business goals. Gaining an understanding of what makes security policies fail and looking into the life cycle of security polices.

■ HOW TO USE THIS BOOK

If you have a question about a certain Internet security topic, look that topic up in the table of contents or in the index at the end of the book. Refer to the page indicated for the help you are seeking. If you cannot find the topic, look it up in the glossary. You may discover that it is included in the book but is referred to in a way you did not anticipate. For example, a *URL* (Uniform Resource Location) is also called an *Internet address* or a *domain name.* Information security is a complex field: Don't feel bad if you have to use the table of contents, index, and glossary frequently.

■ HOW THIS BOOK IS ORGANIZED

The first three chapters of *Safety Net* provide an overview of the risks associated with a web-based business and offer some important advice on how to evaluate the security level of your system.

Managers seeking solutions to pressing information security concerns can refer to the pertinent section of the book to immediately get the information they need. This approach can be supplemented by use of the resource center located at the back of the book, which lists Internet-based sources of information.

Managers can also choose to read this book from cover to cover. When possible, the simplest information about security issues is detailed first, whereas more complex threats are covered later. The book concludes with useful guidelines for developing an effective security policy for a web-based business. This information brings the reader full circle to the beginning chapters of the book.

■ SPECIAL FEATURES

Protecting your online business is a never-ending competition between security systems and/or technologies and the sophistication of those seeking to thwart them. This means that protecting your web site business consists of more than finding the solution to just one security problem. It requires the development of effective security policies based on clear-minded risk assessments and strategies. *Safety Net* includes concise explanations that can assist managers in analyzing and evaluating the security hazards of their web-based businesses. Each chapter includes descriptions of the types of attacks managers can expect and the countermeasures—such as prevention, detection, and recovery—they can employ. At the conclusion of each chapter is a checklist that can assist managers in focusing on the chapter's primary issues. Most chapters include descriptions of hardware and software tools that can assist mangers in protecting their web-based enterprises against security breaches. The book concludes with an extensive resource center, which is useful for additional study, and a glossary, which can help managers become familiar with the definitions of information security words.

Chapter 1

Top Security Troubles for Online Businesses

In this chapter

- ➤ Risk Management, Security Policies, and Information Security
- ➤ Starting in the Right Direction
- ➤ Recognizing Why Security Is Important to Your Web-Based Business
- ➤ What Makes the Internet Marketplace So Vulnerable?
- ➤ Getting to Know Your Enemy
- ➤ Becoming Aware of Common Internet Security Mistakes
- ➤ Achieving Web-Based Business Security
- ➤ Uncovering the Risk Management Cycle of Web-Based Businesses

Internet-based enterprises that suffer security breaches usually experience monetary and production losses, as well as a loss of confidence that can lead to customer defections and reduced sales; for some companies, just one security breach can mean the end of the business. The Internet was not designed for commercial transactions. Consequently, the very infrastructure of the Internet is vulnerable to hackers. Would-be intruders can even acquire the training they need to gain unauthorized access into your web sites, computers, and networks on the Internet. Given the inherently open nature of the World Wide Web for online businesses, the question often is not when an intruder will attack, but rather how the inevitable attack will be made. Therefore, to succeed in the e-marketplace, managers must become fully aware of Internet security threats, take advantage of the technology that overcomes those threats, and continually earn and renew the trust of customers.

This chapter shows how web-based businesses need to identify what they are protecting; it also presents profiles of the most likely intruders. You will discover the most common mistakes of web-based businesses so that you know what to avoid. The chapter includes a discussion of the differences between the information technology (IT) department's concerns and management's role in the security of a web-based business. The chapter concludes with a powerful example of an iterative management framework for managing the security risk assumed by the web-based business. Successful managers recognize and understand the business risk of an Internet-based business; they create ways to tap into the expertise and best judgments of the IT department, system support staff, business managers, and security specialists to gain support for needed controls. The end of the chapter explains how the iterative enterprises risk management process can help managers to create a consensus for assessing the greatest threats to the enterprise and to communicate those results via the firm's security policy.

■ RISK MANAGEMENT, SECURITY POLICIES, AND INFORMATION SECURITY

Today it is essential to ensure the consumer rights of online customers in the networked environment. Managers who understand the importance of security can provide their web-based companies with a competitive advantage by ensuring that each customer feels that his or her privacy is protected. According to authors Simson Garfinkel and Eugene Spafford (1996), since 1991 the population of Internet users has significantly increased and reflects both the good elements and bad elements of today's society. In some situations, the Internet has become like the Wild West, despite a greater reliance on information technology and computers connected to the World Wide Web. Many government agencies, businesses, and academics are aware of the Internet's vulnerabilities, but they work around those difficulties rather than address the issues directly. More enlightened managers are seeking efficient ways to ensure that they fully understand the security risks affecting their Internet-based enterprises, and they want to implement appropriate controls to mitigate such risks.

The future well-being of the enterprise rests with the chief executive officer (CEO) and the executive team. Each member of management, including the chief information officer (CIO) or senior information (IS) executive, needs to be fluent in modern strategic planning and in developing an effective security policy. The enterprise's security policy allows the organization to reach a consensus on what is important regarding the value of security, details what the organization is protecting and why, states the priorities of what is to be protected first (and at what cost), and provides the IT department with a mandate for certain information security activities. In other words, a successful security policy (see Chapter 14 for details) provides a baseline for implementing security controls to reduce vulnerabilities and risks.

For the web-based business, no security measures can guarantee a risk-free environment. The strength of the organization's security is only as strong as its weakest link. Therefore, security is often managed using what is known as an end-to-end method rather than a layered method. Risk is realized when a vulnerability of the Internet-based business is exploited and causes harm to the organization's computers and networks. Technology alone cannot solve the problem. Determining basic security goals can provide the right direction, but an overall security policy is usually the enterprise's key to success. Web-based businesses continue to appear in all kinds of shapes, sizes, and types. Different business models use the Internet in different ways; thus, each web-based business has its own unique set of needs, security requirements, and risk tolerances. One way to develop an issue-specific policy is to break the policy into components based on business or operational requirements. This approach includes conducting risk assessments to determine

➤ The level of threats against the organization
➤ The sensitivity of the organization to the consequences of security breaches
➤ The legal and regulatory issues raised by a security breach
➤ The value of the disclosed, corrupted, or stolen information

These risk assessments become part of the web-based business's risk management program and can assist managers in determining how well the organization's security policy is working. Keep in mind that the risk management and security of the enterprise is an iterative process; by continually sustaining the process, the web-based business can both maintain and improve security. If the Internet-based business fails to apply or stops the process, security deteriorates as new threats and techniques emerge.

■ STARTING IN THE RIGHT DIRECTION

Your web site business may be a target for anyone who is bright, persistent, online, and so inclined. As more and more people conduct business online, security threats continue to increase. Managers must be prepared to battle online fraud, ensure privacy for their customers and partners, protect the company's data and systems, and guard the company from charges of negligence. For professional management, the key objectives of the firm's security management are evaluating cyberthreats and managing the risk of those threats. Security of a web-based business is not only a technical matter, but also a business issue that can determine the success or failure of the enterprise. Consequently, managers must maintain the security of their web-based businesses by establishing security priorities, goals, and objectives, and by overseeing an effective security policy.

Randy Marchany states in a recent SANS (System Administration, Networking, and Security; sans.org) presentation, "The Top 10 Internet Security Vulnerabilities—a Primer," that many information security vulnerabilities are the result of increases in computer network and program complexity. Moreover, computer programs that may be up to 25 years old are now being used in new ways, although many of these old programs were designed to be temporary solutions and are not considered production quality. This may compromise quality control of the entire system—in other words, the system may be weaker than expected because it is difficult to determine what can actually be considered secure.

Listed below are some of the most reliable Internet-based business veterans that have succumbed to security breaches. One of the companies, Network Associates, is even an Internet security firm. Each of these companies has suffered monetary and production losses due to the breaches, and customer confidence may never be the same.

> ➤ CNN (cnn.com) suffered a distributed denial of service (DDoS) attack that was launched by a university computer. Intruders electronically broke into a computer at the University of Cali-

fornia, Santa Barbara, causing a shutdown of the CNN news site for about two hours. Likely using new DDoS (see Chapter 7 for more information) technology, the intruders also used the university computer to paralyze Yahoo!, Amazon.com, eBay, and e-Trade temporarily.

➤ World Economic Forum (weforum.org) had its web server cracked by politically motivated hackers who were protesting not being allowed to demonstrate at the summit meeting. The hackers provided Zurich newspaper *Sonntag Zeitung* with a compact disk (CD) of personal data for 2,700 people who attended the World Economic Forum over the last year. Victims are reported to include Microsoft chairman Bill Gates, as well as top officials from South Africa, China, and other countries. Personal information included detailed travel itineraries and other personal information. The organization's main database was not accessed and information was not vandalized.

➤ Network Associates (nai.com.br and mcafee.com.br), an Internet security firm, recently had two of its web sites defaced by hackers. The intruders, who call themselves Insanity Zine Corp., spattered cyber-graffiti over the Brazilian-based web sites. They gained access to the web sites by hacking the company's host Internet service provider (ISP). Network Associates received what is known as a patch (a small program) to remedy its vulnerability four months before the intrusion, but the company failed to install the corrective software. According to a company spokesman, no actual penetration of the web sites or databases occurred. None of the company's systems or information was damaged.

➤ Travelocity (travelocity.com), an online travel company, exposed the names, addresses, phone numbers, and e-mail addresses of Travelocity customers who participated in an online promotion. For more than a month, 51,000 names could have been exposed by the security breach. According to a company spokesman, the breach was caused by human error and no order information was compromised.

➤ Citibank (citibank.com) was the target of Russian hacker Vladimir Levin, who was arrested in Britain on charges that he used his laptop computer to illegally transfer as much as $3.7 million from New York's Citibank to various international accounts controlled by Levin and his partners. Levin was later extradited to the United States, where he was sentenced to three years in prison and ordered to pay Citibank $240,000 in restitution.

■ RECOGNIZING WHY SECURITY IS IMPORTANT FOR YOUR WEB-BASED BUSINESS

Jeremy Lieb (July 1999) states that results of a CommerceNet study show that the top inhibitors for e-consumers are security and privacy. Consumers are worried about revealing credit card and purchase information online, want to protect themselves from online fraud, and are concerned about their privacy. On a daily basis, however, online businesses are threatened by fraud, sabotage, espionage, piracy, identity theft, and other forms of electronic warfare. This study underscores the importance of information security for an Internet-based business as a critical new area of management. The management team is now responsible for making the business's web site easy for consumers to access and navigate, but difficult and unattractive for vandals, hackers, and industrial spies to attack.

Keep in mind that because all online transactions are based on trust, security is the prime enabler of e-business. As a general rule, the greater the amount of consumer trust, the bigger the web-based business's competitive advantage. Because of the wide variety of web-based businesses, lack of security can result in different degrees of damage to the company. A security breach in one enterprise (such as a not-for-profit web site with low traffic volume) can cause a few whispers; however, a security breach in another enterprise (such as an online bank with high traffic volume) may signal the end of the company. Internet-based businesses that experience security breaches usually suffer expensive downtime and financial losses, as well as humiliation and loss of customer confidence—a consequence that may encourage customers to defect to competitors. Moreover, it may be nearly impossible to determine the exact amount of system damage or to detect the presence of any malicious programs remaining in the system.

■ IDENTIFYING THREATS FROM CYBERSPACE

In February 2000, Stephen E. Cross, director of the Software Engineering Institute (SEI) at Carnegie Mellon University, predicted that U.S. business-to-business (B2B) online transactions would reach $1.3 trillion in 2003. If the projection is correct, about one out of every four B2B transactions will be online. Furthermore, in 1999 about 23 million shoppers spent more than $11 billion online. These statistics indicate that e-business is big business. The only way to participate in the emerging e-market is to have a web-based business. Experienced web-based business managers generally accept the reality that the business is at risk in cyberspace. For example, in July 1999 *Information Security* magazine published the following survey results:

➤ More security threats are being made to web-based businesses. About 57 percent of companies conducting businesses online were more likely to suffer security breaches than companies not on the Internet.

➤ More web-based businesses are attacked each year. Statistics show attack rates to be twice the amount of the previous year.

➤ Each security breach is costly. Companies average a loss of $256,000 for each security breach in the last year. Of the 745 organizations surveyed, 91 estimated losses at a total of $23.3 million.

In the 2001 survey by the Computer Security Institute (CSI) and the Federal Bureau of Investigation (FBI) of 538 IT professionals at Fortune 500 corporations, universities, and government agencies, about 85 percent of the respondents discovered computer security break-ins in the last year, compared to 62 percent in the previous year. Additionally, 64 percent acknowledged financial losses from cyber-intrusions and reported losses of more than $377 million, compared to $265 million in the previous year. Monetary losses are due to the theft of proprietary information and corporate secrets, as well as online financial fraud.

More than 70 percent of respondents state that their Internet presence was the primary point of attack, up from 59 percent in 1999. In the past, it was generally believed that internal computer security was 80 percent of the problem and external threats were 20 percent. The new 2001 CSI/FBI statistics indicate that insider threats are at an all-time low of 49 percent. This may indicate that outsider threats are increasing and web-based businesses need to change their security policies to reflect these changes. Another interesting CSI/FBI statistic highlights how noncriminal employee misbehavior and abuse of Internet privileges are now 91 percent, compared to a abuse rate of 79 percent in 2000.

These statistics show that security for web-based businesses is not just for the IT folks at the operational level; it involves almost every corporate function and all top-level management. No single technology, hardware, or magic key makes organizations secure. The recent wave of cyber-crime has contributed to the need for managers of web-based businesses to develop new ways to evaluate and analyze security risks. Just as they do when protecting the company from burglars, professional managers need to know how to lock the door to their networks and how to make sure the door is strong enough to fend off invaders. Additionally, managers need to know the difference between being an e-business pacesetter and being a laggard when incorporating security into their strategic plans.

■ REALIZING WHAT MAKES THE INTERNET MARKETPLACE SO VULNERABLE

In the fourth quarter of 1993 the ban against commercial transactions on the Internet was lifted. Firms using expensive proprietary networks could now use the less costly World Wide Web for transactions with customers, partners, suppliers, and so on. This development became the foundation of the Internet revolution. The high-speed growth of electronic brokerages is a good example of this rapid expansion. According to Gomez Advisors (gomez.com), an independent online research firm located in Boston, in 1996 there were 15 online brokerages, in 1997 there were 33, and in 1998 there were between 60 and 87. The number of individuals using electronic brokerage services has jumped from zero in 1996 to over 8 million online investors in 2001 (about 10 percent of the total number of investors).

In part, this meteoric rise of online investors can be attributed to increased comfort with the Internet, in spite of the fact that the designers of the Internet did not foresee this type of transactional and commercial activity. In the 1960s, the Advanced Research Projects Agency developed a network called ARPANET as a way to exchange military research information. The network was designed to use all types of computers and to function even if sections of the so-called net were lost due to warfare. Over time, ARPANET evolved into today's Internet. Consequently, the Internet is a complex, dynamic world of interconnected computers; it has neither geographical location nor national boundaries. Control of the Internet is unique because it is in the hands of the users; no central control or authority governs it.

The Internet was originally based on trust. Early Internet designers and users did not focus on privacy or security concerns because the system was designed to exchange information primarily meant for use by the military and by academics. Over the years the Internet community has grown and now reflects all elements of society. It includes good citizens, bad neighbors, and even criminals. According to Stephen Cross (2000), because of the unique infrastructure of the Internet, online organizations can expect cyber-threats because

➤ Internet attacks are easy to accomplish. The Internet was originally designed to fend off attacks to its infrastructure (computers, wires, etc.).

➤ Internet attackers are difficult to trace because attackers can lie about identity and location. It is easy to spoof Internet users. *Spoofing* is masquerading to take advantage of the user's trust to gain sensitive information (credit cards, social security numbers, etc.).

➤ Attacks are usually low risk. In the physical world an attempted robbery results in apprehension and a trial; in the cyber-world, however, an attempted robbery is difficult to discover. For example, management may find it hard to determine whether the computer incident was a security test run by the network administrator or an attempted break-in.

➤ Culprits are nearly impossible to apprehend because they do not have to be on the physical site to commit the crime. Consequently, local law enforcement agencies are unsure of how to treat cyber-crime cases and are troubled by jurisdictional issues.

➤ Manpower is lacking and training is insufficient for tracking computer crime and preserving evidence. Local departments often rely on overworked state and federal agencies. Almost all state Internet crime units already have heavy caseloads and many web-based business cyber-crimes are not large enough to attract federal interest.

■ GETTING TO KNOW YOUR ENEMY

The usefulness of the Internet cannot be ignored. The Internet can even help the average computer user find the basic information and techniques needed to become a hacker. Low-skill intruders can easily find hacker information, tools, and techniques on the Internet. For ex-

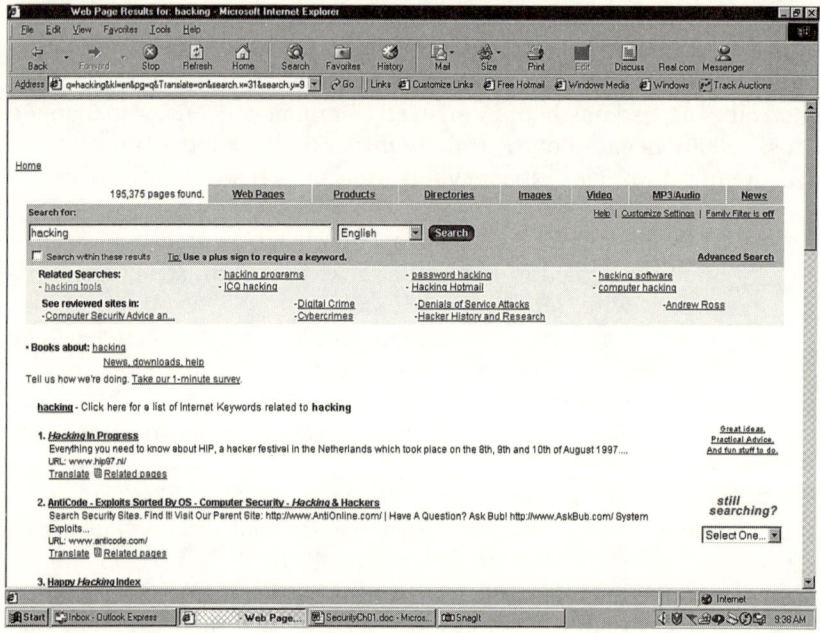

Figure 1.1 Internet search engines help to educate would-be intruders

ample, several hacker groups such as 2600, the Legion of Doom, and Phrack, Inc. share information with each other. Using the search engine Google (google.com) with the keyword *hacking* provides 793,000 responses, and looking for the keyword *password cracking* provides 20,900 responses. Another popular search engine, shown in Figure 1.1, illustrates how the keyword *hacking* provides 195,375 responses with related links to hacking tools, hacking programs, hacking passwords, hacking Hotmail, hacking software, and hacking computers.

A hacking program can be an easy-to-use but sophisticated intruder tool (sometimes called a kiddie script). Intruders can use these kiddie scripts to attack large numbers of web sites simultaneously.

Individuals, not technologies, attack online businesses. These individuals have skill, motivation, and opportunity. Many of these intruders are joyriders looking for stimulation; others seek to commit industrial espionage or are politically motivated. Some intruders just want to eavesdrop or see your most private files. Others are vandals who want to steal or tamper with corporate files. The skill level and motivation level of these individuals is broad. Thomas Wadlow (2000), chief security officer and vice president of Pilot Network Services, Inc., suggests dividing hackers into three categories.

➤ Browsers, campers, and vandals: Browsers just want to break into your system to prove that they can do it. Campers often want to use your resources for free. Vandals are frequently campers who have been thrown out of the system and want to retaliate. The likelihood of this type of attack is high, the number of potential attackers is large, the motivation of the intruders is low to medium, and the skill level required ranges from low to high.

➤ Spies and saboteurs: These intruders are usually individuals who have targeted your company. They know what you do and how you do it; they know your network and maybe even some of your employees. The likelihood of attack depends on your business (do you have a new technology?). The number of potential attackers is low. Motivation and skill levels are medium to high. These criminals are motivated by money and expect to get paid for their efforts.

➤ Disgruntled individuals (ex-employees or ex-contractors): They have expert knowledge of your company because in many cases you have trained them. They are highly motivated because they are angry and frustrated. Access to corporate resources is frequently easy because the individuals still work for the company. These intruders often have contacts or are trusted within the company, which provides them with ready access to sensitive or proprietary information.

■ BECOMING AWARE OF COMMON INTERNET SECURITY MISTAKES

According to Randy Marchany (2001) of the SANS Institute (sans.org), Internet-based businesses have many vulnerabilities and any discussion of Internet security threats can only cover the most common threats at the moment. Managers should strive to eliminate the most common mistakes in order to gain a better handle on securing the entire web-based business. Such measures also make managers better prepared for new threats. The following is a list of the most common mistakes. Keep in mind that the list of high-profile mistakes is constantly changing, and protecting the enterprise from unpredictable threats is always a challenge.

1. Connecting systems to the Internet before hardening them: Hardening your systems can be defined as evaluating and analyzing the web-based business systems (domain name servers, databases, web servers, applications, firewalls) before going online. In other words, the integration of all the elements of your web-based business may provide invaders with a security hole or two.

2. Linking test systems to the Internet with default accounts or passwords: The problem may materialize through loopholes created by this mistake. The default password is blank and users are expected to assign a new password the first time they log in. This loophole allows invaders to use the blank default to access the system.

3. Failing to install updates or patches when security holes are found: Identified system or network security weaknesses often go uncorrected. When software vendors become aware of security holes, they provide small programs called patches. Your firm's security administrator or your Internet service provider (ISP) may be unaware of the new release. Additionally, when a new patch is released, your company or your ISP may be too slow to install the patch. This lag can enable a security breach.

4. Not using encryption security: Not using encrypted protocols for managing systems, routers, or firewalls (i.e., not filtering incoming information from your ISP and other network routing agents) also makes security breaches possible. Today, some security experts see this as a so-called excise tax on network routers; others believe that taking these measures will be a security requirement in the future for all web-based businesses.

5. Not using password security properly: Providing passwords over the telephone, not changing passwords regularly, or changing passwords based on telephone or e-mail requests when the requestor is not authenticated are all mistakes that can lead to security breaches. Weak passwords are selected and easily guessed by would-be intruders. Furthermore, inexperienced or untrained users accidentally violate good security practices and inadvertently publicize their passwords.

6. Not creating and maintaining backup files: The organization

needs to promote the use of sound and reasonable practices for creating and maintaining back-up files. Taking this precaution may mean creating more than one set of backup files and storing them at a different geographical location.

7. Running unnecessary services: When purchasing software programs (sometimes called *shrink-wrapped software*) vendors often include program features that add no value but open additional windows of risk. Sometimes these vendor-provided examples have security holes that can lead to security breaches.

8. Not using firewalls properly: Companies sometimes use firewalls with rules that don't stop malicious incoming or outgoing traffic. Hackers may be able to bypass your firewalls through older versions of master e-mail programs, thereby allowing intruders access to your network to take control of your internal systems.

9. Not implementing or updating virus-detection software: More and more e-corporations use global file sharing. Sometimes these files are misconfigured, allowing viruses to be spread throughout the organization.

10. Lack of security education and training: Not educating users about how to look for potential security breaches or what to do when they see a possible security problem can lead to even greater problems. Lack of training also includes not encouraging uniform high standards of security quality throughout the organization.

■ ACHIEVING WEB-BASED BUSINESS SECURITY

The security of your web-based business is defined in many ways. For example, Cheswick and Bellovin (2001) define computer security as "keeping anyone from doing things you do not want them to do to, with, on or from your computers or any peripheral devices." Another definition of computer security is preventing attackers from achieving their objectives through unauthorized access or unauthorized use of web-based business resources. This definition excludes concerns about user errors, equipment theft, and environmental threats. Rather, the definition focuses on defects in software or system integration; it also concentrates on configuration problems that can be exploited to provide unauthorized individuals access to or use of computers or networks.

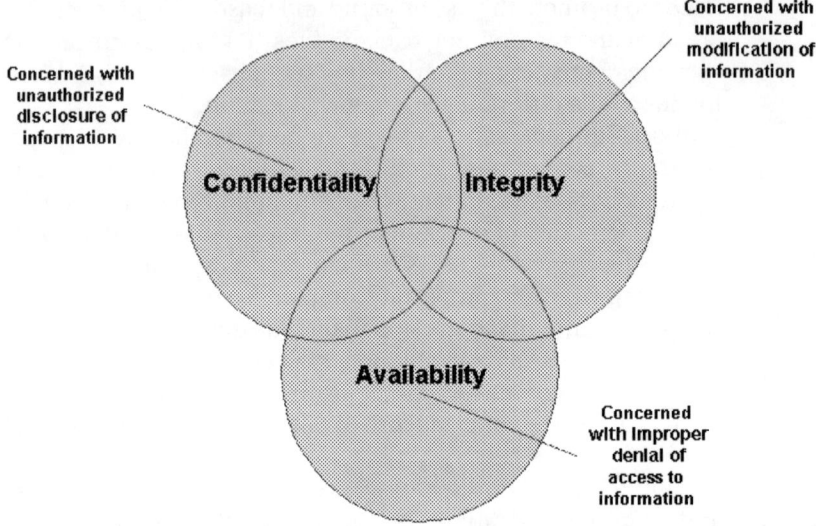

Figure 1.2 Illustration of the CIA information security principles

Both definitions show that information security is not a goal, but rather an ongoing process that involves the entire organization. The definitions also point out management's new role in the area of security. Managers are now involved on a daily basis with the security risk assessment, analysis, and management of their Internet-based enterprises. In contrast, risk management for the technical staff within the organization (security consultants, chief information officers, security administrators, and similar technical managers) is frequently defined by three key security objectives called CIA (confidentiality, availability, and integrity). These overlapping categories are illustrated in Figure 1.2.

➤ Confidentiality

Stop unauthorized disclosure of sensitive information. Such information should be accessible only to designated individuals. *Sensitive information* is generally defined as needing protection from unauthorized disclosure. However, the Computer Security Act broadens this term to "any information, the loss, misuse, or modification of which could adversely affect the national interest or the conduct of federal programs, or the privacy to which individuals are entitled under Section 552a of Title 5, United States Code (the Privacy Act), but which has not been specifically authorized under criteria established by an Executive Order or an Act of Congress to be kept secret in the interest of national defense of foreign policy."

➤ Integrity

Prohibit unauthorized modification of information. Information should remain undamaged by vandals or accidents, and it should be timely, accurate, complete, and consistent. Often organizations divide data integrity and system integrity into two parts. Data integrity means that information and programs are changed only in a specified and authorized way. System integrity means that the system performs as intended and without any deliberate or inadvertent unauthorized manipulation. However, the definition of integrity continues to be debated and will likely change as technology changes and as e-commerce becomes more mature.

➤ Availability

Prevent the improper denial of access to information. The systems should always be accessible to and provide resources to users when needed. The system should always work promptly and service should not be denied to authorized users. Information should be available when required by the business process, in both the present and the future. Resources and related capabilities should be safeguarded.

The IT Governance Institute (July 2000) suggests that IT managers need to add four more overlapping categories to this framework so that IT can better support business objectives or requirements.

Effectiveness deals with information that is important and pertinent to the business process; it also ensures that information is delivered in a timely manner and is correct, consistent, and usable.

Efficiency concerns the provision of information using the most productive and cost-effective resources.

Compliance deals with externally imposed business requirements such as laws, regulations, and contractual arrangements.

Reliability of information relates to providing suitable information for the management of the enterprise and for the management of financial and compliance responsibilities.

➤ The Changing Structure of IT Management

Overall, an organization's IT department is responsible for developing, implementing, and maintaining information security within the enterprise. This *process-level security* within the organization is often divided into three sections: management control, operational control, and technical control. To date, no standardized requirements have been set for establishing, implementing, and documenting information security systems. Specific control objectives vary from organization to organization. Many professional and governmental groups, such as the Center for Internet Security (cisecurity.com/charter.html), are currently trying to develop process-level security requirements for information systems. The following is a sampling of the security standards that are currently available:

➤ British Standards Institute Code of Practice (includes more than 80 control objectives)

➤ CobiT: Control Objectives for Information and Related Technologies (318 control objectives established by the Information Systems Audit and Control Association)

➤ General Accounting Office FISCAM (Federal Information Systems Controls Audit Manual)

➤ Information Security Policies Made Easy (730 controls written by Charles Cresson Wood, Baseline Software, Inc., 1995)

The reason that so many groups are developing international benchmarks, standards, or objectives is that the use of such standards illustrates that the organization uses due care based on the reasonable safeguards of similar organizations with similar resource limitations and priorities. Furthermore, standardization can assist examiners performing enterprise-wide security audits. This type of analysis focuses on process-level security and is often called a baseline comparison.

➤ The New Role of Management for the Web-Based Business

In cyberspace, successful web-based businesses are often what are called first movers, like Amazon.com (amazon.com), which bills itself as "the largest online bookstore in the world," or Internet-based businesses with the latest business model; such businesses seem to rise from almost nowhere, such as Dell Computer Corporation (dell.com), where customers can design their own computers online. These two businesses are only a few years old and are already considered seasoned Internet veterans. Consequently, successful web-based businesses are often one-of-a-kind enterprises with no meaningful comparable baselines. Web-based businesses must therefore rely on risk assessment and management to manage the union between business processes and information systems.

Risk management of the firm's information security (with the assistance of the IT department and others) is one of many duties of executive management for web-based businesses. Management must determine what is the right level of financial investment and organization expenditure in terms of time and talent for IT; the correct level should support the objectives of the web-based business. In the past, many companies viewed the security of their Internet-based businesses as a type of utility. Web-based businesses that rely on information technology to stay open for business cannot afford to be so cavalier.

Successful Internet-based business managers fully understand the information security risks affecting their operations. This knowledge allows managers to implement the appropriate controls and to mitigate business security risks. Today it is the executive manager's role and responsibility to determine what is the acceptable level of risk for the organization, as well as how much of the enterprise's resources to invest for security and control.

■ UNCOVERING THE RISK MANAGEMENT CYCLE OF WEB-BASED BUSINESSES

Successful Internet-based business managers develop and implement enterprise-wide risk management frameworks to protect their businesses on the Internet. The General Accounting Office publication, *Information Security Risk Assessment: Practices of Leading Organizations* (November 1999), suggests the risk management framework illustrated in Figure 1.3. Risk management in the past was often considered a separate form of management. The integrated risk management approach, as illustrated in Figure 1.3, can assist the organization in becoming more proactive than reactive to threats; it also allows for strategic planning. The risk management framework is an iterative process that focuses on five elements of the risk management cycle.

1. Assess risk and determine needs (discussed in detail in Chapter 2). Management should recognize threats and the possibility of their materialization, as well as detect and rank impor-

tant assets and operations, assess the likely damage if a threat does materialize, pinpoint cost-effective ways to protect assets, and keep a record of the enterprise's risk assessment findings.

2. Develop a central focal point. Groups and individuals should be designated as focal points to manage and guide the risk assessment process. These focal points oversee the planning, performance, and reporting of the organization's risk assessment programs.

3. Implement appropriate policies and related controls. Based on the risk assessment team's analyses, management should formulate workable security policies.

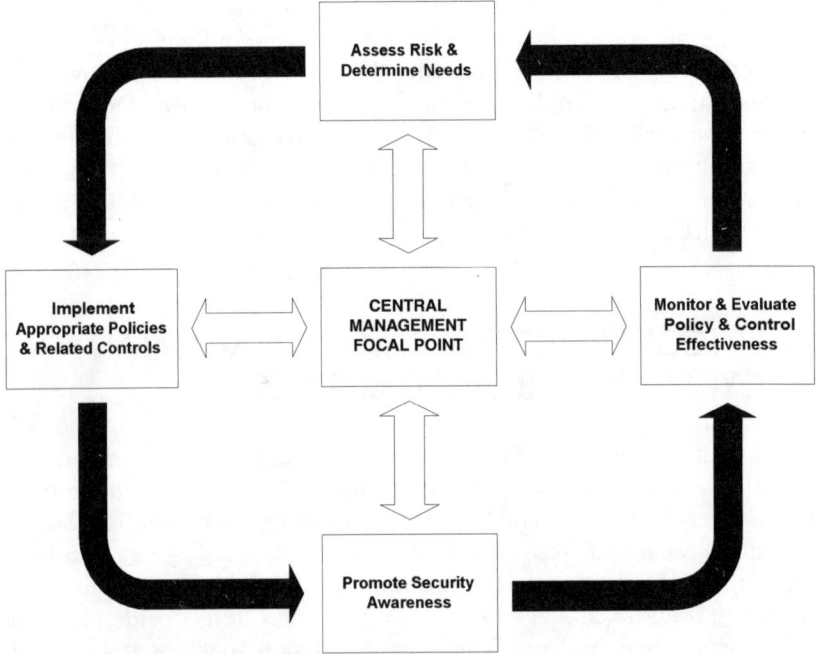

Figure 1.3 Web-based business risk management cycle
Note: This illustration is adapted from the original work of an anonymous author.
Source: General Accounting Office (GA). 1999. GAO-AMID-00-33 information security risk assessment: Practices of leading organizations, a supplement to GAO's May 1998 executive guide on information security management, November.

4. Promote awareness. People are often aware of security only when breaches inconvenience them. However, management should stress that security is everybody's business.
5. Monitor and evaluate policy and control effectiveness. The risk management framework shows how this process is iterative and how information is a security process that affects all aspects of the web-based enterprise.

Figure 1.3 shows an overview of a risk management approach for the Internet-based business. A comparison of Figure 1.2 (IT concerns) to Figure 1.3 clearly demonstrates the uniqueness of management's role. In the web-based business, it is now the responsibility of executive management to assure customers, partners, and investors that the greatest risks to the web-based business have been identified and addressed.

■ REFERENCES

Cheswick, William R., and Steven M. Bellovin. 1994. *Firewalls and Internet Security: Repelling the Wily Hacker.* Reading, Mass.: Addison-Wesley.

Economic Cyber Threats: Stephen E. Cross. Congressional Testimony. 23 February 2000. Available at [http://www.fas.org/irp/congress/2000_hr/000301sc.pdf].

Garfinkel, Simson, and Gene Spafford. 1996. *Practical UNIX & Internet Security.* 2d ed. Cambridge, Mass.: O'Reilly and Associates.

General Accounting Office. 1999. GAO-AMID-00-33 Information security risk assessment: Practices of leading organizations, a supplement to GAO's May 1998 executive guide on information security management, November. Available at [http://www.gao.gov/special.pubs/ai00033.pdf]. 28 November 2001.

IT Governance Institute. 2000. *CobiT Control Objectives.* July. 3rd ed. Published by the Information Systems Audit and Control Association, Rolling Meadows, IL (www.isaca.com). Available at [http://www.itgovernance.org/cobitmg.htm]. 2 February 2001.

Krebs, Brian. 2001. Costs, frequency of computer intrusion on rise—report. *Newsbytes,* 19 March. Available at [http://www.newsbytes.com/news/01/163036.html]. 28 November 2001.

Lieb, Jeremy. 2001. *Getting Secure Online—an Overview.* Corporate publication of CommerceNet. 8 January. Available at [http://www.commercenet.com/research/technology-applications/1999/ecs1.3-03secureonline.html].

Marchany, Randy. 2000. *The Top 10 Internet Security Vulnerabilities—a Primer.* Presentation, SANS Resources—how to eliminate the ten most critical Internet security threats. December. Available at [http://www.sans.org/topten.htm]. 2 February 2001.

Parker, Donn B. 1998. *Fighting Computer Crime.* New York: Wiley.

Poore, Ralph Spencer. 1999. *Generally Accepted System Security Principles: Release for Public Comment,* International Information Security Foundation (www.isaca.org). Available at [http://www.auerbach-publications.com/white-papers/gassp.pdf]. 2 February 2001.

Violino, Bob, and Amy K. Larsen. 1999. Trends security: An e-biz asset. *InformationWeek.* 15 February. Available at [http://www.informationweek.com/721/security.htm]. 28 November 2001.

Wadlow, Thomas A. 2000. The Process of Network Security: Designing and Managing a Safe Network. Reading, Mass.: Addison-Wesley.

Wright, Rob. 2000. How to avoid an online breach, the right tools to fight cyber crime, new technology helps e-business fight online security breaches. *VarBusiness.* 13 November. Available at [http://vb.channelsupersearch.com/news/VAR/21493.asp]. 28 November 2001.

Chapter

Assessing Your Security Level

In this chapter

➤ Assessing Information Security Risks in Your Web-Based Business

➤ Planning and Documenting the Assets That Need Protection

➤ Gathering the Right Risk Assessment Information

➤ Identifying Threats and Potential Vulnerabilities

➤ Qualitative and Numerical Approaches to Security Risk Analysis

➤ Doing Risk Assessments by the Numbers

➤ Mitigating Risks and Taking Corrective Actions

➤ Creating Risk Assessment Reports and Following-Up

➤ Determining the Frequency of Your Assessments

This chapter explores how managers can determine the security level of their Internet-based organizations. You will discover why risk assessments are important and become aware of the three phases of assessing information security risks in a web-based business. Gain an understanding of how to select the right personnel for the risk assessment team and develop the scope of the project and information requirements. Discover how to oversee risk assessment activities to gain the most insight. Learn how to perform both qualitative and quantitive risk analyses. Become aware of the limitations of risk analysis and uncover how to implement the most effective corrective actions. This chapter concludes with a discussion of the importance of following-up on information security recommendations; it also suggests some ways to decide when to start the next information security risk assessment.

■ ASSESSING INFORMATION SECURITY RISKS IN YOUR WEB-BASED BUSINESS

Managers are forced to juggle business requirements, schedules, and strategic objectives while avoiding event failures and security problems. Add constantly changing risk factors to this mix and it becomes clear that assessing information risk is more difficult than assessing other types of risks. For example, consider the following:

➤ It is hard to determine how the web-based business may be attacked; determining the value of the assets stolen, copied, or adulterated is also difficult.

➤ Ascertaining the true value of hardware may be complicated. For example, a $55,000 computer may process $2 million in monetary transactions per day. Therefore, the value of the computer is more than that of the hardware.

➤ It is not easy to determine the cost of training and integrating new security controls to business processes in order to prevent security breaches.

➤ Risk assessment information can become outdated quickly as a result of changes in hacker methodologies or technologies.

Risk assessments are a critical component of information security and are used to highlight exposures, to validate existing security controls, and to communicate risk management results. According to a publication of the General Accounting Office (GAO), "Information Security Risk Assessment: Practices of Leading Organizations" (1999), risk assessment programs are effective in supporting business activities for three reasons.

➤ They identify the greatest threats. Risk assessment programs continually help identify the greatest threats to business operations; they also tap into the best in-house judgments and expertise to develop reasonable ways to prevent or mitigate the vulnerability.

➤ They develop agreement on what is valuable. Risk assessment programs assist organizations in developing a consensus on which security measures are important to business operations; such agreement improves communication within the organization and informs the employees of the information security issues that are important.

➤ They heighten employee awareness of security. A risk assessment program promotes the awareness of threats to business operations and provides the support needed for controls, reducing the likelihood that employees will unwittingly disclose passwords or sensitive information.

Ideally, risk assessment begins before the web-based business's computer network becomes operational; in this way no defective software is included in the system, and system vulnerabilities can be identified and remedied. External security defenses, such as firewalls (see Chapter 11 for more information) are verified before any connection to the Internet exposes the system to potential hackers, vandals, and spies. Because of constraints on time, talent, and finances, managers of Internet-based businesses in the real world are often forced to use existing computer networks and external Internet connections. Consequently, organizations tend to focus scarce resources on prominent vulnerabilities rather than invest in risk assessments of the entire system to determine the greatest threats to the web-based business.

Today's web-based businesses are generally complex and interconnected, making them interdependent and accessible to more people. Internet-based businesses that do not perform risk assessment are flying blindly in cyberspace. The following are a few examples of common problems:

➤ Supplementary features (sometimes called *feature creep*) that are added continuously to the Internet-based enterprise may cause both configuration and integration errors that can be exploited by intruders.

➤ Older computer systems that may not be entirely secure due to upgraded new programs which create unknown security holes.

➤ The web-based business may purchase plug-ins that are independently run applications that operate within the web-based business. These add-ons may not live up to the security guarantees promised by their vendors.

Managers need a true understanding of the points of origin and the scale of threats their enterprises may encounter. To develop and manage effective security programs, managers first need to identify and rank risks to their web-based businesses. The risk assessment of an Internet-based business can be divided into the three phases illustrated in Figure 2.1.

The three phases of the risk assessment program shown in Figure 2.1 can be summarized as preparation, risk assessment, and risk analysis with corrective actions.

➤ Preparation includes determining assessment objectives and methods, deciding on the composition and size of the assessment team, and determining information requirements.

➤ Risk assessment activities include gathering information via interviews, questionnaires, and so on from employees with business operations or process expertise; information resources and other resources can also be consulted.

➤ Risk analysis and corrective actions include choosing someone to analyze the data and calculating the necessary costs of effective actions to mitigate risk to the web-based business.

■ PLANNING AND DOCUMENTING THE ASSETS THAT NEED PROTECTION

Determining the objectives and deciding who should perform the risk assessments for your organization is an important first step in risk assessment. The risk assessment team can include five to eight members, be multidisciplined, and may include a hired consultant to avoid biases. To ensure objectivity, many enterprises make certain that risk assessment team members do not evaluate coworkers, supervisors, or their own business units. The assessment period can vary from a few days to several weeks, depending on the complexity of the system. Some companies have risk assessment programs that have grown more robust over the last several years. Others have risk assessment software written by in-house programmers; such programs assist managers in handling the extensive amount of data that the risk assessment team harvests. Other data-gathering tools may include questionnaires, standard report formats, lists of threats, and control objectives.

The risk assessment process helps the company identify threats

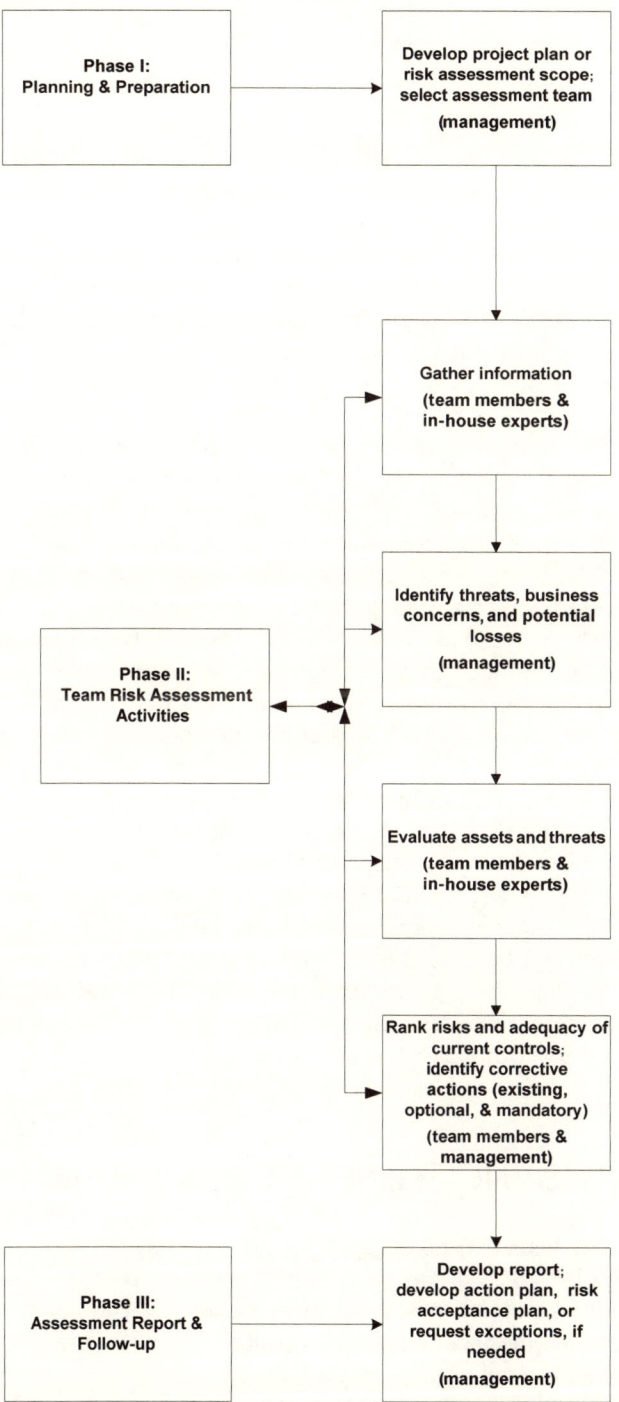

Figure 2.1   Overview of the risk assessment process
Source: General Accounting Office (GAO). 1999. GAO-AMID-00-33 information security risk assessment: Practices of leading organizations, a supplement to GAO's May 1998 executive guide on information security management, November.

and estimate the likelihood of their materialization. The company therefore needs to identify and rank critical assets and operations. Assets can include software, databases, customer information, proprietary business processes, and so on. Software developer Internet Security Systems (iss.net) divides enterprise vulnerabilities into three groups; the company provides the following samples of the types of vulnerabilities that web-based businesses of different sizes can expect:

➤ Emerging businesses are generally smaller organizations. These organizations are frequently start-ups with limited budgets; consequently, they often have vulnerable infrastructures, lack a security control environment, and are unwilling or unable to develop a security control environment.

➤ Middle-market businesses are undergoing rapid growth. These enterprises have annual revenues of between $10 million to $500 million; they frequently have a limited security infrastructure, are under significant threat from internal misuse, and may be subject to significant financial loss if operations are disrupted.

➤ International or large businesses are highly dependent on Internet resources. These corporations are high-profile targets for hackers and frequently have a hardened security system, but their security policies are often inefficient or unenforced. The business may be a bricks-and-mortar organization (a traditional business) with a clicks-and-mortar operation (Internet business). Intruders often aim for critical business infrastructure and use the company's resources to launch attacks against other targets.

■ GATHERING THE RIGHT RISK INFORMATION

The risk analysis can take approximately two days to a week. Sometimes a preliminary risk analysis report is released for comment and a final report is published several months later. Based on the data collected, management can develop a number of scenarios and can ask in-house experts to rank the threats to the organization in order to develop an enterprise-based baseline. Data-gathering tools can include questionnaires, standard report formats, and software to facilitate documentation and analysis. Some organizations may use lists of control objectives and risk factors. Risk factor lists detail major threats, concerns, and objectives; they can include data from both internal and external sources (see the Resource Center for more information about online resources). Team members can use these risk factor lists to guide the interview process.

■ IDENTIFYING THREATS AND POTENTIAL BUSINESS LOSSES

All Internet-based enterprises have some level of visibility through the domain name server (DNS; this function points Internet users to your web site). If your web-based business has a high level of visibility (Microsoft, CNN, Yahoo!, eBay), opportunistic intruders are more likely to attempt to cause harm. Furthermore, if your web-based enterprise is in the media spotlight or is affected by various external events (business mergers, increases or decreases in stock price, etc.) the visibility of the enterprise changes and the organization becomes more or less visible. For example, after 15 April the visibility of the IRS (Internal Revenue Service) web site greatly decreases.

The amount of security you implement should be equal to the value of what you are protecting. For example, a rock concert web site needs a different type of security from that of a web-based business that completes a large volume of Internet-only sales. A security breach in the former can cause a few comments, but the same type of breach in the latter may signal the end of the company; this means that you have to put a value on how much it should cost to restore the security of your web-based business and to maintain the trust of your online customers.

The web-based company (ideally) classifies information into security categories; this practice lets the organization know what is worth protecting. The risk assessment team may suggest daily cataloging for some types of data and annual classification for other kinds of data. When profiling risks and dividing information into data security categories, managers and IT professionals should note the following:

➤ The most severe threats to the most valuable information
➤ The sensitivity of the organization to the consequences of security incidents
➤ The legal and regulatory issues raised by a security breach

➤ The value of the disclosed, adulterated, copied, or stolen information

➤ The criticality of the information to business operations and assets

■ QUALITATIVE AND NUMERICAL APPROACHES TO SECURITY RISK ANALYSIS

Based on the data gathered, team members and management can evaluate and assess threats to the web-based business. Scenarios often are used to illustrate certain vulnerabilities. Many organizations assign costs to what they see as the worst-case scenario. Risk assessment team members then rank the threat according to the severity and likelihood of its occurrence. For example, the risk assessment team may determine that the Internet-based business is subject to a denial of service threat (see Chapter 7 for details) similar to the one suffered by Microsoft. The risk assessment of the real-life Microsoft scenario might look like this:

> Scenario: Microsoft (microsoft.com) and (msn.com) experienced a distributed denial of service (DDoS) attack against the routers that divert traffic to different Microsoft web sites. The attack did not target the web server; rather, it targeted the hardware switches that route data. Hackers barraged the switches with information requests so that the web servers could not process legitimate requests. The attack, which exploited a flaw in the network design, lasted for about two hours. Microsoft is the Internet's third most popular web site, with 54 million unique visitors in December of 2000.

One way for the risk assessment team to analyze this scenario is to use a risk assessment matrix similar to the one illustrated in Figure 2.2; many organizations in different industries use this approach for decision-making under conditions of uncertainty. Using the static risk assessment matrix in Figure 2.2, team members can rank the risk of the Microsoft scenario.

Static analysis, as shown in Figure 2.2, takes a snapshot of the enterprise at a point in time. This static analysis involves the systematic evaluation of the potential impact of each vulnerability (or risk factor). Each potential vulnerability is ranked by the severity of its effects to allow for appropriate corrective actions to eliminate or control the high-risk items. The process is iterative so that managers can determine whether system vulnerability is decreasing or increasing.

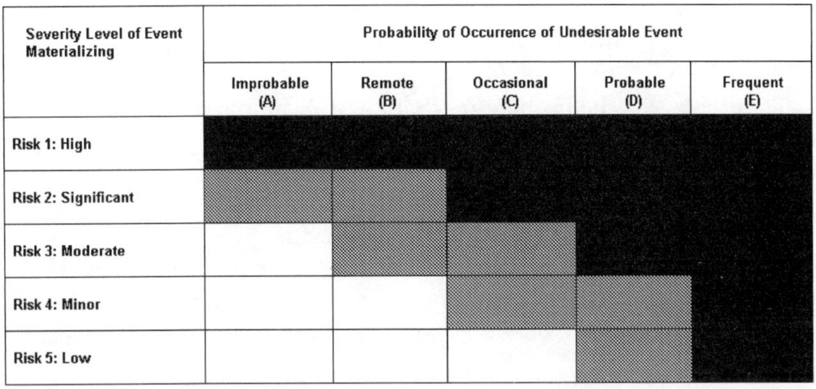

Severity Level of Event Materializing	Probability of Occurrence of Undesirable Event				
	Improbable (A)	Remote (B)	Occasional (C)	Probable (D)	Frequent (E)
Risk 1: High					
Risk 2: Significant					
Risk 3: Moderate					
Risk 4: Minor					
Risk 5: Low					

Figure 2.2 Overview of the risk assessment matrix of a web-based business

In static risk analysis, the probability that the undesirable event will occur can be ranked on the y-axis from low to high. The severity of the possible event is ranked on the x-axis from low to high. Management and assessment team members determine the level of criticality by conducting additional interviews after the areas of vulnerability are exposed. Then risk analysis (using predetermined categories) can be used to estimate the degree of reduced performance or failure of the business in the scenario being analyzed. For example, the static risk analysis matrix in Figure 2.2 lists the severity of a possible undesirable event on the y-axis. The different threat levels are listed as

➤ Risk 1, *high:* Considerably negative impact requires immediate corrective action. High-level information security losses may include great financial loss due to the information's value or the enterprise's high profile.

➤ Risk 2, *significant:* Moderately negative impact requires corrective action with management discretion. Security breach may result in significant downtime and financial loss; extensive recovery time and expenses may be required.

➤ Risk 3, *moderate:* Some negative impact requires management review. Security breach may include significant financial loss and liability exposure.

➤ Risk 4, *minor:* Minimal negative impact is acceptable with management approval. Minor probability exists for a security breach with low-level or outdated information.

➤ Risk 5, *low:* No negative impact requires no management review. The web-based business might not provide a high return for the effort required to breach the firm's security.

On the x-axis the probability that an undesirable event will occur is divided into five categories.

- ➤ Category A, *improbable:* Practically impossible
- ➤ Category B, *remote:* Not likely to occur
- ➤ Category C, *occasional:* Chance of occurring sometime
- ➤ Category D, *probable:* Chance of isolated incidents
- ➤ Category E, *frequent:* Possibility of repeated incidents

Based on the limited information provided about the Microsoft attack, the scenario receives a grade of D1 using the static risk analysis matrix in Figure 2.2. Microsoft's high profile results in a high probability of repeated attacks; therefore the firm receives a score of D for the undesirable event's probability. The severity of the incident is ranked at 1 (on a scale of 1 to 5, with 1 as most severe). The DDoS attack forced Microsoft to turn away hundreds of customers by being off-line for two hours. This hiatus resulted in high financial and productivity losses, not to mention the loss of customer confidence.

■ DOING RISK ASSESSMENTS BY THE NUMBERS

There are many approaches to information security. One approach is to divide risk into two categories: probability that an undesirable event will occur and the consequences if the undesirable event materializes. This approach is similar to methods used to analyze the likelihood of failure for large, one-of-a-kind projects. The data collected by risk assessment team members can assist the firm in placing a value on the assets that need protection and in exposing potential threats and vulnerabilities. This data is then used to create scenarios or risk factor (vulnerability) questionnaires that in-house specialists can evaluate. In-house experts assign numeric values to the likelihood (probability) that the undesirable event will occur and the severity (consequences) if it does materialize.

The combination of these factors provides a relative gauge for the risk factor (probability assessment of the risk posed by the scenario). Analysts can use these elements to develop a risk assessment model

Consequences of Materialization of Undesirable Event		Probability of Occurrence of Undesirable Event				
		Improbable (A)	Remote (B)	Occasional (C)	Probable (D)	Frequent (E)
Risk 1: High	0.90	High 0.91	High 0.93	High 0.95	High 0.97	High 0.99
Risk 2: Significant	0.70	Significant 0.73	Significant 0.79	High 0.85	High 0.91	High 0.97
Risk 3: Moderate	0.50	Moderate 0.55	Significant 0.65	Significant 0.75	High 0.85	High 0.95
Risk 4: Minor	0.30	Minor. 0.37	Moderate 0.51	Significant 0.65	Significant 0.79	High 0.93
Risk 5: Low	0.10	Low 0.19	Minor 0.37	Moderate 0.55	Significant 0.73	High 0.91
		0.10	0.30	0.50	0.70	0.90

Risk Scale
High = Greater than 0.80
Significant = 0.60 to 0.79
Moderate = 0.40 to 0.59
Minor = 0.20 to 0.39
Low = 0.19 or less

Figure 2.3 Numeric risk assessment model for web-based businesses

for the web-based company's information security. Figure 2.3 shows how the risk assessments can be conveniently scored so that management can easily prioritize them.

For some web-based businesses, such as online brokerages, banks, and mortgage lenders, the consequences of even one security incident are very high and can result in extensive legal or regulatory problems, expensive downtime, and recovery and restoration costs. In contrast, even the most sensitive web-based entity may have areas where a successful attack will not cause harm (e.g., duplicate outdated records of low-level information on obsolete operating systems). Therefore, the organization needs to evaluate the value of the asset and consequences of allowing the vulnerability to remain.

The second element to consider is the likelihood or probability of attack. Again, in-house experts use their judgments to reach a consensus about the value of the threat. In some cases, the likelihood of the undesirable event's occurrence is improbable, but its effects can be devastating if it does materialize. In other cases, the web-based company may be constantly attacked but impervious until a small change in the system's configuration makes the web-based business vulnerable. The numeric risk scores are determined using the following formula:

Risk Factor Formula
$(Pf + Pc) - (Pf \times Pc) = R$

Example: Microsoft scenario using numeric scores
0.90 = Microsoft suffers frequent attacks from intruders due to high visibility (Pf)
0.70 = The severity or consequences of the undesirable event materializing are significant due to the large volume of visitors (Pc)

Legend
Pf = probability risk factor = 0.90
Pc = probability consequence factor = 0.70
R = risk factor

Formula
$(Pf + Pc) - (Pf \times Pc) = R$
$(0.90 + 0.70) - (0.90 \times 0.70) = R$
$(1.60) - (0.63) = R$
$0.97 = R$

Risk factor analysis is a simplification of reality. Any real-world system contains controllable and uncontrollable variables, behaviors, and phenomena that cannot be duplicated even by the most detailed model (Morgan and Henrion, 1990). The risk assessment model therefore focuses on the company's own baselines, generating comparisons with the enterprise's requirements, expectations, and previous performance. This allows the comparison of risk factor scores to establish security policies and controls, to assist in the development of security policies, and to assign the responsibilities of developing and implementing proactive mitigation plans.

After the risk assessment team identifies scenarios (or risk factors) that need risk reduction, in-house experts need to determine several remedies or corrective actions for the vulnerability. A corrective action may be as simple as enforcing a current security policy or as complex as purchasing and configuring new hardware and software into the system, establishing new types of security controls, and estimating the costs of those controls.

■ MITIGATING RISKS AND TAKING CORRECTIVE ACTIONS

According to Peter G. Moore (1983), when an immediate problem is recognized, managers can make one of three types of actions: interim, adaptive, or corrective. *Interim action* is a stopgap procedure intended not to interrupt daily operations; such actions allow the organization time to develop a long-term solution. *Adaptive action* occurs when the manager discovers the cause of the problem and realizes either that the cause of the problem cannot be corrected or that the problem solution is not feasible. Adaptive action lets the organization minimize the problem and live with the effects of the dilemma. *Corrective action* attempts to eliminate the problem by removing its cause. This type of action can be used only if the source of the problem is known. It is the best type of action because a problem is not likely to return if its source is removed. Although this solution is the optimum approach, it may not be implemented due to cost or business constraints. Remember that risk mitigation plans and corrective actions are based on the effectiveness of reducing (at minimum cost) the probability or the severity of the undesirable event's occurrence; the ultimate goal is to identify cost-effective actions to mitigate or minimize risk. These actions can include

➤ Putting into action new organizational policies (a relatively low-cost solution)
➤ Implementing new technology (which may be costly and time-consuming)
➤ Putting into operation physical controls, such as creating backups of files and purchasing duplicate hardware

■ CREATING ASSESSMENT REPORTS AND FOLLOWING-UP

Using a qualitative or quantitative risk analysis of information can assist management in reporting risk assessment results. Web-based companies that use this approach will quickly discover that this type of risk assessment facilitates communication and can reduce the cycle time of decision making by making it possible to

➤ Know the status of vulnerabilities on a continuing basis
➤ Identify new threats in a timely manner
➤ Pinpoint area-specific deterioration
➤ Evaluate the effectiveness of risk minimization plans

A draft of the risk assessment report is written by the assessment team (which is often disbanded soon after completion of this task). The draft risk assessment report should first list high-risk scenarios (or risk factors), and then provide recommendations for corrective actions. Risk mitigation plan recommendations may include new or strengthened controls, new ways to identify threats or vulnerabilities, resource requirements, assignments of trained personnel for each corrective action, and schedules of completion dates. Executive management can approve the plan and assign management to monitor the status of recommendations until all of the recommendations are completed.

Remember that corrective actions and risk mitigation plans need to be continually updated due to the constantly changing environment of the web-based business. For example, expensive corrective actions can become obsolete overnight due to

➤ New knowledge about a threat that is available now but was not available earlier. For example, new e-mail viruses are available today that did not exist six months ago.

➤ The risk assessment team or managers of the risk management focal point did not know about a threat or vulnerability or were unaware of the importance of this threat or vulnerability. For example, Microsoft was aware of the vulnerability that brought down its web site but did not think it was important enough to fix.

➤ In earlier times, the knowledge about this threat or vulnerability was not considered necessary or important. For example, domain name servers (DNSs) have existed almost as long as the Internet, but until recently they were never used for attacking web sites.

■ DETERMINING THE FREQUENCY OF YOUR ASSESSMENTS

Security requirements usually change over time. Risks to information and to its value, as well as the probability, frequency, and severity of possible attacks also change. Therefore, managers need to make periodic risk assessments using the GAO risk management model in Figure 1.3 or a similar risk management model. These periodic assessments should identify and measure new or emerging risks from new risk management decisions. Many enterprises set a predetermined time to perform a risk assessment. For example, many government agencies perform information security risk assessments every three years. According to the *Generally Accepted System Security Principles* (Fall 1999), events that could trigger the need for risk assessment can stem from a significant change

- ➤ To the information system. Considerable changes in hardware or software should trigger a new risk assessment.
- ➤ In the information or its value. Some information quickly becomes outdated and loses it value. Other information may become more valuable and need additional protection.
- ➤ In the technology. Improvements in hacker technology may require the purchase of new hardware or software.
- ➤ To the threats or vulnerabilities. Unwanted intruders may discover new ways to attack old systems.
- ➤ To the available safeguards. Organizational changes may make old safeguards obsolete and require new safeguards.
- ➤ In the user profiles. Rapid growth, wireless communications, and telecommuting may require the organization to reassess ways to organize user access to the network and computers.
- ➤ In the potential loss of the system. Expansion of the web-based business may create weaknesses in certain areas.
- ➤ To the organization or enterprise. A security breach should automatically trigger a risk assessment of the organization.

■ REFERENCES

General Accounting Office (GAO). 1999. GAO-AMID-00-33 Information security risk assessment: Practices of leading organizations, a supplement to GAO's May 1998 executive guide on information security management. Washington, D.C.: General Accounting Office, November. Available at [www.gao.gov/special.pubs/ai00033.pdf]. 29 November 2001.

Marchany, Randy. 2000. *The Top 10 Internet Security Vulnerabilities — a Primer.* Presentation, SANS Resources — how to eliminate the ten most critical Internet security threats. December. Available at [http://www.sans.org/topten.htm]. 29 November 2001.

Moore, Peter G. 1983. *The Business of Risk.* Cambridge, England: Cambridge University Press.

Morgan, Grange M., and Max Henrion. 1990. *Uncertainty: A Guide to Dealing with Uncertainty in Quantitative Risk and Policy Analysis.* Cambridge, England: Cambridge University Press.

National Institute of Standards and Technology. 2001. Internet security policy: A technical guide (draft). Available at [http://csrc.nist.gov/isptg/]. 29 November 2001.

Sindell, Kathleen. 1996. *The Handbook of Real Estate Lending.* Chicago: Irwin Professional Publishing.

Wadlow, Thomas A. 2000. *The Process of Network Security: Designing and Managing a Safe Network.* Reading, Mass.: Addison-Wesley.

Weins, Richard. 2000. Vulnerability assessment survey. *Security Focus.* 29 September. Available at [http://www.securityfocus.com/infocus/1263]. 29 November 2001.

Chapter 3

Determining the Impact of Security on Your Bottom Line

In this chapter

- ➤ How Much Security Is Too Much?
- ➤ How Much Risk Can You Afford to Take?
- ➤ Diagramming the Organization to Spot Vulnerabilities
- ➤ The Costs and Benefits of Performing Security Audits

This chapter focuses on how the interruption of a web-based business can affect the organization's profitability, productivity, and perceived reliability. You will discover the hidden costs of security breaches and gain an understanding of the acceptable downtime for an Internet-based business. Included are suggestions about how to allocate a first-year security budget. You will see how managers must balance security threats and exposures, as well as why this type of decision-making is so difficult. You will learn that information security losses are divided into two categories, quantifiable and nonquantifiable. This chapter shows how diagramming your Internet-based business can assist you in spotting business and security risks. It covers what you can expect in a security audit and the types of support, services and products managers can require from their IT departments or outside consultants. A discussion of the monetary benefits of performing an in-house security audit concludes this chapter.

■ HOW MUCH SECURITY IS TOO MUCH?

Economic disruption of a web site can vary. Web-based businesses that rely on monetary online transactions are more vulnerable to potential losses than are other types of Internet-based enterprises. However, security incidents can cause both types of organizations to suffer losses from lost transactions and from reduced customer confidence. Financial losses resulting from security break-ins are expensive in terms of both hard costs and public relations. The Yankee Group, an Internet research organization located in Boston, Massachusetts, estimates the price of cyber-crime by placing a value on productivity losses and the cost of dealing with security breaches, plus costs for security upgrades, consulting fees, and losses in marketing capitalization caused by negative impacts on stock prices.

Although the executive management and the board of directors may recognize the danger of security break-ins, funding for information security may not be sufficient. Worldwide research of 250 major companies by Datamonitor, an Internet research firm (datamonitor.com) located in New York City, indicates that as more businesses rely on the Internet, more fraud and security breaches occur. The report, "E-Security: Removing the Roadblock to E-Business," estimates the worldwide cost of security breaches at $15 billion. However, investment in security is about half this amount.

A study by IDC (www.idc.com) supports Datamonitor's conclusions. IDC, a division of IDG (International Data Group) is an Internet and technology research firm located in Framingham, Massachusetts, predicts that between 1999 and 2003, worldwide e-commerce spending will be $1.6 trillion with a compound annual growth rate of 88 percent. Additionally, U.S. Internet advertising revenue will reach $10.8 billion in 2003 according to *U.S. Internet Advertising Forecast* (September 1999). All industry participants recognize that trust is the enabler of e-commerce. According to IDC, however, the worldwide Internet security market, including software and firewall appliances, is forecast to represent less than one percent of the value of e-commerce business transactions in 2003.

The advantages of web-based business often stem from low-cost distribution channels and a lack of overhead. Many web-based businesses benefit from an extra bonus—they get paid before they have to pay vendors and shippers. However, some costs do offset these advantages. Figure 3.1 shows how management must balance the cost of security with threats and security levels in an uncertain environment.

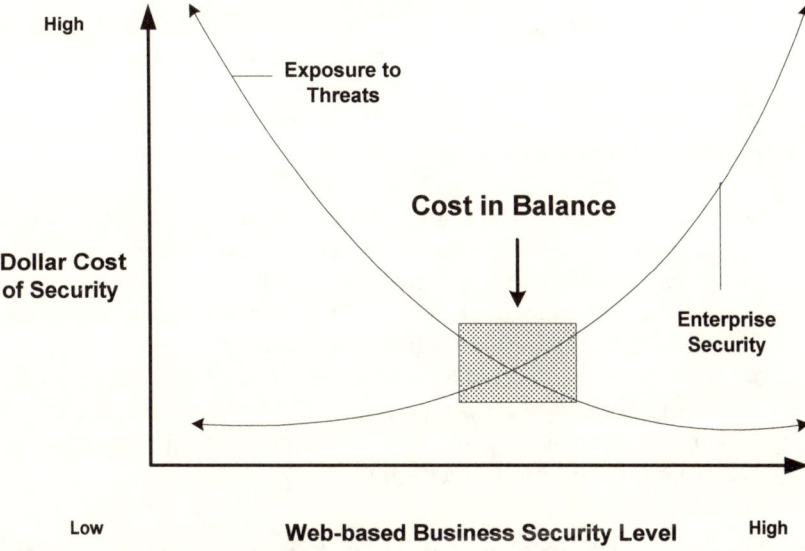

Figure 3.1 Management balances exposures to risks and controls investments in security in an unpredictable environment

For example, if the threat is low or the information asset has little value and the organization is paying top dollar for protection, then the enterprise is paying too much for security. On the other hand, if the threat to the enterprise is high and the level of security is low, then the organization is paying too little and is vulnerable to attacks. The shaded area in Figure 3.1 shows management's goal of balancing security investment costs and risks.

Figure 3.1 indicates that managers should balance the cost of security by matching the value of the asset and the likelihood of the threat. In other words, the cost of securing the information should not be greater than the value of the information itself. This type of cost-benefit analysis is often difficult because some losses are quantifiable and others are nonquantifiable.

Overall, Figure 3.1 highlights the importance of clearly defining the web-based business's security policy. Information security risks are frequently defined as the probability and consequences of an undesirable event occurring. Threats are defined as likely sources of security troubles. Threats include human and natural events (user errors, fire, flood, etc.) that cause harm to the system. Enlightened managers know that to keep the operations running, they must be aware of the different types of attacks their online businesses can experience. Risk management is balancing the cost of protecting an enterprise versus the cost of exposure to security threats. Therefore, it is important for the Internet-based business to know (if possible)

➤ How much will it cost an intruder to attack us? Highly visible web sites, like the Department of Defense (defenselink.mil/pubs/dod101/) receive thousands of both unskilled and sophisticated attacks each day. Therefore, the Department of Defense makes a high investment in security.

➤ How much will it cost to counter an attack? Knowing the value of the asset you are protecting and the cost of the security to protect that asset can assist in the creation of cost-effective risk management mitigation plans.

➤ Understanding the Relationship of Security Costs and Reliability

According to Henry Baltazar (2001), a writer for *eWeek,* the *five 9s* goal of information security is expensive but necessary for most web-based businesses. For example, a 99 (two 9s) percent guarantee allows for a couple of days of downtime per year, a guarantee of uptime of 99 percent and one or two days of lost productivity per year; this level may be acceptable for large enterprises with low-priority static pages primarily used by the company. For example, MCI World Com (mci.worldcom.com) has over 10,000 web pages used by employees. It is likely that MCI has security policies that include contingency detailing what employees should do during this downtime.

The next security level could be considered as three 9s. This level ensures an uptime of 99.9 percent of the time and reduces downtime to several hours per year; this means that disaster recovery services are ready to kick in at a moment's notice. Disaster recovery services can assist managers in hardening mission-critical networks for companies of all sizes by providing standby servers to revive web-based businesses quickly. Costs can vary from several thousand dollars to more than $1 million per year, depending on the amount of data that must be recovered. Frequently, recovery services are subcontracted tape-backup and restoration arrangements. The recovery service monitors all backup activities and stores redundant backup copies at geographically scattered locations.

For web-based businesses, the goal is 99.999 (five 9s) percent because the business is often the technology. High-volume web sites must guarantee 99.999 percent reliability, called the *five 9s goal*. Frequently, web-based businesses consider the price of security to be part of the cost of doing business in cyberspace. Numerous industry analysts agree that web-based businesses will pay for information security either now or later, and that it is better to pay for it before an incident causes a public relations crisis.

➤ Suggestions for Allocating the Security Budget

The five 9s goal may be one reason that organizations do not report security breaches to law enforcement. Both managers and IT professionals fear negative publicity and rival companies' exploitation of security incidents for a competitive advantage. Additionally, some Internet-based businesses (especially cash-strapped start-ups) do not adequately fund information security budgets because security measures are expensive and the return on the investment is not clear until it is too late. Patrick McBride, a writer for *Computerworld* (November 2000), suggests that Internet-based companies of all sizes should divide each dollar of their first-year security budgets as follows:

➤ Policy $0.15 (fifteen cents): The web-based enterprise's security policy provides leadership, consensus, and guidance. Management's clear statement of the organization's security policy assists in interdepartmental communication and lets employees know what is important.

➤ Awareness $0.40 (forty cents): Many organizations suffer security breaches due to social engineering. Education and support can stop employees from posting passwords in work areas and from unwittingly providing field manuals to unauthorized users. Additionally, education can help the organization stay informed about new internal and external threats.

➤ Risk assessment $0.10 (ten cents): Risk assessments show which assets the organization considers valuable and point out which are vulnerable and need protection. Ongoing risk assessments encompass all aspects of the system (see Chapter 2 for more information).

➤ Technology $0.20 (twenty cents): Technology cannot solve all of the enterprise's problems but it can provide many valuable tools such as firewalls, vulnerability scans, intrusion detection systems, and access controls. However, these useful tools, if misconfigured, can cause more problems than they solve. Additionally, new security software may have flaws that make the web-based business more vulnerable than before the addition of the security software.

➤ Process $0.15 (fifteen cents): Information security is an ongoing process that combines management and technical expertise. As the web-based business adds more products, features, and utilities, new security processes are added or modified and old processes are deleted. Consequently, information security involves each individual within the organization.

■ HOW MUCH RISK CAN YOU AFFORD TO TAKE?

Each web-based business has a different risk tolerance level. If the enterprise wants to open its doors to affiliates and partners, the Internet-based enterprise is creating a passageway into another IT environment that is owned and controlled by another entity. However, the benefits of these types of collaborations are hard to ignore. For instance, I provided additional customer value at one of my web sites, kathleensindell.com, by including direct links to other organizations. The first is to Pico (pico.com), which assists users in searching my web site. The second is InvestorWords (investorwords.com), a very large financial and investor glossary. The third is to Amazon.com (amazon.com), an online bookstore. Finally, my web site users can access Zacks (zacks.com) for free online company reports, which are helpful to investors.

Defining what is tolerable risk can vary from industry to industry. Writer Gregory Dalton (August 1998) quotes a 1998 Ernst & Young Survey as stating that a three percent loss from online credit card fraud might be tolerable. However, in the chemical industry the same loss is not acceptable and may be considered a disaster. Dalton goes on to quote the following from the 1998 Information Week/Price Waterhouse Coopers Global Information Security Survey completed by 1,600 IT and security professionals:

➤ Approximately 59 percent of all web sites selling products report at least one or more security breaches in the past year, compared to 52 percent of web sites that are not used for monetary transactions.

➤ Roughly 22 percent of web sites conducting Internet sales experienced information losses, compared to 13 percent of web sites not selling products or services.

➤ About 12 percent of the survey's respondents conducting Internet sales reported the theft of data or trade secrets, compared to 4 percent of online enterprises not selling products or services.

➤ Many of those surveyed, about 49 percent, conceded that they did not know whether intruders stole high-value information without their knowledge, and only 28 percent are certain they did not suffer any monetary losses resulting from undetected security breaches.

➤ Verifying Information Security Quantifiable Losses

The greater the firm's dependence on information systems, the greater the potential for monetary loss if any part of the network becomes unavailable for business operations. Assessing monetary losses is difficult because the organization often finds it hard to reach a consensus on the value of the information residing in one section of the system and the value of that business process to the web-based business. As the Internet-based enterprise gains more knowledge about and experience with the negative impact of security failures, a knowledge database can be developed to assess the value of business processes and information; this database allows the organization to use cost-benefit analysis to support increases in the information security budget.

According to the *Sixth Black Box Network Industry Survey* (1998) of 1,220 IT professionals, completed in the United Kingdom, network crashes are more frequent than expected. One in four organizations suffers a major network crash at least once a month. In one out of five cases, downtime is one-half day; and for one in ten cases, downtime is a day or more. The survey goes on to state that downtime is greater for larger enterprises. Approximately 28 percent of large organizations take one-half working day to become operational again after a crash. About 18 percent of medium-sized organizations and 20 percent of small enterprises need one-half day to resume operations. Around 10 percent of the organizations take over one day to recover. The survey authors come to the startling conclusion that on average, organizations experience six major network crashes per year, leading to three hours of downtime. Assuming that a third of the 25 million people who work in the United Kingdom are affected, *network crashes are the cause of 20 million man-days of lost productivity each year.*

The recent *Ernst & Young Information Survey 2001* indicates that the situation is improving. The survey uses a representative sampling of 273 professionals (chief information officers, information technology directors, and business managers) in Europe. Results indicate that respondents from the United Kingdom continue to report more problems with network crashes than do other international respondents. About three out of every four U.K. companies surveyed experienced a business systems failure in the past 12 months. According to the U.K. respondents, most incidents are results of software and hardware troubles; 31 percent are attributed to a third party.

➤ Looking into Information Security Nonquantifiable Losses

According to author Tim Braithwiate (2001), several nonquantifiable losses increase the difficulty of assessing monetary losses resulting from security breaches.

➤ Loss of business opportunities: Companies with reputations for poor security lose untold business opportunities both immediately and in the future. Future business opportunities may include partnerships, affiliations, mergers with like companies, and other opportunities that have yet to be invented (products or services that are available in cyberspace but not in the real world).

➤ Loss of customer confidence: If the company has a reputation for poor security, customers may create false identities to protect their privacy, a practice that over time can distort data about customer needs and desires. Such inaccurate data can cause expensive customer relationship programs to miss their marks and aim marketing campaigns at imaginary customers.

➤ Loss of reputation or brand equity: When high-profile web sites have security breaches, web-based enterprises suffer humiliation and damage to their reputations. The immediate and long-term costs of the loss of reputation and its effects on brand equity are impossible to calculate. For example, Figure 3.2 shows how hackers distorted the home page of the U.S. Department of Justice in 1996. Photos of the vandalized Department of Justice web site were flashed around the world. More than five years after the event, U.S. citizens still remember the security break-in.

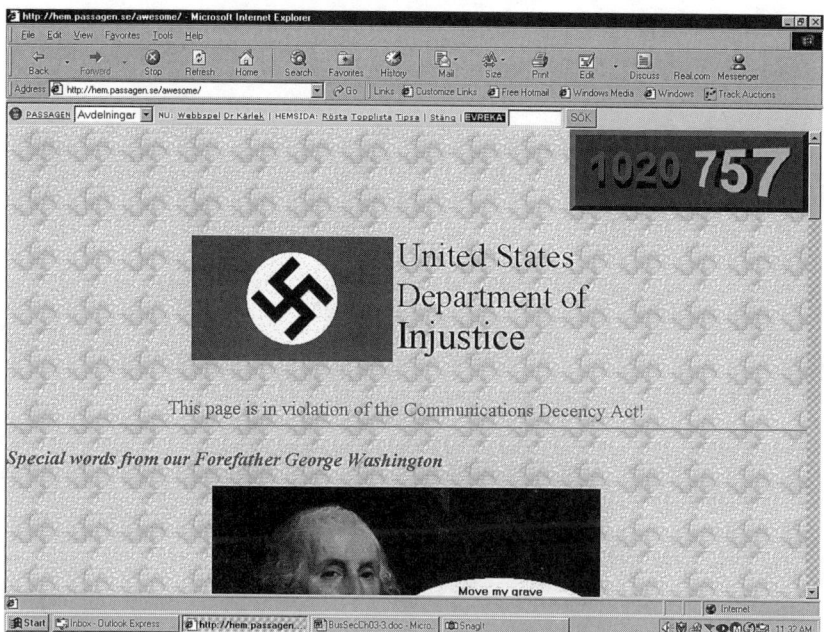

Figure 3.2 The 1996 defacing of the Department of Justice web site has not been forgotten

■ DIAGRAMMING THE ORGANIZATION TO SPOT VULNERABILITIES

Information security is a major concern of web-based businesses. In the past, organizations had paper-based transactions. Internet-based businesses have electronic transactions, and often the information system is the business. Technology makes business operations less costly but more complex due to the interconnectivity between different types of computer platforms, environments, and networks. This complexity makes security information decision-making far from trivial. Consequently, the task of understanding and controlling the security of the Internet-based business can seem overwhelming if it is not visually divided into manageable sections. Figure 3.3 shows the diagram of an order-taking web-based business.

Many managers have never seen a diagram of their web-based business, often because of communication difficulties and the rapid in-

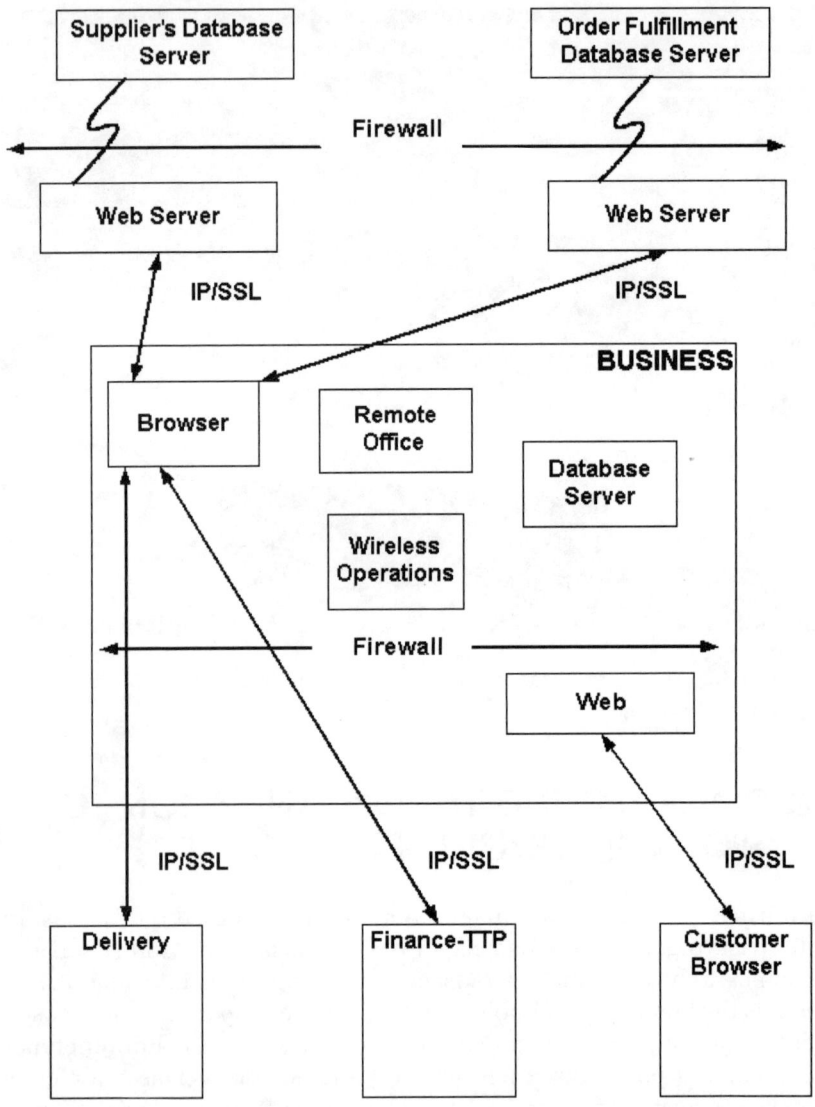

Figure 3.3 Example of the architecture for the order- taking web-based business model
Note: TTP = Trusted third party (finance).

creases of features, hardware, and software in web-based business. After all, the IT department's first priority is to keep business systems running 24-7 (24 hours a day, 7 days a week), not to draw pretty pictures of how everything works together. Accordingly, it is difficult for the executive team to imagine how all the technological pieces of the organization fit together. This difficulty can be exacerbated if a trusted third party (TTP) is used for credit card transactions, or related support of the web-based enterprise's physical facilities are scattered throughout the United States or the world.

The diagram of the web-based business in Figure 3.3 shows the relationship between security and business risks; it also points out the impracticality of solving security issues on a piecemeal basis. For that reason, information security should be part of the organization's strategic plan and should be incorporated into the firm's security policy. Figure 3.3 indicates the placement of IP (Internet Protocol), SSLs, and firewalls for special security tools. *SSLs* are security sockets layers, developed in 1994 by Netscape; they encrypt and secure data for transmission over the Internet. Debate still continues today over the best type of an encryption methodology. Therefore, SSL is not the only choice for web-based businesses. A *firewall* is a system or group of systems that enforce an access control policy between two networks. Figure 3.3 shows how the IP/SSL is placed between web browsers and the enterprise's web servers to prevent unwanted intruders from eavesdropping and from intercepting and distorting data traveling in both directions. For example, competitors could change pricing before the consumer receives that information, or identity thieves could intercept credit card information.

The hypothetical order-taking company shown in Figure 3.3 is similar to 1-800-Flowers (1800flowers.com) and netGrocer (netgrocer.com). Many order-taking firms use a TTP for processing the payment of transactions. A company can use a TTP for up to five types of transactions:

1. New order business: A single database transaction, often using a shopping cart, provides a fast response to the online customer and supplies the business with the number of completed new orders.
2. Payment of the business transaction: This transaction updates the customer's balance (credit verification and consumer authentication) and reflects payment. The order is sent to the

supplier's database server, and the order fulfillment database server generates statistics for the business. At this point, credit terms may be offered to certain customers (multiple billing alternatives, cash-on-delivery options and so on).

3. Order status of the business transaction: Queries the customer's last order on the order fulfillment database and fills the current order. After the order is shipped, the customer's credit card is charged, and the TTP for the business transaction credits the web-based business to complete the monetary transaction.

4. Delivery of the business transaction: A database is accessed and executes the delivery of the business transaction for order fulfillment.

5. Stock level of the business transaction: For reporting purposes, another business database determines the number of recently sold items, noting stock levels below a specified threshold.

■ THE COSTS AND BENEFITS OF PERFORMING SECURITY AUDITS

Many progressive managers seek out the vulnerabilities of their networks before unwanted intruders take advantage of unknown weaknesses. These managers are keenly aware of the losses that can occur and believe that it is common sense to prevent attacks before they happen. Several surveys indicate that some IT professionals have an idealistic attitude towards the information security of their web-based businesses. They are aware of vulnerabilities but do not feel pressured into taking immediate action. For example, IT professionals at Microsoft were aware of network vulnerability but continued to delay the upgrade. This oversight was the source of the successful DDoS attack Microsoft suffered in 2001. An impartial audit takes away many of the misconceptions about the security level of the enterprise. In some instances, IT professionals find their beliefs validated; in other cases, IT managers are forced to face some disturbing realizations. Therefore, a good audit must be well managed, so that if it is painful, it will not cause IT professionals and other employees to hide defects in the future.

According to Laura Sioma in an article written for the SANS Institute (2000), a good audit analyzes the three Es: *efficiency,* the smooth performance of the system; *effectiveness,* the ability of the system to meet business requirements; and *economy,* the system's ability to use resources at the most favorable level. Generally, a security audit is divided into four phases.

➤ Planning: Management should determine the focus and scope of the audit. Different types of web-based businesses require different types of audits. Additionally, the audit program is distributed to the organization.

➤ Analysis: Employees are interviewed, general background information is gathered, and tests are performed. A *penetration audit* is one in which the auditor actually attacks the web-based business. A *configuration analysis* examines the network from inside using a detailed checklist. If the auditor discovers too many discrepancies, then the network has failed.

➤ Reporting results: Audit results and recommendations are communicated in a written audit report. Don't be surprised if vulnerabilities are described to business and IT managers in a shocking manner contrived to achieve maximum effect. A management response memo is developed, detailing a formal action plan to address each audit recommendation. Explanations of why certain recommendations will not be pursued are included.

➤ Following-up: Follow-up by the auditors and management provides verification that the recommendations have been implemented. Of the four steps, this one is the most important.

➤ Selecting the Right Auditors for the Right Web-Based Business

An information security audit provides a metric the web-based business can use in the future. If performed by an outside organization, the audit can avoid the pitfalls caused by internal politics, scheduling problems, and limitations of resources; it can also access the knowledge of individuals in the IT department and internal system users, affiliates, and partners who are not usually interviewed. Auditors use a formal (and repeatable) methodology. Good auditors have studied hundreds of networks and can offer advice, alternatives, and solutions that no one in the organization may have considered. For example, by comparing the byte size of images, one security auditor discovered that an employee was disclosing company secrets. With further investigation, the security auditor learned that when he placed a piece of colored acetate over the company's home page logo, proprietary data was readable.

There are three types of auditors. The first group is composed of independent auditors who come from a variety of backgrounds. These individuals may be full-time employees who are moonlighting, experienced independent consultants, or covert hackers using a type of social engineering to get inside your web-based business. The second type of auditor is an individual from a security firm that is a private business specializing in the analysis of information systems. Again, the expertise of these individuals is difficult to quantify. For example, the individual with 40 years of security experience with whom you signed the contract may not be the individual who evaluates your system. The third type of auditor comes from a special division of one of the so-called big six audit houses. These large auditing firms now include special divisions for information security audits.

According to Thomas Wadlow (2000), typical areas of the network that are audited include

➤ Network design: If the network was poorly designed or in a piecemeal fashion, it may be vulnerable to a security breach.

➤ Network implementation: Integrating new applications may have opened new security holes.

➤ Architecture of the host system: The vulnerabilities in the architecture of the host system could leave your web-based business open to attack.

➤ Physical security: Facilities, hardware, and software issues can also affect a web-based business's vulnerability. For example, hardware and software could be damaged by human error, sabotaged by disgruntled employees, or destroyed by natural disasters (e.g., fire, rain).

➤ Disaster recovery: Disaster recovery may be an in-house plan or subcontracted; it often includes creating backup files and tapes that are stored at another location.

➤ Process and procedures: Tests the firm's ability to match the current security policy (if one is in effect) to actual business practices. Additionally, auditors look for security vulnerabilities in business processes.

➤ Response time for problem resolution: The firm's security policy must clearly state the desired response time for particular problems. Auditors compare desired times to actual response times.

➤ Emergency response: Emergency response times are measured. Auditors note the lack of an emergency response plan or an outdated emergency response plan.

➤ Off-hours response: Off-hours response times are measured. Sometimes when IT professionals are not aware of a computer incident that occurs on a Friday, the problem is not remedied until Monday.

➤ Focusing the Audit and Getting It Right

Before entering into an agreement for a security audit, it is important that both parties agree on the scope of the audit and on what the deliverables are. Additionally, can the project be realistically completed within the current budget? The following is a generic list of areas that auditors should examine and the kinds of metrics you may want to use for measuring the effectiveness of the organization's information security:

➤ What are the organization's most critical security exposures and how should they be addressed?

➤ Where should the organization place the firewall system in relation to the Internet and the web-based business system, the network, business partners, and telecommuting employees?

➤ What are the vulnerabilities of the internal business infrastructure (DNS servers, file servers, mail servers)?

➤ Do the organization's business processes and procedures effectively support the enterprise's security policy?

➤ Can private data be accessed by someone on the Internet?

➤ Can somebody break into the web-based business's system from the Internet? Can unauthorized employees break into the system from inside the organization?

➤ What key technologies should play a role in the system architecture?

➤ Getting Your Money's Worth

Lisa Vass of *PC Week* (August 2000) notes that companies usually pay between $30,000 and $75,000 for help in developing a security policy. A network security audit (with on-site interviews and examination of the web server) can range from $50,000 to $150,000. For security architecture development, you get the first two items as well as recommendations on addressing existing problems for $50,000 to $200,000. Vass concludes by stating that managed security (checking the firewalls and monitoring intrusion detection) is generally $2,000 to $15,000 per month. According to Benjamin Haidri (February 2001), security consultants who perform penetration tests of the network and discuss network details thoroughly with individuals inside the company charge between $100,000 to $250,000 for one security audit. Haidri therefore suggests that web-based enterprises, especially small start-ups, conduct their own risk assessments before calling a consultant or security firm. First, in-house personnel should test everything that can be tested. Next, determine vulnerabilities and document weaknesses. Each problem should be fixed; after the problems have been remedied, in-house personnel should test again.

■ REFERENCES

Baltazar, Henry. 2001. Adding 9s to the uptime can add up. *eWeek,* 5 March. Available at [http://www.eweek.com]. 29 November 2001.

Braithwaite, Timothy. 2001. Executives need to know. *FMN Online: Business Process Improvement,* 7 January. Available at [http://www. fmnonline.com]. 29 November 2001.

Clyde, Rob. 2001. Enterprise security: Built on sound policies. *Axent,* 3 March. Available at [http://axent.se.com.com]. 3 March 2001. No longer available online due to merger with Symantec.

Dalton, Gregory. 1998. Trends: Acceptable risks. *Information Week,* 31 August. Available at [http://ask.elibrary.com]. 29 November 2001.

Datamonitor. 2000. E-security removing the roadblock to e-business. *Datamonitor,* November. Available at [http://www.Datamonitor.com].

Ernst & Young. 2001. Information security survey 2001. *Ernst & Young,* January. Available at [http://www.ey.com]. 6 March 2001. Currently not available online.

Ernst & Young. 1999. Second annual global information security survey. *Ernst & Young.* Available at [http://www.ey.com]. 6 March 2001.

Haidri, Benjamin. 2001. Self-assess, then get advice. *eWeek,* 25 February. Available at [http://www.eweek.com]. 29 November 2001.

IDC. 1999. The daily graphic. A slide taken from the U.S. Internet Advertising Forecast, 1999–2003 Report , *IDC #20159,* September. Available at [http://www.idc.com]. 7 March 2001.

ITC Forecaster. 2000. Is security getting its fair share? *ITC Forecaster,* 29 February. Available at [http://www.idc.com/itforecaster/ itfarchive.htm]. 29 November 2001.

Jutla, Dawn, Ma Shaohua, Peter Bodorik, and Yie Wang. 1999. WebTP: A benchmark for web-based order management systems. Proceedings of the 32nd Hawaii International Conference on Systems Sciences.

Koerner, Brendan. 2000. Finally, and arrest. *U.S. News and World Report,* 1 May. Available at [http://nl4.newsbank.com]. 29 November 2001.

McBride, Patrick. 2000. How to spend a dollar on security. *Computerworld,* 9 November. Available at [http://www.computerworld.com]. 29 November 2001.

Sioma, Laura. 2000. A generalized application security audit program for any computing platform with comments. *SANS Institute,* September. Available at [http://www.sans.org]. 29 November 2001.

Telecom Fraud Review. 1998. Network crashes cause 20 million days lost productivity every year. *Telecom Fraud Review,* August.

Vaas, Lisa. 2000. Security checkup. *eWeek,* 13 August. Available at [http://techupdate.zdnet.com]. 29 November 2001.

Wadlow, Thomas A. 2000. *The Process of Network Security: Designing and Managing a Safe Network.* Reading, Mass.: Addison-Wesley.

Chapter *4*

Your Online Business and Intrusion Detection

In this chapter

- ➤ Protecting Your Systems from Intruders
- ➤ Safeguarding Data Transmitted on the Internet
- ➤ Managing and Ensuring the Safety of Your Web Portals
- ➤ Understanding Network Intrusion Detection Systems
- ➤ Selecting the Network Intrusion Detection Software That Is Best for You
- ➤ Controls That Make Line Management Accountable for Intruders
- ➤ Online Business Intrusion Checklist

Transmitting data on the Internet can be dangerous to the well-being of your online business. In this chapter you will discover how access controls and intruder detection can assist you in protecting your web-based business. You will gain an understanding of the different types of access controls that are available and how to use technological solutions to spot intruders who are trying to hide their real identities. This chapter can assist you in establishing how to manage the security of your extranet and intranet web portals. You will learn the basics of network intrusion detection systems and discover how to select the intrusion detection solution that works best for your web-based business. The chapter concludes with a discussion of the limitations of intrusion detection systems and of the importance of line management for filling in the gap.

■ PROTECTING YOUR SYSTEMS FROM INTRUDERS

Successful web-based businesses are harnessing the Internet's power to integrate and accelerate business interactions. The new business processes used by these companies are quickly replacing well-known processes and infrastructures with networks that enable rapid, secure transactions and communication. Consequently, web-based businesses need the ability to share sensitive resources (forecasting systems, sales tools, pricing models, ordering histories and systems, customer feedback, inventory records, etc.) with partners, suppliers, distributors, customers, and service providers in order to achieve the greatest gains in productivity and effectiveness. These developments create heightened security and information management concerns. The challenge is to allow access to restricted back-office operations and proprietary information, applications, and sources without limiting the value of the Internet by creating security holes or technological bottlenecks.

One way to resolve this dilemma is to *trust but verify.* For web-based businesses this solution requires implementing access controls and intrusion detection systems. Access controls use two approaches. The first approach is to require user authentication (i.e., identifying the individual who is requesting access to your data); the second approach is to require validation of the claimed identity. *Intrusion detection* is often defined as the process of identifying an intrusion incident that was or is being attempted. Intrusion detection systems improve visibility into the inner workings of the network to assist management in identifying security issues. Therefore their effect is different from that of firewalls, which usually prevent all traffic from entering certain areas of the network.

■ SAFEGUARDING DATA TRANSMITTED ON THE INTERNET

The protection of your enterprise's information from unwanted intruders can be divided into two areas. The first area involves information that is transmitted on the Internet to the web-based business; the second area involves enterprise information that is already stored. The following sections discuss the vulnerabilities of the Internet and how you can protect information that is transmitted on the World Wide Web.

➤ Access Management Based on Domain Name

Web servers can also restrict access by using the browser's domain name to determine whether to accept the connection. Access control based on domain names is similar to admission control based on IP address, but the server accepts or denies a connection based on the domain name (instead of the IP address). Also, the server can be fooled by DNS (domain name system) spoofing, in which the server is tricked into thinking a trusted domain name belongs to an alien IP address. Consider the following hypothetical example: A discount computer peripheral reseller called XYZ Company generates the majority of its sales leads online (xyz.com) and subcontracts the maintenance of its web server. The web server host company installs security patches and enforces the use of passwords for access to the system. One day the web site is vandalized with cyber-graffiti mocking XYZ Company. After several hours of testing, the host company discovers that customers are being redirected to the web site of an attacker organization. What happened? The attackers corrupted the DNS entry at XYZ's authoritative DNS server.

This type of attack bypassed XYZ's corporate firewalls and its intrusion detection system, again proving that no single approach is a "silver bullet" to safeguarding your enterprise. Figure 4.1 shows how double reverse lookup can be one solution to this problem. Normally, to verify host names and IP addresses, the web server looks up the IP address using the returned host's name. If the web server looks up the IP address using the returned host's name, then the user is granted access. The double reverse lookup approach adds one more checkpoint. If the IP address returned by the DNS server does not match the IP address, then the connection is dropped. This type of activity may indicate that an attacker organization was trying to hide its true identity. One limitation of this approach is that double DNS lookups can cause problems with e-mail systems of legitimate users. Some e-mail servers are not programmed to respond to the reverse lookup.

Double reverse lookup can reduce troublesome requests and provide more in-depth security. Additionally, the technique is inexpensive and easy to deploy, although it is not foolproof. For example if the precaution does fail, intruders still have to contend with gaining access by using a user name and password.

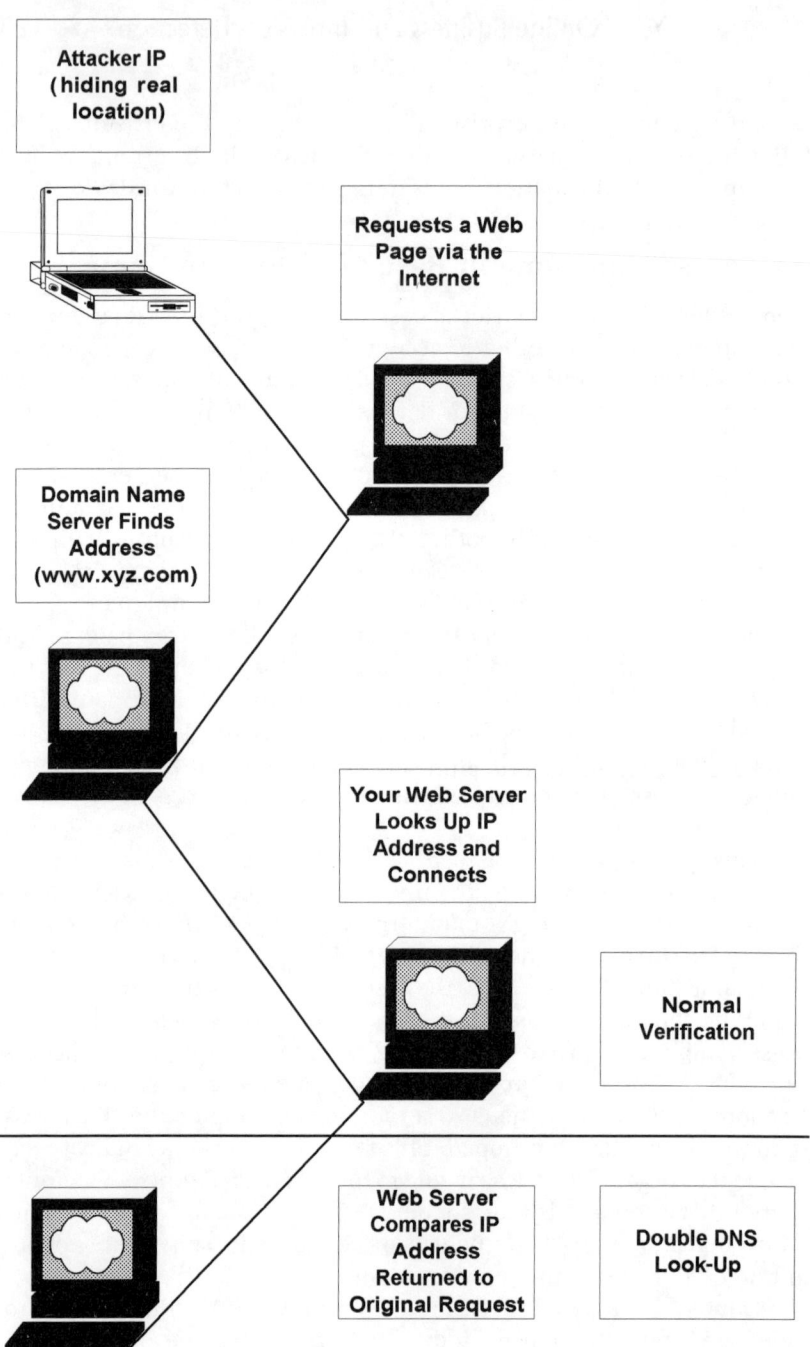

Figure 4.1   Double DNS lookups can assist you in avoiding DNS spoofing

➤ Entry Control Based on User Name and Password

Anup K. Ghosh (1998) notes that historically, passwords have been the frontline defense for protecting information systems and networks. The web site administrator creates a database and access control list (ACL) of legitimate users. Each user is assigned a user ID and password for restricted access to certain parts of the web site. The system refers to the ACL file whenever a client requests a document that is restricted. Web servers provide an option for a centralized or a distributed access control file.

Centralized access control lists include all the directories, databases, and files that require access control. Whenever the user requests access to a restricted web page, he or she must enter the correct combination of user ID and password. These two items are compared to those on the centralized ACL list. If the information matches, the web page is then delivered to the user's browser.

Distributed access control lists are dispersed across the resources that need protection. This approach supports remote users who do not have access to the web server configuration file; for example, sales personnel can use this feature to create their own web pages for specific clients. Each time access to a protected resource is requested, the distributed ACL file is reread and reevaluated. For example, this feature allows sales personnel to make and implement immediate changes. The new files are often partitioned and stored in areas of the network that are separated from normal business operations, reducing the likelihood of creating security vulnerabilities.

Of the two types of ACLs, the distributed approach is more costly and less error-free. After all, it is more difficult to maintain the security of 10 ACL lists, for example, than that of one list. Additionally, the web pages created for partners and customers may be deleted inadvertently or moved by local web site maintenance personnel.

Restrictions based on user ID and passwords can restrict access to intruders, but they have several limitations that create security concerns. For example, in September 1998 the General Accounting Office reported in testimony before the Committee on Governmental Affairs that 23 of the 24 federal agencies had serious access control weaknesses. Insufficient access controls ranged from physical protections, such as gates and guards, to restrictions on access from remote locations and software controls. The needed software controls included authentication and limits on file and other resource usage. In general, the most common types of access control weaknesses include

➤ Easily broken passwords: Individuals often use their birth-days, social security numbers, middle names, and pet names as passwords. Most web servers (unlike UNIX servers) do not disconnect after a certain number of attempts. Intruders therefore can guess repeatedly until they are successful.

➤ Peeking and stealing passwords: Many employees leave their passwords on sticky notes around their computers or in their desks, making it easy for fellow employees to gain access to parts of the network they are not authorized to use.

➤ Social engineering: Some times employees are willing to help individuals who are posing as consultants or contractors by unwittingly providing them with passwords to restricted data.

➤ Password sniffing: Password-sniffing programs are often used by hackers to break into systems. This type of technology is considered breaking-in using brutal force, so to speak. The sniffer program keeps trying password after password until it finds the password that cracks the system.

➤ Not frequently changing the password: Disgruntled employees or former contractors may use old passwords to vandalize the system.

➤ Not changing a password after a remote log-on: Passwords are vulnerable to interception as they are transmitted from web browser to server. Additionally, passwords are transmitted each time a restricted document is accessed.

➤ Access Control Based on Client Certificates

Access control based on client certificates is often considered the best way to control access. In this situation, the user is issued a crypto-graphic certificate (this is called a digital signature). A trusted third party or the web-based business can issue the certificate. When the user contacts the web server, the digital signature is attached to the re-quest and is recorded. If the certificate is valid and authenticated, the user gains access (for more about client certificates, see Chapter 5).

➤ Access Restraints Based on Network Security Protocols

Transmission Control Protocol/Internet Protocol (TCP/IP) allows web-based businesses to link local systems, local area networks (LANs) and wide area networks (WANs) as intranets to work with web browsers and the enterprise's web servers. This system allows all users to communicate with all other users, regardless of location; however, this also means that every single system is susceptible to unauthorized access and vandalism. Several ways to reduce this problem are intrusion detection systems (discussed later in this chapter) and firewalls (detailed in Chapter 11).

■ MANAGING AND ENSURING THE SAFETY OF YOUR WEB PORTALS

Portals are integration points that access a variety of databases, software applications, spreadsheets, documents, and presentations. This information can reside on a wide range of hardware platforms. Sophisticated software programs use a variety of technological mechanisms to make the data available to users. Portals provide users, customers, employees, and partners with easy access to internal information via a web browser. For partners, portals are an effective way to access data, reports, applications, and processes. For customers, portals provide an easy way to access online customer service areas (ordering, repair tracking, service performance, and bill presentation), health records, and personal financial information.

Traditionally, networks were designed to keep people either in or out; today, however, the need for more sophisticated tools is increasing. Depending on the software application and type of transaction, access control often is based on multiple sign-on procedures. Sensitive data usually requires higher levels of security, but authorized users should be able to access this data based on a predetermined set of rules. Portals save users time by providing a single point of access to everything they need. The technology supports single log-ons, reducing the need for support staff to obtain, manage, and administer the security of the information.

The portal access control technology links directly with the company's web server and user authentication directories. Using your web site as a portal is one way to attract new customers and retain existing customers. Additionally, the portal technology can assist you in presenting data via a web browser (from a variety of databases and hardware operating systems) in a manner that is consistent with your corporate image. Portal control access products assist the IT department in controlling access to all areas of the web site. This allows managers to decide who can see what web pages. The benefits of access control technology include

➤ The ability to allow the enterprise to show different web page content to two visitors looking at the same web page: Access control plays a major role in personalization for web-based businesses.

➤ Providing clients with a reduced number of times they have to log in: Often web-based businesses can gain a competitive advantage offering consumers the convenience of so-called one-click access.

➤ Offering access control solutions that work well with extranets, portals, and intranets: These features are especially useful when one partner should not see the data of another partner.

The following is a sampling of access control solutions that provide access control to web sites, portals, intranets, and extranets. All prices listed are subject to change and may vary according to the number of users.

➤ Baltimore's Select Access (baltimore.com) offers a terrific management interface, as well as useful and unique resource discovery features. Prices start at $20 per user.

➤ Entegrity Solutions Assure Access (entegrity.com) offers strong authentication features. The software includes built-in support for client certificates and tokens; its prices range from $15,000 for 1,000 users on a single server to $45,000 for unlimited users on a single server.

➤ Netegrity's SiteMinder (netegrity.com) provides detailed component-level access control and offers broad server and application support. Reverse proxy capabilities are available for web servers using Apache software. Prices range from $2,000 to $4,000 for 200 users.

➤ Securant Technologies ClearTrust Secure Control (securant. com) offers excellent directory integration features; this software has a good interface and unique antihacking features, as well as relatively easy implementation. It is priced between $2,000 and $4,000 per 200 users.

■ UNDERSTANDING NETWORK INTRUSION DETECTION SYSTEMS

Most medium- and large-sized web-based business have some type of intrusion system. As you will recall from earlier in this chapter, many professionals define intrusion detection as the process and identification of an intrusion incident that was or is being attempted. According to Paul E. Proctor (2001), intrusion detection allows the incident to be categorized as the *detection of misuse* (an explicit pattern of misuse), *anomaly* (change from acceptable behavior), *false positive* (an alarm that is not a misuse), and a *false negative* (misuse that is not detected or brought to the attention of management). However, intrusion detection systems appear in a variety of shapes and sizes. Additionally, not all types of intrusion detection systems are appropriate for all types of Internet-based businesses.

Overall, intrusion detection technology can assist you in protecting your web-based business by expanding the options available to manage the risks of an online business. Proctor (2001) points out the difference between security audits (discussed in Chapter 3) and intrusion detection. A security audit is a static analysis of your systems at a point in time. It often provides a baseline for comparison and verifies password polices, security patches, and so on. Intrusion detection, on the other hand, looks for patterns of behavior. For example, the auditor verifies that passwords are properly in place on a target computer. The intrusion detection system often looks for three failed logins to verify that someone has acted suspiciously. Additionally, many networks without intrusion detection systems do not make use of log and audit data. In 1996 Ross Anderson, a professor at Cambridge University, England discovered that for Solaris, Sun System's operating system that passed many governmental audits, did not provide any documented formats or tools for reading logs. Therefore, the system administrator could not detect attacks in progress or those that had already taken place.

➤ Network-Based Intrusion Detection

Figure 4.2 is a conceptual drawing of how standard network intrusion detection works. As a general rule, intrusion detection sensors are placed at mission-critical points in the system. These sensors alert the IT department and trigger an automatic response to the threat. The process is as follows:

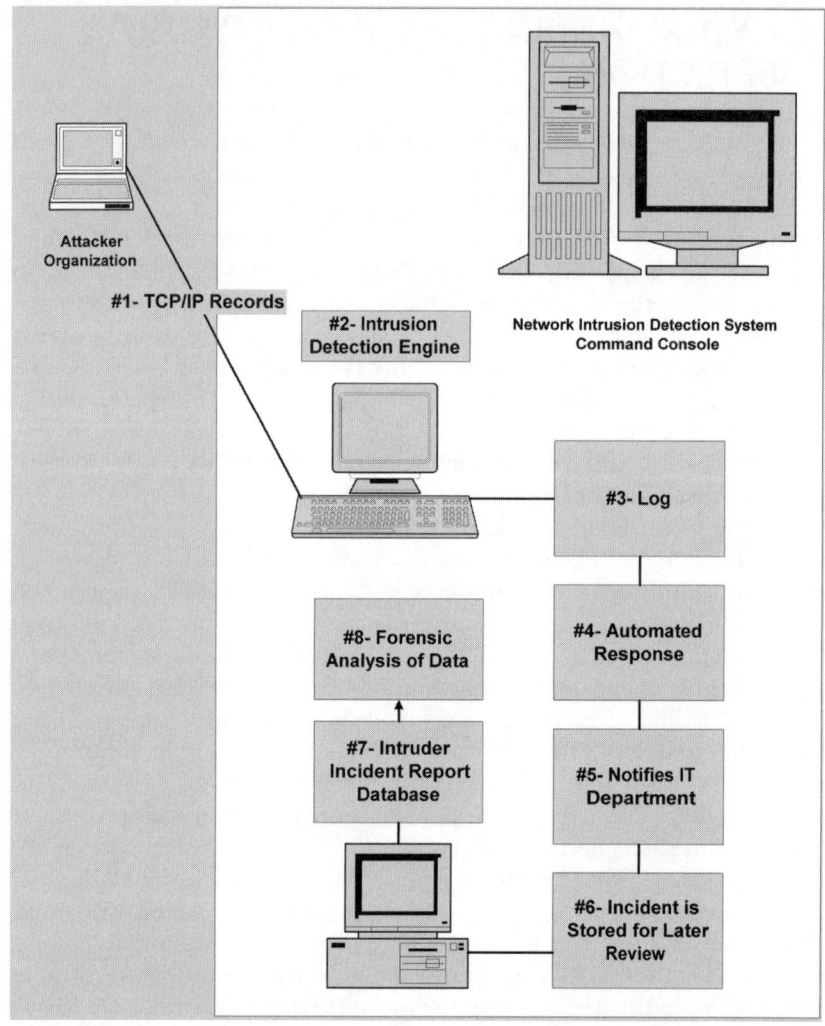

Figure 4.2 Flowchart of traditional network intrusion detection architecture
Source: Adapted from Proctor, Paul, *The Practical Intrusion Handbook* (Upper Saddle River, NJ: Prentice Hall, 2001).

1. The attack organization attempts to communicate with your organization by creating a network packet.
2. In real-time the intrusion detection system sensor reads the packet before it connects with your system. The sensor can be a stand-alone computer or a network device.
3. The intrusion detection sensor identifies a predefined pattern of misuse and generates an alert.
4. The IT department is notified using a pager, e-mail, or other communication device.
5. The intrusion detection system generates a reply to the threat; the reply is either based on a set of predetermined responses or is directed by the IT department.
6. The incident is recorded for later review.
7. The IT department creates a report that summarizes the incident, alert, and response.
8. Forensic analyses are used to spot long-term trends and other similar attempts to attack the organization.

Note that the primary difference between web server-based and network intrusion detection is the origin of the data. Network intrusion detection analyzes TCP/IP packets. Web server-based intrusion detection systems analyze event logs from operating systems and software applications (additional information about intrusion detection for distributed networks is included in Chapter 11).

➤ The Benefits of Intrusion Detection

Your web-based enterprise may already have an intrusion detection system or have several rudimentary ways of preventing intruders from gaining unwanted access to your systems. As your business becomes more sophisticated and expands, it is likely that you will need to increase the security level of how your online enterprise interfaces with the Internet and with customers, vendors, and partners. Each day, attack organizations develop new ways of disrupting web-based businesses; therefore, your organization requires state-of-the-art in-depth security, including policies, controls, and technical solutions. Intrusion detection systems can effectively increase the security for different types of web-based enterprises. Lawrence R. Halme and R. Kenneth Bauer authors for the SANS Institute (sans.org) provide the following insights about how intrusion detection systems can be used to deflect, deter and respond to unwanted intruders. Depending on the nature of your web-based business, your organization may find just one, two, or all three ways of using intrusion detection invaluable to the overall security of your organization.

Intrusion deflection: Intruders think they have succeeded in breaching your security, but they are actually held in specially controlled environments. Special limited-access or decoy accounts prevent damage to your systems but allow you to watch the intruders activities.

Outsider deterrence: The system deters the initiation or continuation of break-ins by increasing the effort for an attack to succeed. In other words, the system checks for anomalies, misuse, and combinations of misbehaviors and uses this information to discourage intruders.

Automated response notification: Automated responses and alerts provide IT staff with immediate notice of an attack. Countermeasures may include booby-trapped files and alarms to lure intruders into revealing their techniques and possibly their identities.

■ SELECTING THE INTRUSION DETECTION SOFTWARE THAT IS BEST FOR YOU

When selecting a technological solution, you should always ask "What makes sense for us?" and "What is necessary to keep information secure?" Different businesses have different information security needs. One way to judge your requirements is to evaluate the impact of past intrusions—what was the impact on your bottom line? Next, look at the types of recent intrusions and hacking activities—are these attempts the same as those from last year? The answers to these questions can help you start your investigation into what type of intrusion detection solution is best for your organization.

➤ Types of Intrusion Detection Solutions

Although intrusion detection systems have been available for several years, they are still considered first-generation technology. Three types of intrusion detection solutions are currently available: network only, host server, and hybrid (a combination of the two). In the future we may see a combination of the intrusion detection solution and firewalls.

> ➤ Network intrusion detection listens to all network traffic addressed to the system. As a general rule, all network intrusion

detection software products seek so-called attack signatures and provide automated alerts and notifications to the IT department. The intrusion detection system can include an integrity checker that examines changes in files; additionally, some include a log monitor that gathers and analyzes log files.

➤ Host server intrusion detection listens to the traffic addressed to the computer where it resides or watches traffic processed inside the host server. Some host server intrusion detection systems are stand-alone entities. Host-based intrusion detection systems frequently include integrity checking and monitoring of critical systems files, such as web pages and user ID databases. Alerts are sent when files are altered.

➤ Hybrid intrusion detection integrates host-based and network intrusion detection systems. Both are supervised and monitored from a single system. This combination is often ideal for web-based companies with high-speed networked environments. Hybrids only listen for traffic coming to them; therefore the sensor deals with less traffic and is easy to tune, resulting in fewer false positives.

Host and hybrid intrusion detection are discussed further in Chapter 5.

More than a dozen vendors offer intrusion detection technological solutions. Today, more than 500 attack signatures tip off misuse of network resources. Many vendors claim they have the ability to analyze more attack signatures than their competitors. Many of these attack signatures, however, are outdated, so such claims should not influence your decision-making. Additionally, the quality of new attack signatures is often poor, resulting in more false positives than in the past and sometimes leading to additional intrusion detection administration costs.

Vendors offer packages of intrusion detection solutions with many features. Six primary features often appear in network intrusion detection products. Depending on the specific needs of your web-based business, the solution you select may include several or most of the following features:

1. Monitoring network traffic: All network traffic is monitored as it enters the system. Each sensor is used to investigate IP packets as they enter your systems.

2. Packet reassembly: The intrusion detection system, in an effort to neutralize intended attacks, includes network packet reassembly; if an attack is sent using several packets, it can be identified (before it can harm the system) when it is reassembled.

3. Real-time alerts: The intrusion detection engine sends alerts to the IT staff when misuse and unauthorized activities are uncovered.
4. Automated reponses: Responses to misuse and unauthorized activities are automatically activated. Automated responses may include denying access, quarantining attackers, and ending sessions. For serious attacks, routers and firewalls may be reconfigured.
5. Notification of IT department personnel: The intrusion detection system uses rules to analyze traffic into understandable accounts of events directed to IT personnel.
6. Data forensics and built-in reports: Intrusion detection solutions have the ability to archive original traffic for replay sessions. This analysis can be used for management reports and for determining long-term trends.

➤ Examples Network Intrusion Detection Solutions

The following are several examples of intrusion detection solutions. Each technological solution includes a product description, operating system information, and current price. Figure 4.3 provides a summary of the major features of the products listed. The network intrusion detection solutions are listed in alphabetical order.

➤ Symantec (www.semantec.com): Net Prowler 3.5 and Intruder Alert manager can form a combination that scans the network and provides automated responses to threats and alerts. Responses can be set to low, medium, or high, and alert notifications can be made via pager or e-mail. In addition to being able to capture sessions, kill processes, launch program commands, and disable user accounts, the combined programs recognize over 400 predefined attack signatures. The programs do not include packet reassembly. (Keep in mind that TCP/IP allows a single message to arrive at your web-based business in many different packets. When these packets are reassembled, they may harm your systems. Therefore, the software programs with packet reassembly have many benefits. However, solutions that allow packet reassembly may slow down your systems and reduce efficiency.) Netprowler 3.5 uses Windows X, NT/2000 operating systems. Netprowler 3.5 sells for $7,995 and Intruder Alert Manager is $1,995.

	Axent Netprowler	Cisco Secure Intrusion Detection Systems	Computer Associates Sessionwall	Internet Security Systems Real Secure	NetworkICE IceCAP/ BlackICE Guard	NFR IDS Network Flight Recorder
Real-time monitoring	X	X	X	X	X	X
Packet re-assembly	O	O	X	O	X	X
Policy based-alerts	O	X	X	X	X	X
Automatic responses	X	X	X	X	X	O
Automatic IT department notification	X	X	O	X	O	X
Pre-built management reports	O	X	X	X	X	X

Figure 4.3 Summary of network intrusion detection features
Note: X = intrusion detection system feature included; O = intrusion detection system feature not included.

➤ Cisco (cisco.com) Secure Intrusion Detection Systems (IDS; formerly Net Ranger) provides real-time scanning of network traffic. It is designed to detect, report, and terminate unauthorized activity throughout the network based on patterns of misuse. The intrusion detection engine uses rules to analyze network traffic into meaningful accounts of events that are directed to IT personnel. Secure Intrusion Detection Systems includes a director that provides a graphic central interface for security management. However, the system does not reassemble network packets. Cisco Secure IDS uses Openview on Solaris or HP/UNIX operating systems and sells for approximately $12,000.

➤ Computer Associates (computerassociates.com) Sessionwall 3.40 is easy to install and relatively inexpensive at $2,000. Sessionwall provides real-time, nonintrusive detection, policy-based alerts, automatic prevention features, and built-in reports. Sessionwall has packet reassembly and uses Windows 95/98 and NT/2000 operating systems.

➤ Internet Security Systems (iss.com) RealSecure provides a

terrific management interface. Real-time network traffic monitoring is effective at capturing attacks. This system allows administrators to watch network-based attacks, port scans, and remote buffer overflow-based attacks with system-level events such as failed logins. However, the system does not reassemble network packets. ISS RealSecure uses the Windows NT/2000 operating system and costs approximately $10,000.

➤ Network ICE (networkice.com) offers many products including the ICEcap Management and Reporting Console. ICEcap manages BlackICE Guard. BlackICE Guard monitors all network traffic and in real time stops hostile traffic from entering or exiting a protected area of the network. The ICEcap Management Console archives suspicious data for forensic analysis; ICEcap can also send security alerts based on which system reports an incident, and ICEcap management reports include analysis of network security. Network ICE has packet reassembly and uses Windows X, NT/2000 operating systems. Prices vary.

➤ Network Flight Recorder (nfr.com) has packet reassembly and is a traditional network intrusion detection product. The software includes remote administration from a UNIX workstation, advanced query capabilities, and an extensive library of attack signatures, updates for which are typically available for download within 24 hours of their identification. The solution allows the IT department to perform ad hoc queries, make graphs, and create custom reports. Network Flight Recorder is $3,500.

■ CONTROLS THAT MAKE LINE MANAGEMENT ACCOUNTABLE FOR INTRUDERS

Effective intrusion detection requires more than technology. According to Amoroso (1999) almost all reported events in which intruders have been caught in real-time involve manual intrusion detection methods used by well-trained IT department personnel. Moreover, these incidents often involve locally developed intrusion detection tools and traps rather than commercial intrusion detection systems. Early versions of intrusion detection software often struggled with problems created by the lack of IT staff and expertise to manage the system appropriately.

Some organizations do not see the benefits of intrusion detection because they have unrealistic expectations of an intrusion system's capabilities—for example

➤ It only takes one vulnerability in one computer to allow access to an intruder. When security is breached, intruders can wreak havoc on the entire network and leave a backdoor open so that they can return and do it all over again.

➤ Intrusion detection systems cannot compensate for a lack of access controls. Strong methods of identifying and authenticating users are needed for effective information security.

➤ The intrusion detection system is not able to compensate for irrelevant data or the quality of information the system provides. In other words, "Garbage in, garbage out."

According to Ross Anderson (2001) intrusion detection systems have a success rate of 60 to 80 percent in laboratory tests and a high false alarm rate. Reasons for poor performance of intrusion detection systems include

➤ Too many false alarms due to bad network packets caused by software bugs

➤ Too few attack alerts

➤ Vulnerabilities of old versions of software that are frequently the focus of attacks

➤ Opportunistic exploitation

Effective line management is critical to protecting the web site from threats from intruders. All web-based businesses have a number of vulnerabilities that add to the hacker's toolkit. According to a white paper titled "State of the Practice of Intrusion Detection Technologies" (2000) written at the Carnegie Mellon Software Engineering Institute, "the security implication of each business goal needs to be identified and transformed into organizational security requirements." Meeting these requirements, which can reduce the likelihood of intrusion, becomes part of the line manager's responsibilities. A sampling of the line manager's suggested security responsibilities includes

➤ Carrying out additional security training: Line managers are responsible for conducting periodic security awareness training and for updating the staff on changes in the security policy. These tasks may require meetings or corporate events to promote security awareness.

➤ Closely following the organization's security policy: Some departments develop their own security measures or make modifications to the network to meet their own business needs. Each department needs to follow a formal plan so that security breaches are not unknowingly created.

➤ Communicating the need to follow new security procedures: Often employees object to changes in security procedures. Managers must make certain that staff members understand the rationale behind new security procedures and the ramifications of not following them.

➤ Disseminating the security policy: Line managers are responsible for making all employees in their departments aware of the firm's security policy. Requiring employees to indicate their agreement by signing off on the policy can help reinforce awareness.

➤ Enforcing password and other security policies: Intruders frequently gain entry to web-based businesses by social engineering—for example, a helpful employee provides a password over the telephone or to a coworker. Management must visibly enforce security policies.

➤ Including stakeholders in developing the information security policy: To ensure employee cooperation for changes, updates, or a new security policy, line managers need to meet with staff, develop the policy, and achieve their commitment.

➤ Performing follow-up activities: The most expensive, state-of-the-art security measures are not effective unless they are maintained and pursued. Frequently, after IT staff and line management install an intrusion detection system, they move on to other tasks. New hacker tools are created every day and new security holes are being discovered regularly. Therefore, managers need to ensure that log files are being reviewed for possible security breaches and verify the installation of security patches to applications and operating systems.

■ ONLINE BUSINESS INTRUSION DETECTION CHECKLIST

This checklist details some of the steps for determining whether your system has been compromised. This checklist can be used to look for several types of break-ins. Modifying your systems can close potential weaknesses.

- ✓ In an effort to understand where to focus your security efforts, explain how you know whether intruders are likely to have physical access to a machine, access to the system (possibly beginning with low-level access privileges), or are able to penetrate the system remotely.
- ✓ Describe the real-time processes you have in place that can assist you in determining who (either insiders or outsiders) are misusing your system.
- ✓ Put in plain words the technological solutions and security policies you have implemented that let you know if an unauthorized entity is monitoring your network traffic.
- ✓ Have any web-based businesses similar to yours been attacked by intruders? What was the impact on those enterprises? How are those online businesses fending off future attacks?
- ✓ Have you formulated any preplanned responses for different types of attacks? Do you have an intruder detection system that launches an automatic response to an attack?
- ✓ Explain how the IT department is notified of an intruder. Does your intrusion detection system automatically notify the IT personnel of unauthorized activity on the network?
- ✓ Describe how your organization collects and archives evidence that can be used to understand the nature of an intruder's attack.
- ✓ Describe the information you require in management reports that detail an intruder incident or attack.

■ REFERENCES

Allen, Julia, Alan Christ, William Fithen, John McHugh, Jed Pickel, and Ed Stoner. 2000. State of the practice of intrusion detection technologies. Carnegie Mellon Software Engineering Institute, January. Available at [http://www.sei.cmu.edu]. 3 December 2001.

Amoroso, Edward. 1999. *Intrusion Detection.* Sparta, N.J.: Intrusion Net Books.

Anderson, Ross. 2001. *Security Engineering: A Guide to Building Dependable Distributed Systems.* New York: Wiley.

Deveau, Denise. 2000. Overly friendly access sets off company alarm. *Computing Canada* 26:13.

Ghosh, Anup K. 1998. *E-Commerce Security: Weak Links, Best Defenses.* New York: Wiley.

Halme, Lawrence R., and R. Kenneth Bauer. 2001. AINT misbehaving: A taxonomy of anti-intrusion techniques. SANS Institute, 21 August. Available at [http://www.sans.org/newlook/resources/IDFAQ/aint.htm]. 3 December 2001.

Oblix. 1996–2001. Meeting the e-business imperative: Secure and scalable web access management. Oblix Identify Based Security Solutions (www.oblix.com). Available online at [http://www.oblix.com/docs]. 4 April 2001. No longer available online.

Proctor, Paul E. 2001. *The Practical Intrusion Detection Handbook.* Upper Saddle River, N.J.: Prentice Hall.

Rapooza, Jim. 2000. Access control tools add site security. *eWeek,* 17 July. Available at [http://www.zdnet.com/products/stories/reviews/0,4161,2602508,00.html]. 3 December 2001.

Rapooza, Jim. 2001. Shielding nets from prying eyes. *eWeek,* 22 January. Available at [http://techupdate.zdnet.com]. 3 December 2001.

SANS Institute. 2001. Intrusion detection FAQ (version 1.52). SANS Institute, 21 October. Available at [http://www.sans.org]. 3 December 2001.

Stein, Lincoln D. 1998. *Web Security, A Step-By-Step Reference Guide.* Reading, Mass.: Addison-Wesley.

Sun Microsystems. 1994–2001. Protecting from within. Sun Microsystems, published in 1999. Available at [http://www.sun.com/software/white-papers/wp-security-intranet/protectingfromwithin.pdf]. 3 December 2001.

Vigilinx. 2001. Security monitoring realities and futures. Vigilinx, 9 April. Available at [http://techlibrary.networkcomputing.com]. 3 December 2001.

Chapter 5

Your Vulnerable Web Server

In this chapter

- ➤ Understanding Web Server Risks
- ➤ Protecting the Server with a Proxy Server
- ➤ Looking into Web Server Threats from CGI Scripts
- ➤ Spotting Attackers with a Host Intrusion Detection System
- ➤ Anatomy of a Typical Intrusion Scenario
- ➤ Implementing Secure Remote Access to Monitor Your Server
- ➤ Common Vulnerabilities of Web Servers
- ➤ Understanding Web Server Threats
- ➤ Web Server Security Checklist

Attackers often focus on an organization's web server to achieve unauthorized entry to confidential documents, to gain improper access to private information (such as patient records, social security numbers, and customer card numbers sent to the web server by clients via their web browsers), and to reveal the web server's operating system defects and system vulnerabilities to provide other intruders with clues about how to break into the web-based business.

Often, attacks are the result of operating system security holes, defects in web server software, and errors in configuring the web server. Web-based businesses that are high-profile targets for web server attacks include the following three examples

1. Financial institutions, which may be probed and attacked in an effort to commit fraud.

2. ISPs (Internet service providers), because of their ready access to the World Wide Web and their ability to move large amounts of data over the Internet. Additionally, many ISPs host consumer databases for large corporations. These databases often include sensitive customer information such as credit card numbers. Attack organizations can copy this information, and then sell it to the victimized companies.
3. Pharmaceutical companies, which may be victims of industrial espionage attempts. In this situation, skilled hackers are paid large sums of money to steal research and development data.

Experts agree that it is only a matter of time until intruders come knocking at the door of your web server. Web servers that catch the attention of attack organizations are frequently those that appear to be weakly protected or are suspected of having a known vulnerability. Intruders can use any number of methods to attack your web server. Some methods are designed to watch and record your activities passively. Other methods are designed to prevent customers from using your services; the aim of certain approaches is to annoy users and destroy data. Frequently, attackers use the systems they have compromised to hide their tracks when they launch attacks against other web sites and systems. Today, even low-skilled intruders can use hacking technology to exploit web server vulnerabilities and gain root access to your organization's web server. If attackers gain root access to your web server, then they have won. Your only recourse is to reinstall. This is time consuming and costly; it also can disrupt business operations.

■ UNDERSTANDING WEB SERVER RISKS

Web servers are data providers to many clients. A client is a piece of hardware or software that is used to communicate one-on-one with a server. Servers and clients can be on one computer but are usually on separate machines connected by a network. The Internet uses this client-server relationship to allow millions of users access to web sites. Web servers and clients use a basic set of rules called Hypertext Transfer Protocol (HTTP) to transmit information. Think of clients as Internet users with web browsers connected to your web servers to conduct different types of transactions. Information is stored and accessed using HTML (Hypertext Markup Language). Once a connection is established, the web server responds by sending the document or image to the requesting client via HTTP. One of the benefits of this approach is that the client does not care where the web server gets its information; this means that you can change your database from one type to another or even use two different types of databases, as long as the web server is acting as a "front end" or user interface. A few examples of different types of databases are Sybase, Oracle, and Microsoft.

When the Internet user enters a URL (uniform reference locator) address in the web browser (for example, www.Microsoft.com), the destination is a web server (with a numerical destination or IP address). In addition to this IP address, the browser must supply an access port number, usually accessed by port 80. Port 80 tells web servers which "channel" to use when sending to the user and where on the server to look for the data. To sum it up, port 80 is the default destination for sending and receiving data in HTML. E-mail would use a different port number, but the same IP address and possibly the same URL.

HTML is a small text-based language that tells the web browser what to display when the Internet user visits a web site. In the early days of the Internet, port 80 was selected as the default port for HTML traffic. No particular significance rests in the number, but if you decided to run your web server on another port, no one would be able to locate your HTML data.

A large number of hackers are opportunists who probe the Internet looking for web server vulnerabilities. These individuals are often patient and persistent. When a victim organization is located, the intruder will attempt to gain root access to the web server, and then install a back door so that they can return. *Root access* is the highest level of access to the network. Keep in mind that the web server and the PCs on your network have a trust relationship; root access therefore means access to every machine in your system.

■ PROTECTING THE SERVER WITH A PROXY SERVER

As a general rule, web sites are protected by a perimeter defense often called a DMZ (demilitarized zone) that includes a router or a firewall. The perimeter, however, no matter how complete, may not be sufficient to protect the organization. Attached to this protective barrier are your web servers. Usually port 80 is open in this protective shield to allow HTTP traffic to your web server. Any data not located on your web server is obtained from supporting servers inside the firewall (for more details on firewalls, see Chapter 11).

➤ Using Proxy Servers to Protect Your Web Server

As shown in Figure 5.1, a proxy is often the "middleman server." In other words, it is an intermediary between the client and the web server. Like a bodyguard, proxy servers sit behind the organization's firewall and in front of the organization's real web server.

The most common users of proxy servers are large corporations and ISPs like America Online. The benefits of proxy servers include

➤ Caching: Users can quickly download data from local proxy servers. This can increase the speed, accuracy, and scope of information you can deliver over the Internet. Additionally, users are not receiving access to a full web server that contains all of your data.

➤ Load balancing: If multiple requests are made for the same web page, a proxy server can prevent a traffic jam.

➤ Sharing IP addresses: Large corporations may share IP addresses within a group a clients. This protects the network from being identified by the public. In other words, the organization has an internal identity and an external identity. This makes it difficult for intruders to monitor and target specific machines directly.

➤ Content filtering: Examples are accepting only HTTP requests, restricting access to certain areas of the web site, or providing personalized content.

➤ Maintaining security: Proxy servers prevent unwanted intrud-

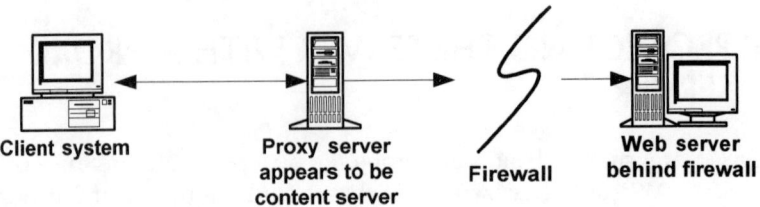

Client system   Proxy server appears to be content server   Firewall   Web server behind firewall

Figure 5.1 A proxy server can appear to be the real web server

ers' access to the web server; they prevent scans by intruders because they will not pass these types of requests on to your internal web server.

The downside of proxy servers is that they make audio and video streams less efficient for internal users. Proxy servers check each request before they respond, affecting the quality of audio and making movements jerkier, such as forcing sound and lip movements to be out of synchronization. Proxy software is available from many software developers. The following are two examples:

➤ SymantecWebthority (semantec.com) provides centralized management and strong authentication, replication, and load balancing features; it works with any type of web server. The product starts at $25,000 and runs on Windows NT and Solaris using the Sun-Netscape Alliance's iPlanet Web Server.

➤ Tivoli SecureWay Policy Director (tivoli.com) includes centralized management and strong authentication. The solution simplifies the administration of access control across multiple applications and reduces the need to deploy a redundant, parallel access-control solution. It is compatible with OS; HP-UX; Sun Solaris; IBM OS/390; Digital Open VMS; IBM AIX; MS Windows NT. Prices vary.

■ LOOKING INTO WEB SERVER THREATS FROM CGI SCRIPTS

The Internet is a *packet-switched network*. All Internet requests, messages, e-mail, HTTP, and so on, are broken into small pieces called packets. These packets are sent through numerous computer routes across the Internet. The packets arrive in a different order, and then are reassembled into the correct order at their destination. Frequently, incoming requests for data are not checked for malicious codes. Hackers can embed different types of data into normal-looking packets aimed at your web server. The tainted packets can contain information for which your web server is not prepared, possibly resulting in an unforeseen security breach that provides the intruder with access to information about how the web server operates and allows further access into your system.

Today, web servers are sending more than just HTML code on port 80. They are including video and audio, embedded CGI (Common Gateway Interface) scripts, and all sorts of things because it is easy and inexpensive. According to Douglas Harbrecht (2000), an editor at BusinessWeek Online, this diversity of traffic makes it harder for firewalls to do the job of discovering and filtering tainted packets of code. This makes it easier for attackers to breach the security of a web-based business. If security is breached, companies that share files can be hit hard but limiting the use of applications served over Port 80 can negatively affect productivity.

Information technology (IT) management often assumes that CGI programs are correctly written for the tasks for which they are designed. When a CGI script executes, it usually has the privileges of a user account—which often includes access to the enterprise's network, hardware, and file systems. When CGI scripts are good, they are very good; they can quickly access database connections, write customers orders, send e-mail, and so on. When CGI scripts are bad (i.e., when they are written incorrectly or maliciously), they are very bad; they can lead to security breaches, corrupted data, and other problems. For example, a faulty CGI script might not verify that a return e-mail address contains only the customer's address. If additional, malicious commands are included in the return e-mail address, they can bypass the router and firewall. According to Lincoln Stein (1998), three categories of risk can arise from poorly written CGI scripts.

1. Flawed CGI scripts can leak information that is helpful for intruders to gain access to confidential documents, corporate secrets, and proprietary information.
2. Defects in CGI scripts can assist attack organizations in making unauthorized modifications to files on the web site and on the web server.
3. Poorly written CGI scripts can be used to execute attack organization commands on the web server.

■ SPOTTING ATTACKERS WITH A HOST INTRUSION DETECTION SYSTEM

Another way to reduce the likelihood of attack is to test mission-critical web hosts, web servers, and PCs for vulnerabilities. Host intrusion detection solutions analyze data that originates on host computers. Data sources include operating system event logs and application logs for the web server, databases, and so on. In contrast, network intrusion detection (discussed in Chapter 4) analyzes data that originates on the network, such as TCP/IP traffic. Host intrusion detection is primarily used to fend off attacks from inside the organization. Often, the biggest benefits of host-based intrusion detection systems are their abilities to

➤ Detect potential threats: IT personnel identify and prioritize the unique threats to their specific organizations so that these threats can be monitored.

➤ Respond to predefined threats: After likely threats are identified, IT personnel and management can develop appropriate corrective actions.

➤ Deter potential attackers: Internal and external attackers that know their actions are being monitored; they are therefore less likely to tamper with the enterprise's data.

➤ Anticipate potential attacks: An attacker may engage in many preliminary activities before the actual attack. Recognizing these preliminary activities can assist your organization in stopping the attack before it begins.

➤ Assess the damage of a successful security breach: Having the software in place to identify exactly what happened could assist the firm in analyzing the impact of a successful attack. Forensic issues include the computer and files accessed, the attack methods used, and the time period of the attack.

➤ Locating Host Intrusion Solutions

Software vendors have created several applications to assist web-based businesses in detecting threats to host computers by potential vandals, hackers, or thieves. According to Paul E. Proctor (2001), host intrusion detection software includes agents that monitor data and detection engines that match patterns of misuse. Logs are created to archive raw data and alerts are generated when predefined patterns of misuse (attack signatures) are observed. Detection can be periodic, in real time, or based on routine data analysis. In the event of suspicious activity, the IT department can be notified via e-mail, pager, or some other predetermined method. An appropriate response is implemented and management reports are generated.

Over the years, developers have created software that has generated many host intruder detection solutions. The following are a few examples:

➤ Network Security Suite from BlindView Development Products (blindview.com) includes the Business BlindView EMS Enterprise Console for about $1,995 and uses NOSadim and HackerShield products (pricing begins at $695 per server). It scans and monitors host servers. Easy-to-use scanning capabilities and updating features are included. NOSadmin offers detailed security reports that can be customized. It can recommend and automatically implement corrective actions to uncovered security problems. The system has the ability to track who is visiting forbidden web sites and how often. Additionally, the program alerts management to unauthorized language in e-mail messages. Basic security management policies are employed.

➤ ETrust Intrusion Protection from Computer Associates (platinum.com) is priced starting at $1,945 (for up to 125 concurrent sessions) to $19,435 (for an unlimited number of concurrent sessions). The product provides real-time alerts as well as business and security policy management. It offers a wide variety of report formats and allows system administrators to view network usage by user, client, and server.

➤ WebTrends Security Analyzer 2.1. Enterprise Edition from WebTrends (webtrends.com) offers an unlimited number of IP addresses for $4,999. It is easy to navigate through options for scanning the entire network, subnets, or the most critical parts of the network. Analyses and easy access to third-party security tests are provided. Although the analysis is good, the program does not point out potential security threats or violations; the product also does not make recommendations or automatically take corrective actions.

➤ TripWire 2.1 from TripWire Security Systems (tripwiresecurity.com) includes a "bulletproof" internal system security but its report formats are cumbersome. Installation may be difficult. When the product encounters a security policy violation, it sends an e-mail notification. Pricing begins at $495 for one to four seats.

➤ Getting a Grip on Hybrid Intruder Detection Solutions

Firewalls, passwords, and authentication systems are like locks and deadbolts to keep burglars out, but they cannot see everything that is happening on the network. Hybrid intrusion detection software combines network- and host-based intrusion detection solutions. In other words, these programs are good at watching for misbehavior in the system because they constantly scan network traffic or host audit logs looking for anything out of the ordinary. Host-based solutions can show whether an attack actually happened and whether its impact was great enough to warrant corrective action. Network intrusion detection monitors traffic in real-time and can stop an attack in progress before the intrusion causes serious damage. Network and host intrusion detection each serve a specific purpose and can greatly reduce the likelihood that an attack will slip through your defenses. The following are several examples of hybrid intrusion detection solutions:

➤ CyberCop Monitor 2.0 by Network Associates (nai.com) analyzes both system and network events to spot potential attackers. CyberCop includes a multi-role architecture for Solaris-based web servers. Features include the ability to recognize coordinated reconnaissance tactics, real-time responses to intrusions, alerts for IT personnel, auditing functions, and the ability to allow administrators to add customized signatures to increase attack detection of new and evolving threats. The new version is free of charge to current CyberCop users. Pricing for each Solaris web server begins at $1,295.

➤ CentraxIce by CyberSafe 3.0 (centraxcorp.com) provides continuous monitoring of your network, server, and applications. The program uses a central console to reduce administration costs and to centrally manage security policies. CentraxIce includes a customizable security configuration checker, automated audit logs, and management reports. If the program detects a potential misuse, it can launch a TripWire scan as a response to the threat. CentraxIce includes real-time notifications, attack anticipation testing, customizable responses, graphic reporting capabilities, and damage assessment features. It supports Microsoft NT/2000, Solaris 2.5–2.7, IBM AIX v4.2.1 and 4.3.2, and Hewlett-Packard HP-UX v10.20, 11.0. Prices vary.

■ ANATOMY OF A TYPICAL INTRUSION SCENARIO

Your web-based business's server gives almost unlimited access to a wide range of corporate resources to users, customers, employees, partners, and suppliers. However, all organizations want to limit access to unwanted intruders. Your Internet-based business has a right to protect its information, reputation, finances, corporate secrets, and proprietary information. You can restrict access to areas of sensitive or confidential information by limiting the number of users who have access. Robert Graham (2000) and Network Security Solutions (1998) provide an overview of a typical intrusion scenario.

➤ External reconnaissance: The attacker organization uses public resources such as press releases, annual reports, and news articles to find out as much as possible about your web-based business. Next, the intruder looks up your registered domain name. The attacker may even use utility programs to find the names of your network computers, use HTML on your web servers to identify other hosts, and view documents on your FTP (File Transfer Protocol) servers. Using this information, the attack organization can build a list of IP (Internet Protocol) numbers for internal machines on your network and start to understand the relationship between them. For example, there are five classes (A to E) of TCP/IP addresses. An IP address from Class C can be any one of up to 256 addresses attached to the network. Knowing the possible IP address of an internal host computer can assist an attack organization in bypassing your firewall.

➤ Internal reconnaissance: As it becomes bolder, the attack organization looks for trusted network components to attack and may walk through your web site looking for web pages with CGI scripts that are easy to hack. The intruder may use utilities like *rcinfo* or *showmount* to see what is available. At this point, the hacker is checking your doors and windows but has not broken in.

➤ Exploiting vulnerabilities: The attack organization can start building lists of your organization's internal and external hosts using scanners to spot specific remote vulnerabilities. The intruders start exploiting holes in targeted computers. The weaknesses in the CGI script may be compromised. The attack organization may focus on cracking passwords with easily guessable words or empty (guest) passwords. The persistent intruder may use a root kit and go through several stages of intrusion in an effort to gain access to your root directory. As an example, a hacker may gain unauthorized access to a web server with a high-speed connection, install a root kit, and gain prohibited and undetectable access to the host.

➤ The foothold: At this point the intruder has broken in and will likely attack your web server after working hours. Such timing gives the intruder the opportunity to install sniffers and back doors programs without having to worry about being observed by system administrators. As a general rule, intruders encounter fewer defenses inside systems than outside of them. After exploiting weaknesses in the web server and network, the intruders may start covering their trails by installing more back doors and Trojan horses (discussed in Chapter 13). Many back-door programs include utilities that allow attack organizations to change or erase logs, dates, and permission files. For example, activities in event logs can be erased and audit trails can be changed. The attacker then verifies that his or her presence is not logged. The back door will allow intruders to return at their leisure.

➤ Reaping their rewards: Now the attack organization can easily steal your proprietary processes, trade secrets, and confidential data. Additionally, intruders can use your systems for launching attacks against other web-based businesses or vandalize your web site with embarrassing cyber-graffiti. If the attack organization's goal is to steal sensitive information on your network, it attempts to gain access by abusing the trust relationship between the web server and the organization's network.

■ IMPLEMENTING SECURE REMOTE ACCESS TO MONITOR YOUR SERVER

Each day web-based businesses are faced with a conundrum—how to keep most people out of the web server while allowing the right people (web administrators, authors, and developers) into the web server so that they can upgrade features, freshen content, and make other needed changes. To complicate this issue, the physical location of the web server is usually in a different geographic location from that of authorized personnel, requiring most Internet-based businesses to use some type of remote authoring or administration. Many web authors use Microsoft's FrontPage and software, such as PCanywhere, for this purpose. For example, my web server is located in Connecticut. At the

Connecticut location, the web site administrator performs local maintenance and I (and the companies I hire) update content, modify capabilities, and add features remotely using Microsoft's FrontPage product
and other remote authoring tools.

To protect your web server from the prying eyes of local and remote users, control access on a need-to-know basis. Additionally, you
may want to make the root directory and its subdirectories readable
only to certain users or groups of users; you can accomplish this goal
by limiting access to certain IP addresses or by requiring remote users
to provide passwords. These measures often provide your first line of
defense for remote authoring.

Many organizations focus their security efforts on the entrances or
so-called front doors of their operations. Consequently, the enterprise's
exits have low levels of security. This vulnerability can be exploited by
attack organizations that can install back-door programs that allow
them to log in to the web server. The following are several of the methods used for remote attacks:

➤ Replacement of the original log-in program: The attack organization replaces the original log-in program with a back door.
The back door allows the attacker to gain access, based on the
incoming IP address, user name, or a combination of both, to
the web server without any authentication.

➤ Trojan horse program: The attack organization installs a program that looks like a remote procedure service. The routine
remote procedure cloaks the installation of a Trojan horse program, which allows the attacker to run arbitrary commands on
the web server.

➤ Installation of a root kit: Root kit programs are designed to allow
attack organizations to gain high-level access to the web servers.
Remotely installed root kits can be used to exploit Windows
NT, UNIX, and other types of web servers. Some of the later versions of root kits are so sophisticated that they do not require
the web server to be rebooted after installation. Attack organizations can use root kits to hide processes, files, and registry entries, as well as to intercept keystrokes and redirect EXE files.
For example, consider an administrator who begins a Microsoft
NT session by typing his or her password in the Ctrl-Alt-Del log-
in screen. Using the features of the root kit, the attack organization can capture the administrator's password in clear text.

After an attack organization has gained root access to your web server, the game is over—the attack organization has won. The only way to be safe is to reinstall; this prevents the intruders from using Trojan horses, entering through back doors, changing log entries, or tampering with mission-critical activities. Backup copies of files may be used but you need to make certain that they are not tainted. Always remember the possibility that the attack organization used root access to corrupt backup copies for several weeks before being discovered.

■ COMMON VULNERABILITIES OF WEB SERVERS

Eric Larson and Brian Stephens (2000) point out that the software for web servers often includes extra programs that you may not need, and software manufacturers may leave ports open. Unnecessary software should be removed from the operating system; unused ports should be closed. Implementation of these measures is called hardening the operating system. Default file permissions and ownership, file-sharing features, command paths, and software patches are all issues that need to be addressed.

Determine the role of each process on the web server. Next, ask yourself whether you require that particular function. For example, does your web server host require the remote log-in function? If the function is not required, then as a security precaution remove it from your system. If you cannot remove this function from the system, ask yourself whether you can use an alternative that will provide you with a more secure method offering the same functionality.

Al Berg (2000), a contributing editor of CMP Net (lantimes.com), recommends checking the Unofficial WWW Hack FAQ (frequently asked questions; nmrc.org) to discover the latest explicit instructions for mounting attacks against web servers and how to repel them. Common vulnerabilities include

> ➤ UNIX web servers include test programs for demonstrating how to write Common Gateway Interface (CGI) programs. These CGI programs can be misused by attack organizations to breach the security of your web server.
> ➤ UNIX and NT web servers often support Server Side Includes

(SSI). SSI directives on HTML web pages can instruct the web server to perform certain commands.

➤ Web servers or their operating systems are often misconfigured, providing security holes for intruders.

■ UNDERSTANDING WEB SERVER THREATS

Your web server can be assaulted in many ways. Throughout this book you will discover many different types of attacks. This chapter focuses on several ways unwanted intruders can breach the security of your web server. Knowing how hackers can intercept all of your enterprise's Internet traffic and all of the traffic traveling across your network is critical to developing a good understanding of how to manage the risk of your web-based business. The following are non-technical descriptions of two ways an attack organization can gain access to your organization's web server.

1. Packet sniffer attacks: Sniffer software passively watches and copies packet transmissions. This allows attack organizations to gather information unobtrusively about your system and its potential vulnerabilities.
2. Spoofing the web: After the attack organization has internal access to your system, it can begin to tamper with restricted and proprietary data. By spoofing the web, the attack organization can create all types of havoc, including modifying legitimate customer orders.

➤ Sniffer Attacks

Data is transmitted over the Internet to the web server and your network in the form of packets. Attack organizations can use utility programs, such as packet sniffers, to passively watch, display, copy and store this traffic. You can find free packet sniffer programs on the Internet. One popular program is called tcp-dump from tCPdump.org. Windows X/NT users can download another free packet sniffer located at netgroup-serv.polito.it/windump/install/default.htm. This packet sniffer is called WinDump and is the Windows platform of tcp-dump.

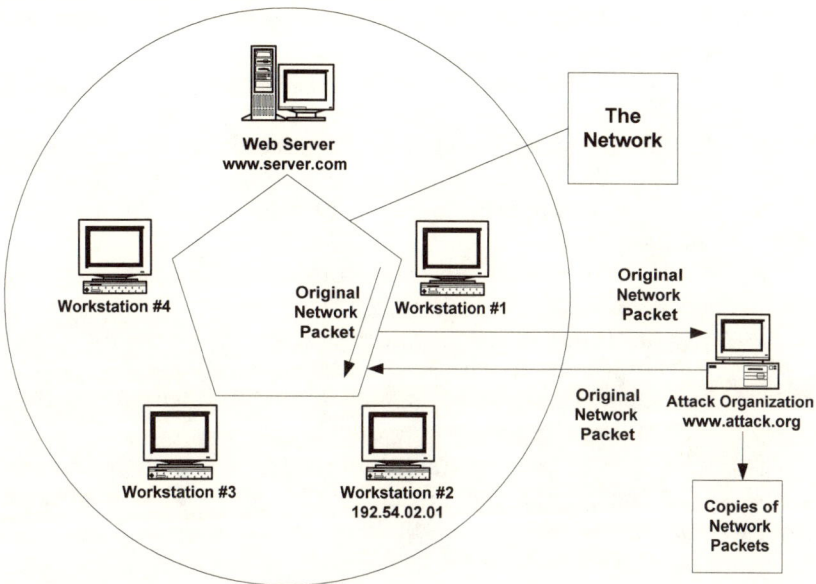

Figure 5.2 Attack organizations often use passive packet sniffers as a first step in gaining access to your web server

WinDump is a network sniffer/analyzer for UNIX operating systems and can run under Windows 95/98/ME, Windows NT, and Windows 2000. WinDump and similar programs can be used to watch and diagnose network traffic according to various complex rules such as focusing on certain ports, on keywords in data, on IP addresses, or on services that require passwords; such programs can also be used to spy on the HTML forms completed on your web site and submitted by customers via the Internet.

Use of these spy tools is often a first step before the attack organization does something malicious. Figure 5.2 is a conceptual diagram of this type of attack. After gaining access to the web server, the intruder gathers as much information as possible. To begin the process, the intruder acquires a user ID and password. To sniff your data, the intruder must access the root file of an internal host server in your network for example, Workstation #2. The trust relationship between hosts and web servers then enables the intruder to eavesdrop and copy all the data transmission of your entire networked organization.

The attack organization now has internal access to the web server and to any information transmitted by the server. This information can include

➤ Confidential data (human resource records, medical histories, credit card information, social security numbers, etc.)
➤ Log-in names for employees, contractors, customers, suppliers, partners, etc.
➤ Password files, such as access control lists for public and restricted areas of the network
➤ Any information that is transmitted over the network (confidential pricing, inventory records, corporate secrets, private correspondence)

This information can prepare intruders for an actual attack on the web server or may provide the intruders with a platform for attacks on other web-based business.

➤ Web Spoofing

Online businesses can be subject to web spoofing. Unlike sniffing, which is a passive activity, spoofing is a tampering activity. At the whim of the attacker organization, user requests can be captured, modified, or dropped. This means that all requests from the user's browser may be monitored and possibly altered. For example, customers may be lured to the attack organization's duplicate of your home page when they are directed from another web site or e-mail newsletter that is suppose to link to your web-based business. Consequently, legitimate customers may be duped because of the hijacked web session.

Figure 5.3 shows how an attack organization can provide a false web site that looks exactly like yours. Note that all customer traffic is controlled by the attack organization—this means that the attack organization is free to exploit the situation in many ways.

First, the attack organization convinces your web server that it is another host computer and that the web server should receive information from the attack organization. Next, the attack organization records the pages visited by the victim. When the victim completes an HTML form (such as a buy order for 100 shares of XYZ stock), the form is sent to the attack organization. The attack organization can modify, delete, or meddle with this information and send it back to the victim. In our example, the attack organization sends back a confirmation for

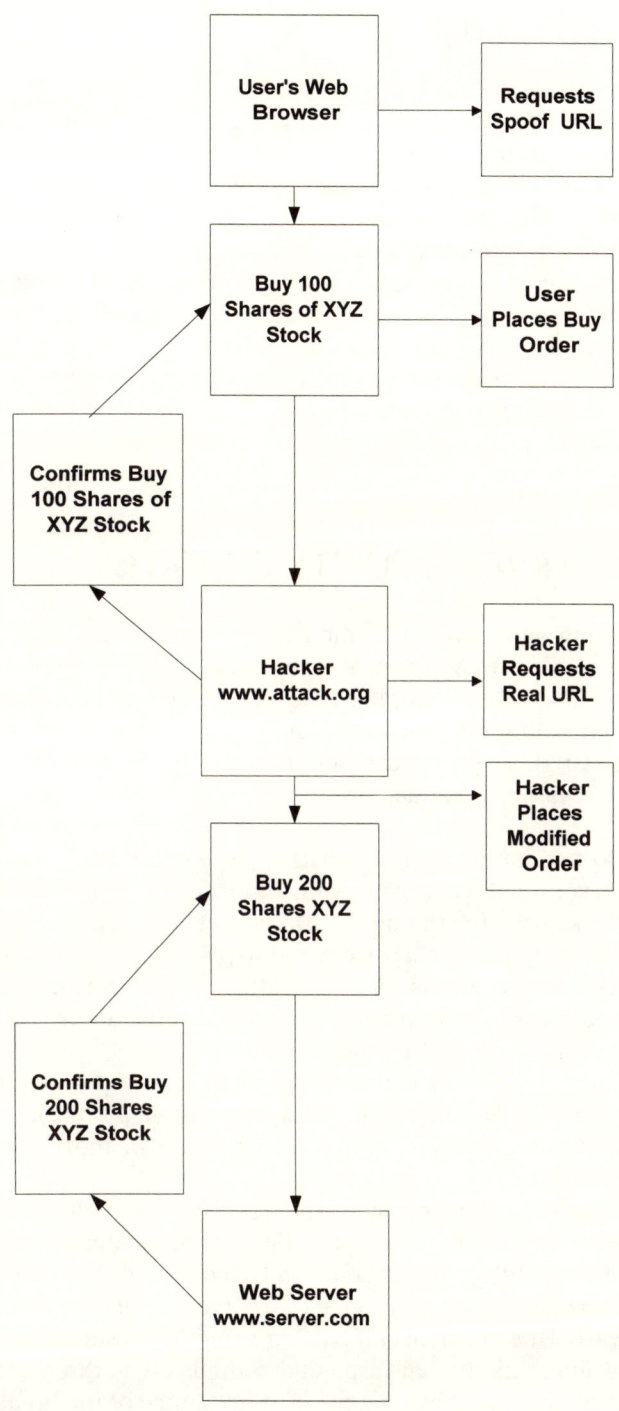

Figure 5.3 Web spoofing occurs when intruders actively tamper with your web site

100 shares of XYZ stock. The order cannot be processed because your organization never received it; this can damage your customer relationships and can force customers to defect to competitors.

However, the attack organization might not stop at this point. Figure 5.3 shows how the attack organization can send the modified order to your web-based business, changing the order, for example, from 100 shares to 200 shares of XYZ stock. This order is confirmed by your organization and notification is returned to the attack organization. If the attack organization continues this type of activity, you may discover that your corporate reputation has been smeared and that customers are filing lawsuits for order errors or other mistakes.

■ WEB SERVER SECURITY CHECKLIST

The following web server vulnerability security checklist can assist you in protecting your web server. Several books are available that include comprehensive lists of complex, defensive tactics and procedures. The items listed below are simple defensive procedures. If management makes certain these procedures are followed, they can greatly increase the odds of evading an attack.

- ✓ Do not connect the web server until everything is ready. Web servers make access to your enterprise's computers and networks easy for the public. Do not let security take a back seat to deployment because of need-it-yesterday time schedules. Attack organizations constantly travel the Internet looking for weaknesses in web-business operations and may take advantage of this security weakness.
- ✓ Use only the core operating system and required application programs. Unneeded features are possible points of attack and should be removed from the web server or moved to another machine.
- ✓ Remove unneeded start-up programs from the web server. Monitor remote administration. Attack organizations may use this capability to gain root-level access to the web server.
- ✓ Consider the installation of web server intrusion detection software. Host, or hybrid intrusion detection systems look for suspicious activity, can respond automatically to threats, notify IT personnel, archive and preserve evidence of the break-in, and create reports for management decision-making.

✓ Apply all relevant security patches. The installation of security patches for operating systems and application programs is an easy, low-cost way to avoid security breaches.

✓ Make certain that the web server is behind a firewall. A firewall protects your web server from unwanted intruders, but it is not infallible. Large enterprises should consider using proxy servers and a perimeter security network called a DMZ (demilitarized zone) for additional protection.

✓ Clean up the web server and keep only the needed files. An attack organization can exploit extraneous files that come with the web server or files that are the unwanted leftovers of web authors.

✓ Keep backup copies of all web pages. When any changes are made on the web site, backup copies should be made and stored in a different location or on the enterprise's intranet.

✓ Test the web server and system for vulnerabilities. When a change is made to the web server and network, it should be tested to verify that the change has not created a security hole somewhere else in the organization.

✓ Manage web server log-ins. Keep a record of log-ins and analyze these records for activity that may indicate misbehavior on the web server. Changes may indicate attack patterns by intruders.

✓ Monitor the system for suspicious activity. New attack methods and technologies are developed every day. Keeping aware of the latest threats. Monitoring the web server and system for misuse is effective for understanding and reducing security risks.

■ REFERENCES

Berg, Al. 2001. Nix web server attacks. CMP Net, Available at [http://www.lantimes.com/handson/97/708a063a.html]. 3 December 2001.

Ghosh, Anup K. 1998. *E-Commerce Security: Weak Links, Best Defenses.* New York: Wiley.

Graham, Robert. 2000. FAQ: Network intrusion detection systems. Version 0.8.3, 21 March 2000. Available at [http://www.ticm.com/kb/faq/idsfaq.html]. 3 December 2001.

Harbrecht, Douglas, ed. A prime port of call for hackers? BusinessWeek

Online, 11 July. Available at [http://www.businessweek.com/bwdaily/dnflash/jul2000/nf00711e.htm]. 3 December 2001.

Karve, Anita. 1999. Can intrusion detection keep an eye on your network's security? ZDNET, 1 April. Available at [http://cma.zdnet.com]. 3 December 2001.

Larson, Eric, and Brian Stephens. 2000. *Administrating Web Servers, Security and Maintenance.* Upper Saddle River, Ill.: Prentice Hall.

Klander, Lars. 1997. *Hacker Proof: The Ultimate Guide to Network Security.* Houston, Tex.: Jamsa Press.

Mourer, Darrin. 2000. Why place your web servers on the web? A look at web proxy technology and architecture. SANS Institute, 8 November. Available at [http://www.sans.org/infosecFAQ/threats/web_servers.htm]. 3 December 2001.

Network Security Solutions. 1998. Techniques adopted by "system crackers" when attempting to break into corporate or sensitive private networks. Network Security Solutions, December. Available at [http://www.rootshell.com/docs/cracker.txt]. 22 April 2001. Not currently available online.

Parnell, Terre'. 1999. Scanning for weak links in server security. NetworkWorldFusion, 30 August. Available at [http://www.nwfusion.com/reviews/0830revsecmon.html]. 3 December 2001.

Proctor, Paul E. 2001. *The Practical Intrusion Detection Handbook.* Upper Saddle River, Ill.: Prentice Hall.

Prosise, Chris, Shah, Saumil Udayn. 2001. Hackers' rootkit for Nt. CNET, CNET Builder.com, 22 February. Available at [http://builder.cnet.com/webbuilding/0-7532-8-4877567-1.html]. 3 December 2001.

Stein, Lincoln D. 1998. *Web Security: A Step-By-Step Reference Guide.* Reading, Mass.: Addison-Wesley.

Chapter
6

Guarding Your Wireless Operations

In this chapter:

➤ The Impact of Wireless Commerce on Your Web-Based Business
➤ The Wireless Web and Your Enterprise
➤ Wireless Security and Your Web-Based Business
➤ Unplugged, Clueless, and Insecure?
➤ Guarding Your Wireless Operations Checklist

Wireless technologies are creating new opportunities and new problems for web-based businesses. This chapter details how mobile commerce, called m-commerce, is changing e-commerce forever. On-line veterans, such as Charles Schwab, AOL (America Online), and Amazon.com are already offering their products and services on wireless hand-held devices. You will uncover the five types of wireless networks and gain an understanding of their strengths and weaknesses. You will discover how wireless business applications can expand your online business. This chapter explores several of the most popular Internet encryption methodologies. Then WAP (Wireless Application Protocol) and IEEE802.1X wireless security standards are both discussed. The SSL (secure socket layer), public key encryption digital signatures, and other tools referenced in this chapter can be used for both wired and wireless operations. The chapter concludes with a wireless operations checklist that can assist you in optimizing the protection of your web-based business.

■ THE IMPACT OF WIRELESS COMMERCE ON YOUR WEB-BASED BUSINESS

In the United States, computers drive e-commerce, but in other parts of the world, cell phones are the preferred way of getting information, overseeing financial transactions, and managing affairs electronically. In Sweden, for example, consumers can use cell phones to make small purchases. If you want to purchase a cola or a car wash, you can use your cell phone and have the charge added to your telephone bill. The name of this new type of activity is *m-commerce.* Most people define m-commerce as mobile electronic commerce, a subset of e-commerce. Mobile commerce includes all commercial transactions by wireless hand-held devices such as PDAs (personal digital assistants), pagers, cell phones, and two-way radios.

Wireless voice communication presently dominates m-commerce. Mark Zohar (1999) of Forrester Research (forrester.com), an Internet research company, notes that mobile information such as access to AOL, e-mail, instant messaging, travel updates, and yellow pages is becoming more available on more hand-held devices; he forecasts that by next year m-commerce will include more products and services, such as one-click transactions, navigational aids, travel reservations and bookings, and online auction bidding. Michel Levy (2000), president of ECNow.com, forecasts that in five years half of all day stock transactions will be completed over cell phones.

Today, companies like Amazon.com and Barnes and Noble are negotiating with telecommunications companies to let mobile shoppers search for books, music, and software on their cell phones free of charge. This would be an important development, considering the fact that the Yankee Group (yankeegroup.com), an Internet consulting and research firm, predicts that in three years more than 30 percent of all wireless users will access the Internet using wireless hand-held devices.

The wired Internet is characterized by high bandwidth, convenient point-and-click navigation, colorful graphics, and speedy downloads of web pages. The wireless web has less bandwidth, a small format, and limited content. Consequently, the wireless web will be part of overall interaction and customer experience with your web-based business. In the past, commerce was based on the paper letters, books, postal mail, paper memos, and so on. Now the voice telephony network is used everywhere—some cell phones allow you travel around the world and communicate using the same device without changing your telephone number. As we go into the future, wireless Internet transactions will drive another set of user experiences. Due to low transmission speeds and the small format of cell phones and handheld devices, customers' profiles will become more important than ever. Mobile communications using cell phone interactions will have to target just a few of the customers' top needs and desires. Nigel Deighton (2001) of the Gartner Group (gartner.com), an Internet research organization located in Stamford, Connecticut, points out that these interests are likely to center on travel, financial task management, entertainment, and shopping applications as one element of a broader customer experience.

➤ Uncovering Business Applications for Wireless Networks

Wireless commercial transactions will force a wider vision of the Internet. This vision is likely to take the form of a component in an information and communications network. Currently, over 450 million people worldwide use cell phones, and it is estimated that this number will increase to 1 billion by 2002. In contrast, about 200 million PCs are connected to the Internet. This relationship shows the potential value of m-commerce. Individuals are mobile and are likely to become more mobile as technology develops. Web-based businesses simply cannot ignore the business opportunities offered by m-commerce. The following are a few examples:

➤ E-mail messaging: Many employees use e-mail as the primary way of communicating with the office, clients, partners, and affiliates. The connectivity of e-mail and the Internet gives individuals and web-based businesses the ability to interact and share information through a wireless exchange. For example, authors can send manuscript illustrations as e-mail attachments to publishers using e-mail messaging.

➤ Mobile instant messaging: Mobile instant messaging allows mobile individuals to check on the availability of people, communicate instantly (nonverbally), and use text chats to exchanges ideas and information. Mobile instant messaging includes telephony software (voice over the Internet), video conferencing, and online games. For example, your brokerage can send stock price alerts to your PDA.

➤ Unified messaging: Unified messaging is currently being developed. After development is complete, users will be able to send all their fixed and mobile voice mail, e-mail, faxes, and instant messages to the same mailbox, accessing different types of messages with any one single interface. This technology requires the availability of text-to-speech and speech-to-text technologies.

These mobile commerce business applications show that nearly everything is likely to go wireless. Wireless commerce gives users a maximum amount of flexibility by allowing them to decide where to complete a transaction. Other benefits are convenience, as well as savings in time and cost. Functions such as bill paying, merchandise purchasing, stock trading, and banking will soon be standard fare for wireless devices. In the not-too-distant future, it is likely that ordinary individuals will make commercial transactions using their cell phones, pagers, two-way radios, and PDAs; this means that web-based businesses must deliver a mixed-mode experience that will be genuinely useful and compelling.

■ THE WIRELESS WEB AND YOUR ENTERPRISE

In the beginning of wireless network communications, one-way information was often basic data about the weather or stock prices; transmission of such information did not require encryption or any other security measures. Over time, demand has increased, and customers want the functionality of the Internet merged with the convenience of the telephone. Partners, affiliates, and employees also want to access the network using handheld devices such as Palm Pilots and cell phones.

Customers, business partners, and employees can connect to your wireless network with today's new technologies, allowing them to complete the same tasks as if they were locally connected. Actually, the ability to work off-line and communicate without any physical wired boundary has existed for some time in the form of e-mail systems. Telecommuting employees can enter new orders, close deals, and make

Table 6.1   Overview of Personal to National Wireless Networking

	Wireless Personal Area Network (WPAN)	Wireless Local Area Network (WLAN)	(LAN-LAN) Bridge LAN-LAN	Wireless Metropolitan Area Network (WMAN)	Wireless Wide Area Network (WWAN)
Area covered	A few feet	Within building or campus	Building to building	Metropolitan area	National
Functions	Alternative to cable	Extension of or alternative to wired LAN	Alternative to wired connection	Extension of wired LAN	Extension of LAN
User fees	No	No	No	Yes	Yes
Typical transmission speed	0.1–20 Mbps	1–11 Mbps	2–100 Mbps	10–100 Kbps	1–32 Kbps

Source: Adapted from the Wireless LAN Alliance [http://www.wlana.com], 1999.

cash deposits through smart cell phones. However, the goal of many web-based businesses is to make m-commerce a full partner of their e-commerce objectives. The wireless network therefore must become an integral part of the enterprise.

Table 6.1 shows the five types of wireless networks. Wireless networks range from WPANs that only cover a few feet to WWANs that cover the nation. Your organization may have one or several of the wireless networks described in the following list:

➤ Wireless PAN (personal area network): Wireless networking connects up to several feet and allows the exchange of information between devices.

➤ Wireless LAN (local area network): Wireless networking connects disparate networks in areas of up to 300 feet, making access easier and more cost-effective.

➤ Wireless LAN LAN (local area network, local area network): Wireless connections between buildings allow users in different locations the opportunity to access the Internet, share files, and access network resources without wires.

➤ Wireless MAN (metropolitan area network): Cellular telephony systems provide wireless networking for specified metropolitan areas. Such systems are useful for virtual private networks (see Chapter 11 for details).

➤ Wireless WAN (wide area network): Satellite or cellular telephony systems connect users across the nation.

Wireless LANs use electromagnetic airwaves (radio and infrared) to communicate information from one point to another without relying on any physical connection. The area they cover is within a building or campus. Many industry experts expect wireless LANs to replace cables and infrared as the primary connectivity solution for applications such as synchronization. Wireless LANs assist rather than replace the enterprise's wired LAN (local area network) system. The following are a few examples of how wireless LANs provide flexibility and power:

➤ Medical practioners use handheld devices to deliver patient information. Consultants and auditors increase productivity with quick network setups.

➤ Enterprises can reduce overhead administrative costs of dynamic environments. Network managers implement wireless LANs to provide backup for mission-critical applications running on wired networks.

➤ Training sites at corporations and universities use wireless LANs to facilitate access to information, exchange of information, and education.

➤ Retail stores simplify network reconfiguration. Trade shows and branch office workers minimize setup requirements by installing preconfigured wireless LANs.

➤ Warehouse and dock workers use wireless LANs to exchange information with central databases in order to help increase their productivity. Restaurant waitresses and car rental service representatives provide faster service with real-time customer information.

➤ Senior executives in public or customer conference rooms can make quicker decisions because they have real-time information.

■ WIRELESS SECURITY AND YOUR WEB-BASED BUSINESS

The need for a wireless e-commerce security tool is rapidly growing. Web-based businesses need to demand stringent security measures for their wireless activities. However, disputes frequently arise between software vendors about the transfer speed, size, readability, and navigation standards wireless security should embrace. For example, most cell phones and web-enabled PDAs have data transfer rates of 14.4 Kbps (kilobits per second) or less. In contrast, typical cable modems or DSL (digital subscription line) connections to the Internet are 56 Kbps. Therefore, a web page that usually downloads in two or three seconds takes an agonizingly long time to download at 14.4 Kbps. Additionally, web pages with high graphic content are often unreadable on the small screens of PDAs.

A delay in developing universal standards could dampen the growth of m-commerce. A knowledge of the different types of encryption security used in e-commerce can facilitate your understanding of the security issues faced by m-commerce. PDAs and cell phones do not allow users to point and click with a mouse. Navigation is somewhat tricky because it requires using one hand to scroll keys. Keep in mind that unlike paper-based information, electronic information can be stolen remotely; the perpetrator does not need to be on the premises. Additionally, electronic data is much easier to intercept and alter than is paper-based data. When data is encrypted, a cryptographic system transforms the electronic information into an unreadable form; the information owner is now assured that the information cannot be tampered with in this form. Because cryptographic systems use a key to determine how the electronic information will be transformed, guarding the key and overseeing access to the key are top management concerns.

Many of the handheld devices that are being used for m-commerce were not invented with security in mind (much like the Internet). For software vendors, traditional mechanisms for TCP/IP, HTTP, and encryption security, such as SSL, PKI (public key infrastructure), and CA (certificate authorities), are too big and cumbersome for low-powered devices or miniature cell phones so small they can slip into a shirt pocket. Additionally, wireless handheld devices have different network configurations (see Table 6.1). Safe wireless access is a serious problem for web-based businesses. Because of the lack of industry-wide standards, network administrators are seeking their own solutions on a company-by-company basis. An examination of how encryption works for information transmitted over the wired Internet can help you gain a better understanding of the security of the wireless Internet.

➤ Understanding Cryptographic Systems

Keep in mind that both e-commerce and m-commerce are based on trust, but the exchange of confidential information and the protection of personal data still must be maintained. Cryptology has existed for centuries, but today it is a commercial commodity and a fundamental building block of a secured network. Technological advances have made cryptology practical and inexpensive to use. Figure 6.1 shows a symmetrical key cryptographic system, the fundamental approach for the first half of the twentieth century. Note that the encryption-locking key and the decryption-unlocking key are the same. Bob writes a message to Alice, and then uses the encryption key to encrypt the message. The information is transmitted over the Internet, where it can be intercepted. If an eavesdropper intercepts the encrypted message, the information will be scrambled and unreadable. Alice receives Bob's encrypted message and uses her decryption-unlocking key to decode the document.

The weakness of this approach is that the sender, the receiver, and anyone else who has the key can decode the encrypted message. Additionally, the two users of this system must agree in advance to use and maintain the same common secret key. The strength of this approach

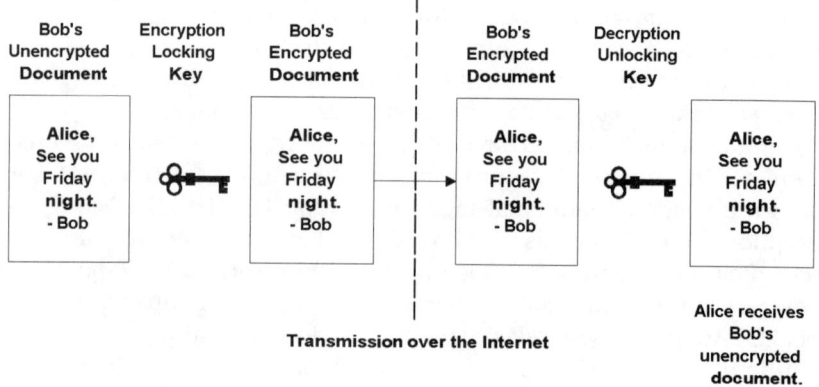

Figure 6.1 Overview of personal-to-global wireless networking

results from keeping the key complex and secret. For small corporations, this approach is effective. For large enterprises (with users distributed over a wide area), a symmetrical system becomes less effective, and the chances of a security breach increase. Ideally, each worker should have a private key. According to experts from Certicom (2000), a firm that specialized in wireless security, any enterprise with 1,000 users would require approximately 500,000 keys to maintain security. Although many software programs can assist you in key management, maintaining a half-million keys is unrealistic.

➤ Public Key Infrastructure

Public key encryption was developed in the 1970s in an effort to reduce the problems associated with key management and possible compromises during the delivery of confidential information. Figure 6.2 is a conceptual view of public key cryptography. Public key encryption does not require shared confidential keys to be preplaced so that users can communicate. Each user has a public and a private key. The public key is published or stored in a publicly accessible directory and the private key is known only to the user and kept separate from public keys. Private keys are based on complex RSA (Rivest-Sharmir-Adelman; the standard was named for its three inventors) mathematics that effectively hide the key or make it indeterminable to intruders who may try to decode the key by using brute force.

Figure 6.2 shows how public key infrastructure works. Bob writes a document, then encrypts the document using Alice's public key. Alice's public key can be distributed to friends and business associates. (Note: Bob does not know Alice's private key. Alice's private key is kept in a secure location on her computer and never released to anyone.) Bob sends the encrypted document over the Internet, where it can be intercepted. If the document is intercepted, the eavesdropper will only get an unreadable scramble of letters and numbers. Even Bob, the sender, cannot decrypt the message; this makes the message a one-way communication. Alice receives Bob's encrypted document and uses her own private key to decrypt the message.

The strength of public key infrastructure is that it eliminates the need to transmit confidential information in a secured channel. The source of the private key is a primary weakness of the public key infrastructure system. If Alice's private key is discovered, an attacker can compromise all of Alice's encrypted messages; moreover, the attacker can sign messages as though he or she were Alice.

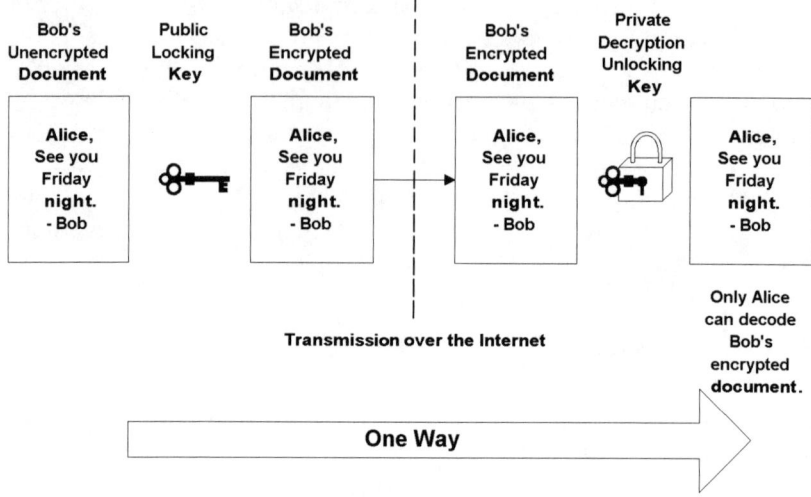

Figure 6.2 Do you know where that public key really came from?

➤ Secure Socket Layer

SSL (secure socket layer) combines client authentication, signed digital certificates, and symmetrical encryption to identify end users accessing a web site. Signed digital certificates come from trusted CA (certificate authority) third-party vendors such as Certicom (certicom.com), RSA (Rivest-Sharmir-Adelman) Security (rsas.com), Entrust Technologies (entrust.com), Baltimore Technologies (baltimore.com), and Verisign (verisign.com), and authenticate that the user and the server are who they say they are.

The SSL method is transparent, and the data load is divided between the client and the server. SSL was originally developed to support encryption and authentication in both directions so that HTTP requests and responses could be protected against eavesdroppers and manipulators. Figure 6.3 is a conceptual drawing of the hand-shaking process of SSL.

1. The client sends a hello message (client-hello) to the server. This message contains the client's name, a transaction serial number, and a random *nonce* (a random number).
2. The server responds with a message (server-hello). The server

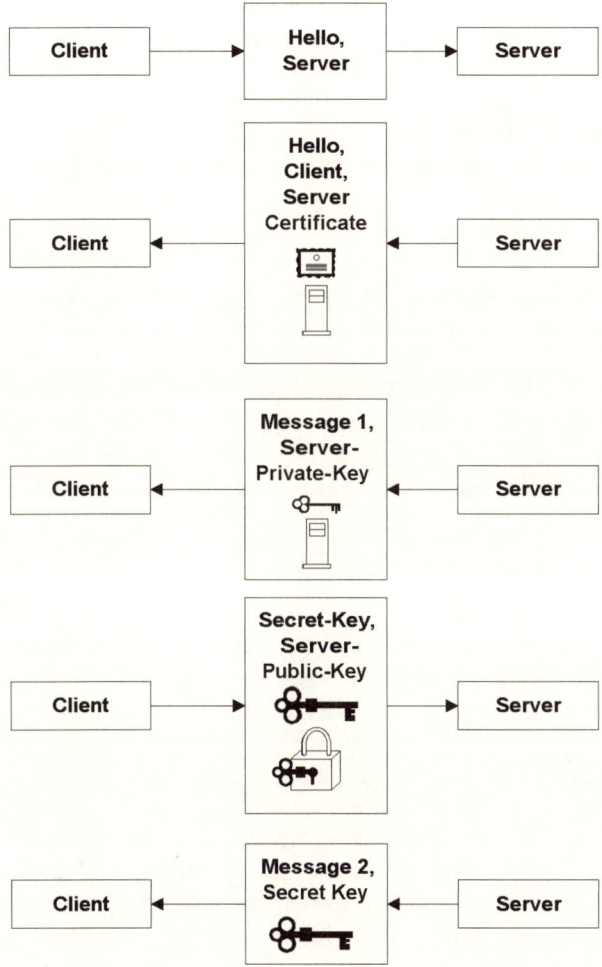

Figure 6.3 Conceptual overview of the Secure Socket Layer cryptographic system

message contains its name, transition serial number, a random nonce, and a certificate containing its public key. The certificate must be digitally signed by a CA (certificate authority) that both the client and server trust.

3. The server authenticates itself by sending message 1, which was encrypted using the private key. The client decodes the en-

crypted text using the server's public key. If the client browser accepts the signed certificate, then the client accepts that the server is who it says it is. The client must also agree to trust the CA. (This trust of the certification authority is discussed in detail later.)

4. Once the client accepts the signed certificate, the client generates a private key that is encrypted using the server's public key. The session key is used for a symmetrical encryption session.

5. All the hand-shaking is done and both the client and the server know the secret key they will use for the session. The server can send message 2 using the secret key.

One of the benefits of SSL security is that it prevents IP spoofing from captured passwords or password files. The mutual authentication of client and server provides each participant in the transaction with positive identification of the other via the trusted third party.

➤ Certificates of Authority

Certificates of authority (CAs) are used to authenticate client and server identity. Without this type of authentication, an attack organization can lure your customers into connecting to the wrong server or into a server spoofing the identity of your web-based business. Customers can be swindled when they request your server's public key and the attack organization sends a fraudulent key. Next, when the client receives the digitally signed message using the server's private key, it can also be a fake. Without the oversight of the CA, the client, after receiving the attack organization's server's public and private keys, may mistakenly believe that it is safe to transmit confidential information. The security difficulty in this example is a problem of mistaken identity; the client is connected to the wrong server. To avoid this difficulty the client needs a way to verify that the server actually is what it claims to be. Certificates of authority are designed to solve this problem because they validate the authenticity of a server or user.

Certificate authorities guarantee that when the client downloads a file sent by your web-based business, your organization (not a fictitious entity like the one described earlier) has signed the file. Digital certificates come from a trusted third-party certificate-authority company. Like public notaries, these organizations put their seal on the document to validate its authenticity.

When visiting a web site using SSL, click on the site's certificate

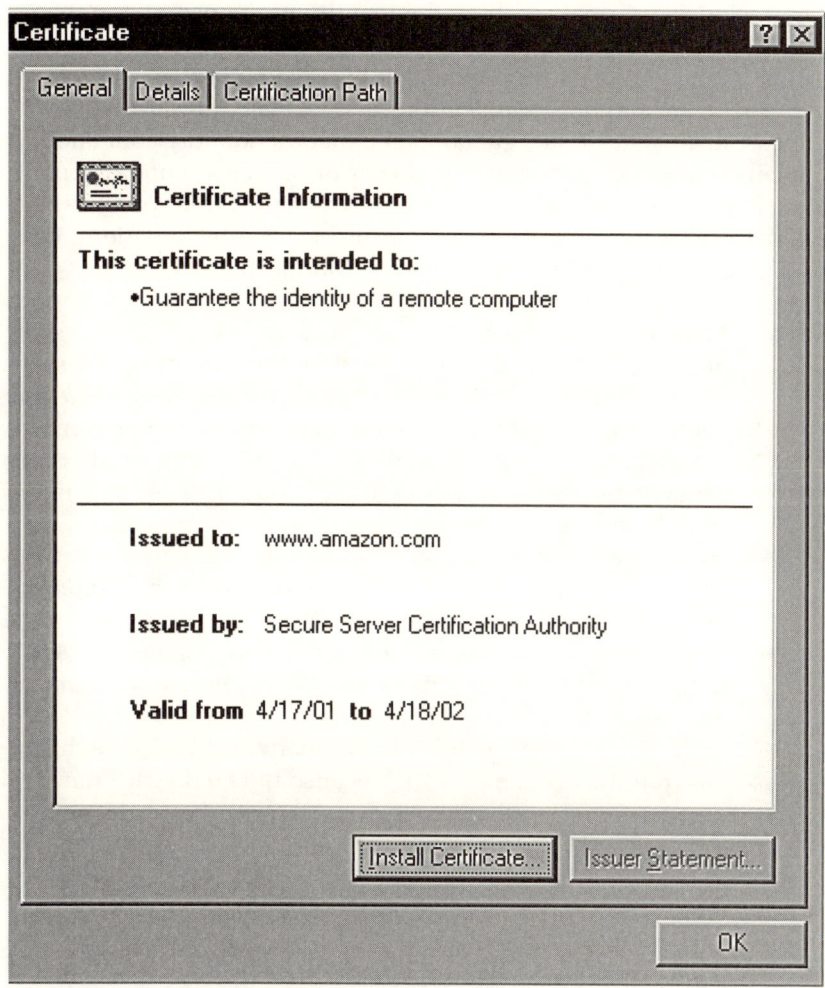

Figure 6.4 Example of certificate information

while you are connected. To indicate a secured web site, Netscape web browsers display a key icon, and Internet Explorer web browsers use a padlock icon in the status bar. For information about certificates while using a Microsoft Internet Explorer browser, click on *Properties* under the *File* menu. Each web has a *Certificate* button that allows you to view the current site's certificate. Figure 6.4 shows how a web site's certificate includes information about the identity of the owner and the issuer, as well as the expiration date. The important part of this message is that it is a guarantee of a remote computer's identity.

Certificate authorities are entities that validate the authenticity of the certificates they issue, guaranteeing that the identity contained in the certificate belongs to the true owner of the corresponding public key. However, the management of certificates by a third party can be difficult and certificates of authenticity do have many limitations. Ross Anderson (2000) provides the following examples:

➤ Many web users disable the security features of their browsers, hoping that this action will speed up their Internet access. If the client check against the root certificate fails, then the client should ask for permission to proceed. However, many browsers are configured to proceed anyway; as a result, their users do not see warnings (and often do not know how to respond if they do see a warning).

➤ Some web browsers are shipped with the software for certificates of authority turned off. Consequently, many Internet users are not aware of this feature.

➤ Many vendor certificates bind a company name to a DNS name, but are not authorities on either. This assists them in denying all liability.

➤ Valid certificates may be for a company or DNS name different from that of the web site because the credit card transaction service was subcontracted; this assists the certificate authority in denying all liability.

■ UNPLUGGED, CLUELESS, AND INSECURE?

It is likely that the next Internet gold rush will focus on m-commerce. As usual, web-based businesses are hurrying to deploy new wireless offerings before competitors. Consequently, wireless Internet commercial transactions will have many of the same problems as wired Internet commerce. In the wireless world, commercial transactions are more difficult because of divergent networks and protocols, as well as the bickering over wireless standards. Moreover, when wireless security concerns are raised, someone is quick to note that SSL encryption did not evolve until a year after the Internet's development and several terabytes of data were transmitted over the Internet. However, that was in the past and today the online world is larger, technologically smarter, and overall more dangerous.

According to Jay Wrolstad (2001) in a recent report from Myers Reports, (myers.com), an Internet research firm, m-commerce revenues will likely reach $4.74 billion in 2004. However, these forecasts are uncertain because of unresolved questions about technology standards, governmental legislation, and consumer privacy rights. Consumer services include one-way communications with news, sports, weather, and stock quotes. Typical wireless two-way communications include credit and debit card payments through cell phones for music, books, cinema tickets, and stock trades. The transmission of basic information such as the weather and news does not require any type of security. The transmission of wireless commercial transactions requires the same level of security as your web-based transactions. Internally, the transmission of corporate information on your wireless network also needs the same level of security that is not in place. The following explores two popular wireless security standards, WAP (Wireless Application Protocol) and IEEE802.1X (the X stands for the version number of the protocol).

➤ Becoming Aware of the WAP Wireless Security Standard

Today the Internet marketplace includes handheld digital wireless devices, such as mobile phones, pagers, two-way radios, smart phones, and communicators from low-end to high-end, that allow Internet access to users from around the world. WAP is a communications protocol and application environment that can be used with a number of operating systems. WAP is one of the many standards for getting Internet data safely to mobile Internet users. The central element of this approach is the WAP gateway. Some call the WAP gateway a virtual gatekeeper between the worlds of WTLS (Wireless Transport Layer Security) and SSL. WAP includes its own WTLS security protocol, which is equivalent to SSL but uses encryption algorithms that are less resource-intensive. Using WTLS, the wireless device communicates with the WAP gateway over a wireless network. Next, the WAP gateway transmits the message over the Internet by communicating with the web server and converting the WTLS message into a SSL message. After the message is in the SSL format, the e-commerce site or corporate network can read the message.

Before the current versions of WAP, a known security hole still remained. This security hole was at the WAP gateway, where the data goes from the wires to the air for wireless transmission. At the WAP gateway, the HTML data must decrypt, then reencrypt itself as WML (Wireless Markup Language); this step is necessary because the data is going from SSL encryption, which supports HTML, to WTLS encryption, which supports WML. If the attack organization can intercept the decrypted traffic before it is rescrambled, then your Internet transmission can be hacked.

➤ Securing Your Wireless LAN with the IEEE802.1X Standard

Support for IEEE802.1X is being added to the next release of the Microsoft for Windows Operating System. The IEEE802.1X standard uses encryption and authentication for wireless security. The Wired Equivalent Privacy (WEP) algorithm is used as the secret key for authentication and encryption. WEP provides encryption services to protect authorized users of a wireless LAN from eavesdropping and provides the physical security attributes comparable to a wired medium. The WEP encryption is a symmetrical cryptographic system that uses the same key to encrypt and decrypt. The standard assumes that the secret shared keys are delivered to the IEEE802.1X wireless station (STA) via a secure channel independent of IEEE802.1X.

At this time, the major weakness of this system is the lack of a key-management protocol. For a large corporation with many stations, this lack of access control may play a pivotal role in breaching the enterprise's security. Herb Bethoney (2001) reports that an attacker can eavesdrop on a wireless network using a wireless LAN analyzer application. The attack organization can capture the plain and encrypted text of shared keys used for authentication, figure out the authentication response, provide a new *checksum* (a simple error detection scheme), and then connect to the network as a valid user.

For enterprises that already have wired networks, wireless LANs can save time and money (keep in mind that wireless LANs are extensions of wired LANs). For example, at the University of North Carolina, Chapel Hill, a classroom in a relatively modern building took $150,000 to renovate with fixed-network connections. The rest of the building cost $15,000 to renovate and was completed in two days. The university used IEEE802.1X-based wireless LAN products because of their flexibility and cost. The system's interoperability and ease of management provide another advantage to the university.

■ GUARDING YOUR WIRELESS OPERATIONS CHECKLIST

The items listed in the following checklist are protective procedures for your enterprise's wireless networks and operations. Keep in mind that technologies as well as operating and security standards are changing every day. Remaining up-to-date with the latest developments is important to the quality of management decision-making.

✓ Make certain that your organization uses SSL (or another encryption method) to prevent confidential information on the server from being intercepted.

✓ The degree of security you use on your wired networks should be equal to the security you use on four wireless networks. Wired and wireless Internet transmissions have the same degree of risk.

✓ Determine which CA signatures are installed in your customer's web browsers and which ones these browsers trust. Avoid little-known CAs that may not stay in business.

✓ Determine the best way to back up your private keys and certificates. If these items get corrupted, you will have to start the whole certification process all over again.

✓ What access-control policies are in place to verify client certificates? Make certain you understand what the software is supposed to do.

✓ Test your wireless security to verify that it is as effective away from home as it is at home.

✓ Develop a wireless security plan. Keep in mind that viruses and other security threats are not limited to the wired Internet.

✓ No single methodology will meet all your wireless security requirements. Review multiple approaches and implement several to be secure. Different levels of security are needed for different types of mobile needs.

■ REFERENCES

Anderson, Ross. 2001. *Security Engineering: A Guide to Building Dependable Distributed Systems.* New York: Wiley.

Bethoney, Herb. 2001. WEP can't stand alone for security. *eWeek,* 15 April. Available at [http://techupdate.zdnet.com/techupdate/stories/main/0,14179,2706267,00.html]. 3 December 2001.

Certicom. 2000. An introduction to information security. Certicom white paper. July. Available at [http://www.certicom.com/research/wecc1.html]. 3 December 2001.

Deighton, Nigel, Ken Dulaney, Bob Egan, Simon Hayward, Daryl Plummer, and Martin Reynolds. 2001. The "supranet" explained. *Gartner Group's Dataquest, Report Number* IX20010212031307242. 29 January 2001.

Field, Benjamin J. 2001. Wireless security overview. SecurityPortal. Available at [http://www.securityportal.com]. 20 May 2001. Currently not available online.

Izarek, Stephanie. 2000. Weaving a wireless web. Fox News, 9 March. Available online at [http://www.regisoft.com/wireless.htm]. 3 December 2001.

Larson, Eric, and Brian Stephens. 2000. *Administering Web Servers, Security and Maintenance.* Upper Saddle River, Ill.: Prentice Hall.

Levy, Mitchell. 2000. Wireless applications become more common. Commercenet.com newsletter, 21 June. Available at [http://www.commerce.net/research/ebusiness-strategies/2000/00_13_n.html]. 3 December 2001.

Myers Reports. 2001. The seamless media survival guide. Myers Reports, 26 March. Available at [http://www.myers.com/research/reports/me_seamless.html]. 3 December 2001.

Nobel, Carmen, and Scott Berinato. 2000. Wireless: Unplugged and insecure. *eWeek,* 2 July. Available at [http://www.zdnet.com/zdnn/stories/news/0,4586,2597657,00.html]. 3 December 2001.

Teerikorpi, Eero. 2001. How secure is the wireless Internet? *Telecommunications,* 1 May. Available at [http://cma.zdnet.com]. 3 December 2001.

Stein, Lincoln D. 1998. *Web Security: A Step-by-Step Reference Guide.* Reading, Mass.: Addison-Wesley.

Zohar, Mark. 1999. The dawn of mobile ecommerce. The Forrester Report, October. Available online at [http://www.itechnopreneur.com/attachments/The_dawn_of_mobile_commerce.pdf]. 3 December 2001.

Chapter

Reducing Denial of Service Attacks

In this chapter

The level and severity of denial of service (DoS) attacks vary. Some industry professionals note that attackers have gone from just one web servers to the core of the enterprises infrastructure. DoS attackers may want to annoy one person by targeting a certain online account, bother several individuals by canceling their credit cards, or attack a large web-based business so they can boast about their success with other attackers. Both insiders and outsiders can cause DoS attacks; however, they are usually initiated by attack organizations. In this chapter, you will discover what motivates DoS attackers and how the popular types of DoS attacks work. You will gain a good understanding of the damage DoS and DDoS (distributed denial of service) attacks can do and find out how your organization can unwittingly be the source of a DoS attack against another business. You will uncover effective countermeasures for DoS attacks. This chapter explains exactly what you should do if your web-based business is attacked. The chapter concludes with step-by-step instructions on how to calculate the severity of an attack.

■ DENIAL OF SERVICE (DoS) ATTACKS: INTERNET WEAPONS OF MASS DESTRUCTION

All DoS attacks have one thing in common; one host communicates with the victim system, then effectively crashes it by sending information the victim cannot possibly process. The first DoS attack happened in 1988. The Robert Morris "Internet Worm" caused a buffer overflow in a UNIX server. This type of exploit was not repeated until 1996, when a paper detailing how to write the program was published in hacker magazine *Phrack* (phrack.com). Over the next several years, attacks have become common, and involve both UNIX and Microsoft products. DoS attackers focus on configuration errors, software defects, and weaknesses in the nature of the Internet.

In June 2001, an unknown attacker hit the Computer Emergency Response Team (cert.org) Coordination Center. CERT is a nonprofit organization that provides information on the latest vulnerabilities in computer systems. The DoS attack flooded the center's web site with useless data requests, rendering the web site useless for 24 hours. Web-based businesses such as Yahoo! (yahoo.com), eBay (ebay.com), Amazon.com (amazon.com), ZDNet (zdnet.com), CNN (cnn.com), MSN (msn.com), and eTrade (etrade.com) have also been victims of DoS attacks.

Brian Lemos (2001) reports that Stefan Savage, a professor of computer science and cofounder of security company Asta Networks (asta-networks.com) found that at least 4,000 DoS attacks happen each week, and the problem is getting worse. The results of the recent 2001 CSI/FBI report support this assertion. According to the 2001 CSI/FBI Computer Crime and Security Survey, 78 percent of the respondents report being victims of DoS incidents in 2001, compared to only 60 percent in 2000.

One of the reasons for this increase may be the ability of attackers to hide their identities. Groups like the Internet Engineering Task Force (ietf.org) are working on a new technology to trace tainted data back to its source; such an undertaking, however, is difficult because DoS attacks may come from hundreds of locations at the same time. Apprehension of the perpetrators requires cooperation from many organizations (law enforcement, the enterprise's ISP, and others).

What motivates these attackers? Scrambray, McClure, and Kurtz (2001) note that DoS attackers are often frustrated individuals who want to get even with those they perceive as the sources of their frustrations. A DoS attack can bring web-based business down in a hurry, and is an excellent way for attackers to overcome a feeling of powerlessness. Additionally, some attackers may be motivated by personal disputes or political vendettas against the web-based business itself or against individuals within the web-based business. This rule has one exception. Some DoS attacks are needed to bring down the system so that the attacker's programs can be enabled (i.e., when the system is rebooted, the attacker's changes are installed). These new changes may grant the intruders systemwide administrator privileges. If the attack organization gains this type of root access, then the attacker has won. Therefore it is very important to make certain that an attack organization has not attacked your web-based business *twice.*

■ KNOWING YOUR ABCS OF DoS ATTACKS

In some situations, attack organizations are not interested in stealing, copying, or vandalizing information from your web-based business. DoS attacks on your web-based business are not to gain access, but rather to prevent others from using part or all of your network. This type of electronic warfare includes jamming, mimicry, and physical attacks on your web-based business.

According to Bennett Todd (2000) of OVEN, a firm that develops web sites and applications to maximize bandwidth, attack organizations take advantage of the two types of Internet weakness. The first is the public Internet, spelled with a capital *I,* which is used by individuals all over the world. Information sent over the Internet can include spoofed (fake) source addresses. After these tainted packets reach their targets, they are difficult (if not impossible) to backtrack to the attack organization because of the IP (Internet Protocol). Second is the Internet, spelled with a lowercase *i.* It is a collection of networks that organizations privately use for transmitting documents and communicating. DoS attackers can use these small "i" connections to exploit the limitations of TCP/IP (Transmission Control Protocol/Internet Protocol) and enterprise vulnerabilities. DoS attacks are designed to bring a network to a standstill by using several methods.

➤ Flooding limited resources with a barrage of useless traffic that is impossible to process. This is often called *resource starvation* and it effectively locks out users for a period of time.

➤ Crashing a network device or host computer. Crashing a host computer prevents legitimate users from interacting with the web-based business. Frequently, attack organizations exploit software defects in the operating system or network services to install malicious codes or programs. When the web server is restarted, the attack organization's programs are enabled.

➤ Reconfiguring a resource to make it useless. Sometimes attack organizations reconfigure enterprise resources with back-door programs. The attack organization then turns on its programs, and the computers of your web-based business become like zombies, launching DoS attacks against unsuspecting victim organizations.

Technological solutions can be installed to limit the damage caused by all known types of DoS attacks. Like all web-based security issues, however, these solutions can stop problems today but cannot anticipate the new DoS attacks that are constantly being created by attackers. Table 7.1 provides an overview of several popular types of attacks, including the names of the attacks and the resources affected.

Table 7.1 shows five categories of resources that are affected by the DoS attacks listed. The following is a detailed explanation of how these resources are affected by DoS attacks:

1. Disk overloads: A disk is a round plate on which data can be encoded. Accessing data from the machine's main memory is faster than accessing data from a disk. Disks retain data even when the computer is turned off and are the storage medium for most types of information. In a DoS attack, the disk is filled with useless information, denying use of this resource to legitimate users.

2. Bandwidth consumption: *Bandwidth* can be defined as the size of the pipe from your network to the Internet. In other words, bandwidth is the amount of data that can be transmitted in a certain amount of time. For digital devices, such as computers, bandwidth is generally measured in bits per second (Bps). For

Table 7.1 Examples of the Resources Affected by Denial of Service Attacks

Attack	Filled Disk	Bandwidth Consumption	Buffer Overflow or Change in Internal Data Structure	Crash or Slowdown of CPU Cycles	Software or Malformed Packet
FTP bounce	X				
Smurf		X			
SYN flood			X		
PING of Death			X	X	X
Teardrop			X	X	X
UDP bomb		X		X	

analog devices, bandwidth is usually measured in cycles per second or Hertz (Hz). Bandwidth is important for web-based businesses because it determines how fast the information can get into and out of the processing server.

3. Buffer overflows or reconfiguration of a resource to make it useless: The buffer acts as a holding area that allows the CPU (central processing unit) to manipulate information before transferring it to permanent storage (your hard drive), your printer, or another type of permanent storage device. Because the process of reading and writing data to a disk is relatively slow; many programs keep track of data changes in the buffer and then copy the buffer to a disk. This process can be compared to what happens when you use a word processing program. Saving each small change you make to disk would make altering the document slow and inefficient; therefore, the buffer keeps track of all the changes you make to your document until you save the file to disk. The computer then updates the disk with the contents of the buffer. If the computer fails, all of the editing changes will be lost unless your word processing program has an automatic save feature. If your buffer overflows before the data can be "saved," your system has been compromised.

4. Crashes or CPU slowdowns: The system is forced to stop (crash) or the CPU is overworked and the timely processing of data is

denied. (Note: Two typical components of a CPU are the arithmetic logic unit (ALU), which performs arithmetic and logical operations for the computer, and the control unit (CU), which extracts, decodes, and executes instructions from memory.)

5. Malformed packets or software defects: Information is transmitted on the Internet via packets. Some clever attack organizations have learned how to create malformed packets that trick routers and firewalls into believing that the packets are normal. When unprepared web servers receive the malformed packets or malicious code, they are likely to stop responding to any requests.

■ TYPES OF DoS THREATS AND COUNTERMEASURES

Businesses have seen many types of DoS attacks (and more are invented each day). Often in a DoS attack, intruders send a steady stream of requests to your web-based business in hopes of exhausting all memory (called resource starvation) or consuming all processor capacity on the server (called bandwidth consumption). Resource starvation happens when the attacker prevents legitimate users from accessing your enterprise's resources—valuable resources such as memory and CPU time are filled to capacity with bogus data preventing legitimate users from using or storing information. Bandwidth consumption occurs when attackers transmit vast quantities of data in a fixed amount of time—in other words, the system is flooded with mountains of junk data than cannot be processed. The following are a few examples of DoS attack techniques. Many of the potential countermeasures listed here are suggested by Joel Scambray and colleagues (2001).

➤ FTP Bounce Attack

An FTP bounce attack causes the disk to fill with useless data (see Table 7.1, first column). A normal FTP (File Transfer Protocol) connection is used to transfer documents and data anonymously. FTP connections are usually made using port 21. The user's ID and password are sent and the user receives the requested data. A FTP bounce attack is designed to slip past the organization's firewall. The attack organization uploads a file to the FTP server and requests that the file be sent to an internal server (in the enterprise's network). The uploaded file contains a tainted software program or malicious script that occupies the internal server and uses up all the memory and CPU resources.

Countermeasures for This Type of DoS Attack

Install firewalls to filter content and commands (see Chapter 11).

➤ Smurf DoS Attack

Smurf attacks cause bandwidth consumption (see Table 7.1, second column). In a Smurf attack, ICMP (Internet Control Message Protocol) packets are sent to broadcast addresses of vulnerable networks. (Note: Administrators can use the ICMP to determine if sections of the network are alive. In other words, normal ICMP packets, like all IP packets, contain both source and destination addresses so that the replies are always sent back to the source.) These Smurf packets are spoofed (have fake identities) so that the target and the source addresses are the same. The target replies to the requests by setting up a continuous look function. This activity quickly amplifies the number of bogus requests and can consume all the available bandwidth.

The mechanics of Smurf attacks are as follows: Smurf attacks can amplify themselves by sending PING (Packet Internet Groper) requests to an Internet broadcast address. These are special addresses that broadcast (relay) all received messages to all the connected hosts. Each broadcast address can broadcast to 255 hosts, so a single PING request can be multiplied 255 times. All the hosts receiving the PING request reply to the victim's (spoofed) address instead of the real sender's address. The targeted victim can receive hundreds or even thousands of these PING messages per second. This barrage of requests can consume all of the victim organization's bandwidth and stop the web-based business.

Smurf DoS Attack Countermeasures

> ➤ Configure routers to deny IP-directed broadcasts from other networks into your own network.
> ➤ Configure external routers to block all outbound packets from your site that indicate a source address not contained within your enterprise's network.
> ➤ Disallow broadcast ICMP packets through your router so your organization can avoid contributing to a DoS attack on another organization.

➤ Configure internal routers to block IP spoofing from the network (i.e., block any packets that do not originate in your network).

➤ Harden your operating system to reduce the risk of this type of attack (see Chapter 3).

➤ Contact your operating system vendor to find out whether an operating system security patch is available for this type of DoS attack.

➤ SYN DoS Attack

SYN attacks cause buffer overflows (see Table 7.1, third column). A SYN attack can be summarized as a stream of connection requests aimed at your server. Figure 7.1 shows a normal Internet connection. The client, via his or her web server, contacts your web server. This "Hello, Server" message is flagged with a SYN code. The server acknowledges this by returning a "Hello, Client" message flagged with a SYN ACK code. In

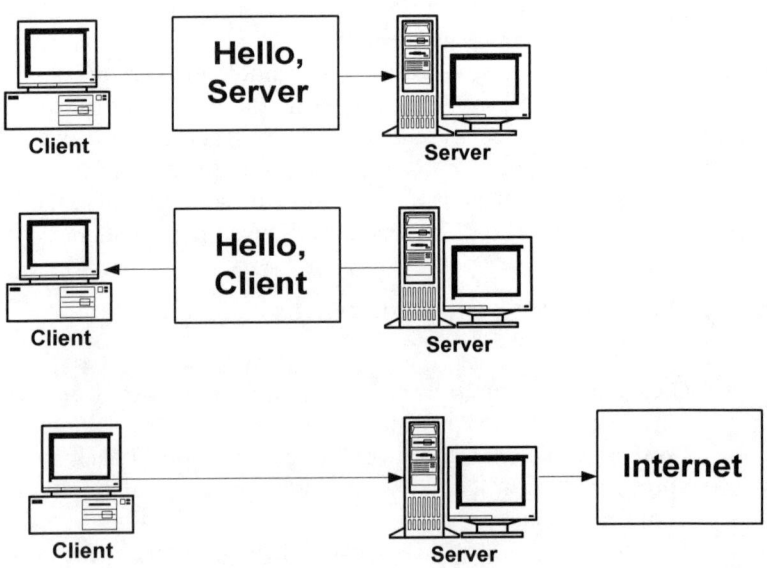

Figure 7.1 Normal Internet connection

DOS Attack

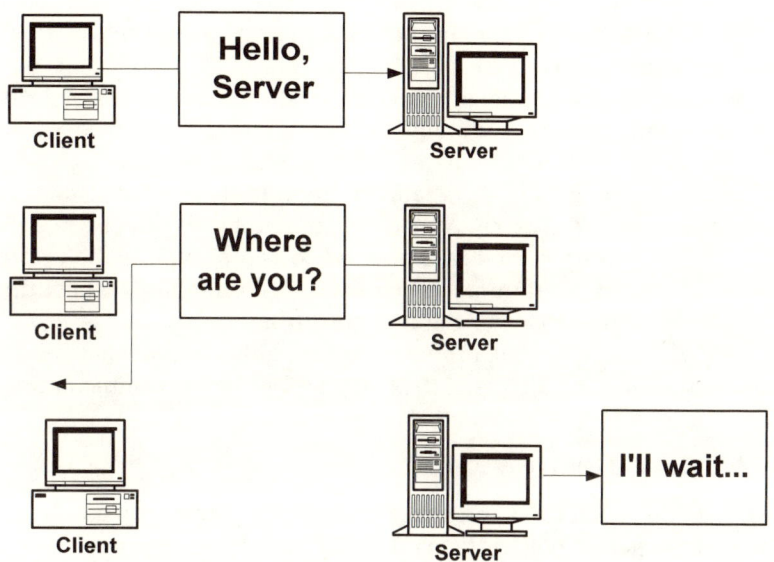

Figure 7.2   Conceptual diagram of a SYN DoS attack

step three, the client must acknowledge this return message. If all goes well, this TCP three-way handshake is correctly completed and the server connects the client to the information requested.

Figure 7.2 illustrates what happens when the victim organization is subject to a SYN flood attack. The attack organization sends the victim server a "Hello, Server" message and requests a response to a non-existent machine or system. The server tries to respond to an incorrect IP address. The three-way TCP handshake cannot be completed. The request remains in the server's queue waiting for a response until the packets begin to expire (about one minute), when the request is dropped. During this waiting period, the victim server is bombarded with more and more fraudulent requests from the attack organization. The connection queue is filled, and TCP services are denied to legiti-mate users. To sum it up, attack organizations can send a relatively small number of malicious requests on many systems to tie up the memory, CPU, and applications on your server. The end result is a server shutdown resulting in denial of service to legitimate users.

SYN DoS Attack Countermeasures

➤ Reconfigure the server to reduce the waiting period for the three-way handshake. Keep in mind that this may impact legitimate users who may be disconnected when they are downloading large documents.

➤ Install service packs to upgrade older operating systems. More recent operating systems are often more resistant to SYN attacks.

➤ In Windows NT, the default configuration directs the server to retransmit the SYN ACK message five times; this means that the waiting period is increased to three minutes before the connection attempts are stopped. Therefore, a good countermeasure is to lower the default setting.

➤ Increase the size of the connection queue. This measure may not stop the effects of SYN attacks, but it can diminish them.

➤ PING of Death Attack

A PING of death occurs when attackers flood the target with malformed data packets (see Table 7.1, fifth column). Administrators troubleshoot the Internet connections of their networks by sending IP (Internet Protocol) PING packets to specific addresses and waiting for a reply. In a PING of death DoS attack, the victim's network or machine is flooded with malformed IP PING packets with command line instructions that cause a buffer overflow that leads to a crash. As many as 18 operating systems are vulnerable to this type of attack, but most can counter it by using security patches. Additionally, many routers and printers are vulnerable to this type of attack. Patches are also available for these devices.

PING of Death Attack Countermeasures

Temporary perimeter protection can be obtained by installing a firewall to block PING floods.

➤ Teardrop DoS Attack

The teardrop attack (sometimes called a fragmented attack) includes a buffer overflow, crash, and malformed packets (see Table 7.1, third, fourth, and fifth columns). To speed up IP transmission over smaller or congested networks, packets are frequently broken up. When the packets arrive at their destination, they are reassembled. However, many routers and intrusion detection systems are unable to discover malicious packets until they are reassembled—the tainted packets can slide under your defenses without examination. When the tainted packet is reassembled, it can overflow the buffer. There may be three end results to this situation. The effected machine can hang or lock up, reboot, or exhibit no ill effects until the attack organization sends a start command for its malicious program.

In a teardrop DoS attack, the reassembled packet starts in the middle of another packet. The operating system is not prepared for this situation and allocates memory to hold the invalid packets. As the machine receives more and more of the malformed packets, resources are starved.

Teardrop DoS Attack Countermeasures

➤ An operating system security patch for this problem is available.

➤ Microsoft users can get either a hot patch (a temporary fix to a software application) or the latest service pack to solve this problem.

➤ UDP Flood Attack

UDP flood attacks are DoS magnification attacks. The attacker sends large numbers of UDP (User Datagram Protocol) packets to the target, thus tying up the network. UDP flood attacks are similar to Smurf attacks. *User Datagram Protocol* is a connectionless protocol that is used for broadcasting messages over a network. Individual attacker machines are used to send tainted packets to overwhelm the victim. To make matters worse, attack organizations can spoof (hide) the true source of their addresses. Consequently, the server cannot find the source of the attack without help.

UDP Attack Countermeasures

Disable unnecessary User Datagram Protocol services.

■ A QUICK GUIDE TO COMMON DoS ATTACKS

The following is a quick guide, listed in alphabetical order, to several common types of DoS attacks. This easy-to-use reference shows the primary differences between the most popular types of DoS attacks.

➤ DNS cache poisoning: DNS (domain name server) is the directory used for mapping domain names and IP addresses (just like a telephone directory). To improve productivity, the DNS server caches the most recent data for quick retrieval. Consequently, this cache can be positioned and the information spoofed to redirect customers or to block access to the web sites.

➤ FTP bounce attack: A hacker uploads a file with malicious software or code to the FTP (File Transfer Protocol) server, then requests that the file be sent to an internal server on your network.

➤ ICMP PING (Internet Control Message Protocol; Packet Internet Groper): These requests have a nonexistent source. Attackers use ICMP PING packets to flood the target's network with bogus requests.

➤ PING of death: This attack floods the victim's network or machine with IP PING packets by using a command line instruction.

➤ Smurf flooding attack: An ICMP magnification attack, this attack is a variation of the PING attack. An attack organization creates an oversized packet that is reassembled past the firewall. The target and the (faked) source are the same, causing a redirected broadcast that consequently magnifies itself, consuming the organization's bandwidth.

➤ SYN flooding attack: The victim server repeatedly responds to faked requests from nonexistent entities. The targeted system must consume resources to keep track of the partially opened connections, resulting in a buffer overflow that locks up the default port for a short period of time.

➤ TCP flooding attack: To launch this type of assault, the attack organization sends a large number of TCP (Transmission Control Protocol) packets to the target system, thus tying up the network.

➤ UDP flooding attack: This magnification attack uses intermediate hosts to generate large amounts of UDP (User Datagram Protocol) network traffic. The tainted UDP packets create a

sort of ping-pong game between two ports. If the process is repeated with multiple hosts, a large traffic stream is generated.
➤ Teardrop (fragmentation) attack: The hacker sends packets that
are reduced in size or broken into small packets. Because the
intrusion detection system often cannot identify these miniature attack signatures, they are passed along to the server.
When the packets are reassembled, they overflow the buffer.

■ DISTRIBUTED DENIAL OF SERVICE ATTACKS

The first distributed denial of service (DDoS) attack was launched in
February 2000. The DDoS targets were Yahoo!, eTrade, eBay, buy.com,
CNN.com, and several other large web-based businesses. DDoS attacks
are generally large-scale attacks manned by persistent individuals who
may or may not have more skills than the average intruder. Like DoS
attacks, DDoS attacks are designed to keep legitimate users from accessing your enterprise's resources.

According to the CERT Coordination Center (2001), several methods can be used to launch DDoS attacks.

➤ Resource starvation: Damage can be caused by the consumption of memory, disk space, CPU time, bandwidth, and even
network connectivity. For example, the web server crashes because it is flooded with bogus requests that are impossible to
process.
➤ Restructure or reconfiguration of information: Intruders can
alter the configuration of machines or networks. For example,
changing routing information used by routers can disable your
network.
➤ Physical destruction or alteration of the network: Unauthorized users should be prevented from physical access to network wiring closets, routers, computers, power and cooling systems, and so on. For example, prevent frustrated individuals
from cutting all of the wires to the network, which can create a
denial of service incident. The physical security of your hardware and software cannot be ignored.

Attack organizations usually use technological penetration tools to
complete port scans and other reconnaissance of thousands of com-

puters. These attack organizations are looking for poorly configured systems or vulnerable software that can provide them with instant access to a handler computer. In just a few weeks, an attack organization can gain control of several hundred systems.

The attackers select the victims and then use tool kits that automatically do the dirty work. The attack organization's tool kit gains root access (as you will recall from Chapter 5, this access is the same high level of access as the administrator) to the handler computers. Usually, owners of the compromised systems are unaware of this activity because attack organizations are good at covering their tracks while installing DDoS attack programs and back doors. (The back doors are used so they can return at their leisure.)

About five types of DoS attacks are currently known to be supported by DDoS programs: Smurf, ICMP flood, UDP flood, TCP flood, and SYN flood (see the preceding section of this chapter, Quick Guide to DoS Attacks, for more information). Newer DDoS attack programs allow the attack organization to select the DoS attack they want to use for a particular victim.

Figure 7.3 is a conceptual diagram of a DDoS attack. A client computer orchestrates the attack. The infected handlers are often little-known, rarely used machines that are not monitored on a daily basis. The client breaks into handler machines and makes them into zombies, so to speak, that control many agents. Software is used to hide the break-in, conceal the attack organization's nefarious activities, and allow surreptitious reentry. This action is frequently called *breaking root*. In other words, the attacker installs a root kit that allows access and privileges equal to those of the system administrator.

The handlers are used for more scanning and security compromises. Installation of the attack organization's programs can take less than five seconds. This means that thousands of DDoS programs can be uploaded within an hour. Installation of these DDoS programs allows the attack organization to control the handlers that control the zombie agents. (Remember zombie agents are small, well defined programs that gather information or perform tasks in the background.)

Agents are hosts that have been burgled and are also running the attacker's program. These zombie agents may be high-speed computers in large organizations or home PCs (personal computers) that are connected to cable modem or DSL lines. At the attack organization's cue, agents start sending hundreds of packets to the targeted server. To start the attack, the attack organization can send out just one command.

Several types of methods have been used to launch DDoS attacks.

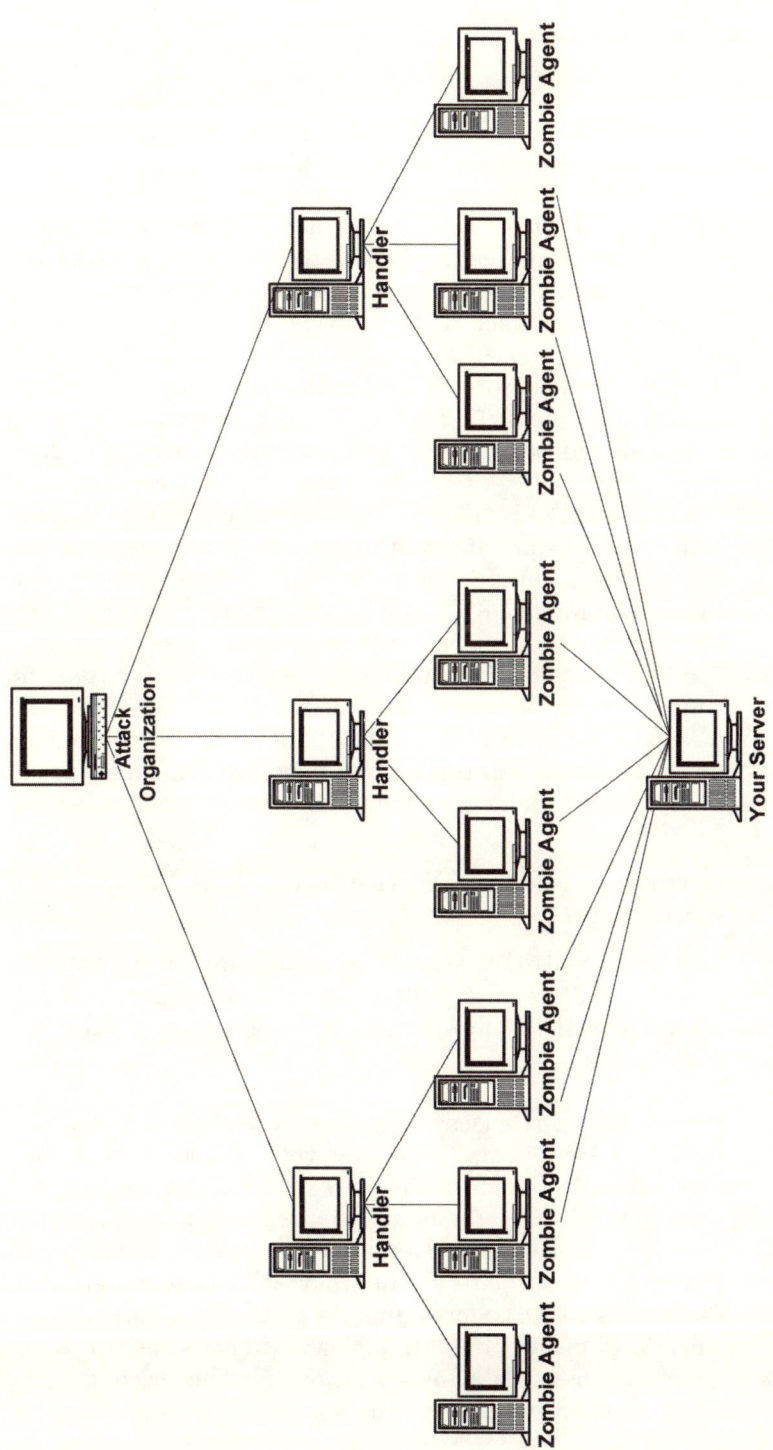

Figure 7.3 Diagram of a DDoS attack

Source: Adapted from Terry William Ogletree, *Practical Firewalls* (Indianapolis, IN: Que, 2000).

Many of these programs are freely available on the Internet. Scambray and colleagues (2001) provide a few of the following examples:

➤ TFN is a UNIX-based DDoS tool with both a client and a server component. This feature allows the attacker to install the DDoS program onto a remote, compromised system and then initiate a DDoS attack. TFN is capable of setting ICMP, Smurf, UDP, and SYN flood attacks.

➤ TFN2K is a successor of TFN that allows randomized communications on ports. This ability enables attackers to sidestep the preventative measure of port blocking on external routers. This versatile DDoS program can launch SYN, UDP, ICMP, and Smurf attacks, and can switch between various types of attacks.

➤ Trinoo is a program that is similar to TFN. Using a remote control program, a master client communicates to handlers, who in turn communicate to agents. These agents then launch useless traffic at an unsuspecting target server.

➤ Trinity v3 targets Linux IRC (Internet relay chat) hosts. The software is installed onto a chat system, where it awaits commands to attack either individual Trinity agents or all agents on the channel. Trinity v3 is capable of setting eight types of flood attacks for any length of time.

➤ Discovering Whether Your System Has Been Compromised

Detecting a DDoS installation may require several different approaches. As with all web-based business security issues, there are no silver bullets or easy solutions. The following are a few suggestions to assist you in your investigations:

➤ Refer to Netscan (netscan.org) to determine whether your network is a Smurf amplifier. Enter your IP address and click *check*. The Netscan program checks the number of responses to an ICMP PING. If the number is greater than one, then the network is misconfigured and needs a configuration change.

➤ Determine which ports are in use on your system and check these ports for DDoS programs. As part of your normal security efforts, make certain that any unused ports are turned off.

➤ Search for the actual names of DDoS programs by conducting a file search or use online detection tools. For example, there is a program called RID (which is available on several Internet web sites) that can help you discover whether an attack organization has installed TFN, Trinoo, or TFN2K in your system. Note, however, that this configurable remote DDoS detector is useful only if the attacker did not change your default ports. Check system logs for suspicious activities. Attack organizations are clever at hiding their tracks, but experienced IT personnel may find a few anomalies that can lead you in the right direction.

➤ Action Steps for When You Are under Attack

The first symptom of a DDoS attack is often a router crash. Routers are devices that connect the enterprise's LAN. Each router determines where a packet should go, and it communicates with other routers to determine the best path between any two hosts (a host can be any computer on your network). You should note that as a general rule routers do not care about the type of data they are transmitting. The primary function of routers is to route packets as quickly as possible.

In the next stage of the DDoS attack, the server may not be working because it is overloaded, tricked by malformed packets, or damaged by malicious software. Further analysis may indicate that the destination addresses of packets are correct, but the sending addresses are random numbers. In this situation it is not possible to trace the malicious traffic to its source or to find the compromised host because the malformed packets include only the address of your organization's LAN router. With luck you can identify the ISP (Internet service provider) who sent the packet. This task is easier in a smaller organization than in a larger organization. Because large organizations may have their own complex internet (see the previous section of this chapter, Knowing Your ABCs of DoS Attacks, for an explanation of this term), tracing the packet to an outside ISP may be almost impossible.

When under a DoS attack, contact your ISP as soon as possible. Have the ISP filter all incoming and outgoing traffic (the ISP controls the traffic flow at its network's points of entry and exit). Such filtering lets the organization eliminate packets with forged IP addresses that are often used in DDoS attacks.

Make certain your security policy (see Chapter 14) provides clear instruction about what to do if you are under attack. Be prepared for the worst-case scenario. For example, if your ISP is unprepared, you will have to shut down your routers and systems to protect yourself. These actions will not stop the attack, but they can assist you in limiting the damage and can help you start tracking down the attacker.

➤ Augmenting Your DoS Defenses

Many software vendors are developing products to help online enterprises deal with DoS attacks. These products assist in the defense of the web-based business and help ensure that the enterprise does not become the source of a DoS attack on another organization. Many of these specially designed products apply filters and inspect the headers of ICMP, UDP, and TCP traffic. Among other things, the software correlates inbound and outbound UDP and ICMP packets while recording certain types of activities.

When your system is attacked, these DoS defense programs are useful for limiting ICMP traffic to a reasonable number. Software developers often use complex algorithms to recognize unusual online traffic behaviors (e.g., high levels of ICMP traffic) in real-time. As the attack occurs, the applications can develop an attack signature (sometimes called the fingerprints of an anomaly). This ability can assist web-based businesses in knowing what type of DoS attack they are fending off; it also provides insight into how to reduce the damage of the attack. The following are a few examples of the latest products:

> ➤ Arbor Network's Peakflow (arbornetworks.com) uses router-specific filtering to identify abnormalities in traffic, and the program automatically reconfigures machines to avoid attacks.
> ➤ Asta Network's Vantage System (astanetworks.com) is a hardware and software combination that surveys and flags traffic for anomalies. Sensors detect unusual behaviors while a coordinator interfaces with the sensors and reports back to the user.
> ➤ Mazu Networks (mazunetworks.com) is a product suite that combines packet analysis and packet filtering with a non–signature-based statistical traffic model to detect deviations.

■ CALCULATING THE SEVERITY OF AN ATTACK

Attack organizations can use many ways to make your web-based business look bad. Frustrated intruders may resort to using DoS or DDoS tactics that crash your network, delay your system's operations, or cause your web-based business to provide less-than-satisfactory service. These attacks can be small and target users, groups of individuals, or large enterprises. For example, a small DoS attack could be a Java applet (a small Internet-based program written in the Java programming language) that uses up memory and CPU resources, thus slowing down the processing of customer orders and service requests. Large attacks can be well-orchestrated, such as the recent DDoS attack against Microsoft, and bring entire enterprises to their knees for over 24 hours. Stephen Northcutt (2000) provides the following mathematical formula for ranking the severity of an attack:

(target criticality + attack lethality) – (system countermeasures + network countermeasures) = attack severity

To determine the severity of a DoS attack, in-house experts rank each item from 1 to 5, with 5 having the greatest negative impact. The maximum score (worst-case scenario) is 8. The minimum score (best-case scenario) is –8 (negative eight). The first element to be ranked is *target* criticality, or how serious the attack will be to mission critical operations. Northcutt suggests a score of 5 if the attack organization takes over the firewall or DNS server. The second element is *lethality,* or the likelihood that the exploit will do damage. Northcutt suggests that if attackers can gain root access, the score should be 5. The third element is *countermeasures,* or circumstances that can affect the severity of the attack. Northcutt suggests a score of 3 for older operating systems with some missing security patches. The following shows the mathematical formula for calculating the severity score.

For example:
    Target criticality: 3
    Attack lethality: 5
    System countermeasures: 5
    Network countermeasures: 2
Score of attack severity:
    Attack severity: $(3 + 5) - (5 + 2) = 8 - 7 = \underline{1}$

The score for the example is 1, midway between the worst score of 8 and the best score of –8. Therefore, the incident should be ranked as having a medium level of severity. Ranking the severity of attacks can be useful for assisting management in preparing an appropriate risk management program for the web-based business.

■ DENIAL OF SERVICE SECURITY CHECKLIST

At this time, the only certain way to prevent a DoS attack is to abstain from using the Internet. For a web-based business, however, this is also a certain way to go out of business. The following is a checklist of some steps that can assist you in making your organization more difficult to attack; taking these steps also can reduce the impact if your organization is attacked.

- ✓ Keep current; continue educating line management and staff about the latest DoS threats. Check the Resource Center at the end of this book for a list of online sources.
- ✓ Check with network equipment and system vendors to learn whether security patches are available for your system.
- ✓ DoS attackers target servers, clients, and routers within a networked environment. Limit the ways in which outsiders can gain access to your network or computer resources.
- ✓ Discover whether your system has been compromised. Using the Resource Center at the back of this book and online resources, look for DDoS installations on your system.
- ✓ Routers and firewalls connecting your enterprise to the Internet should use filters that eliminate packets arriving from external sources with internal source IP addresses.
- ✓ Judge the trade-off between the services offered on specific systems and the risks posed to the security of your web-based business.
- ✓ Monitor network traffic patterns. Be suspicious of changes in use or in types of traffic. Enable detection of unsolicited ICMP PING replies and unusually high traffic levels.
- ✓ Deploy detection software that checks for system configuration changes. Make sure your backup policy includes protection for configuration information.
- ✓ Make certain that line management and staff know what to do in case of a DOS attack.

■ REFERENCES

Betts, William. 2000. Defying denial of service attacks. *Network Magazine,* 5 December. Available at [http://www.networkmagazine.com/article/NMG20001130S0002]. 4 December 2001.

Biggs, Maggie. 2000. Protecting against DOS attacks—take these steps to avoid being a denial of service victim. *InfoWorld,* 14 February. Available online at [http://www.inquiry.com/pubs/infoworld/vol22/issue07/T21–07.asp]. 4 December 2001.

Computer Emergency Response Team (CERT) Coordination Center. 2001. Denial of service attacks. CERT Coordination Center, 4 June. Available at [www.cert.org/tech_tips/denial_of_service.html]. 20 May 2001. No longer available online.

Computel. 2001. Distributed denial of service attacks. Computel white papers. Available at [http://www.computel.com/lb/whitepapers3.htm].

Computer Security Institute. 2001. 2001 CSI/FBI computer crime and security survey. Computer Security Institute, 15 March. Available at [http://www.gocsi.com/prelea/000321.html]. 4 December 2001.

Farrow, Rick. 1999. Blocking buffer overflow attacks. *Network Magazine,* 1 November. Available at [http://www.networkmagazine.com/article/NMG20000511S0015]. 4 December 2001.

Fonseca, Brian. 2001. Warning: DOS attacks on the rise—users need to brace for battle against online floods of debilitating packets. *Info World,* 28 May. Available at [http://cma.zdnet.com]. 4 December 2001.

Lemos, Robert. 2001. DOS attacks: No remedy in sight. *ZDNet News,* 1 June. Available at [http://cma.zdnet.com]. 4 December 2001.

Lemos, Robert. 2001. DDOS attacks—one year later. *ZDNet News,* 7 June. Available at [http://cma.zdnet.com].

Northcutt, Stephen, Mark Cooper, Matt Fearnow, and Karen Frederick. 2001. *Intrusion Signatures and Analysis.* Indianapolis, Ind.: New Riders.

Scambray, Stuart, Stuart McClure, and George Kurtz. 2001. *Hacking Exposed: Network Security Secrets & Solutions.* 2d ed. Berkeley, Calif.: Osborne/McGraw-Hill.

Todd, Bennett. 2000. Distributed denial of service attacks. OVEN Digital white paper, 18 February. Available at [http://www.opensourcefirewall.com/ddos_whitepaper_copy.html]. 4 December 2001.

Chapter

8

The Insecure Employee

In this chapter

- ➤ Understanding Insider Security Threats
- ➤ The Devil You Know: Internal Threats
- ➤ Missing the Click: Accidental Losses
- ➤ Social Engineering Losses
- ➤ Incident Readiness and Inadequate Training
- ➤ Developing and Implementing Security Awareness Campaigns
- ➤ Writing and Stating Guidelines for Employee Practices
- ➤ Your Insider Security Checklist

External security measures are generally the main focus of information security. However, the internal environment must also be secured. In the past, information security was limited to the domain of the IT department, but in today's networked enterprises, all employees must be aware of how they can be maneuvered into voluntarily or involuntarily providing attack organizations with sensitive information. In this chapter, you will achieve an awareness of how frequently the computer systems of enterprises are assaulted by insiders and an understanding of the potential motivations of these attackers. This chapter discusses how employees can accidentally access, modify, and erase proprietary data or disclose sensitive information. You will discover how attackers using social engineering can con sensitive information from unsuspecting employees with which to commit computer crimes that may never be discovered. You will see how incident readiness and training are often better than a technological defense. You will also discover how training employees to recognize security incidents and hazards can save your firm from security break-ins. The chapter concludes with a description of the ingredients for an effective internal security plan.

■ UNDERSTANDING INSIDER SECURITY THREATS

For web-based businesses, Internet security impenetrability is not possible. Consequently, web-based businesses are open to criminal practices that their brick-and-mortar counterparts can easily overcome. In the past, the IT department was staffed by a group of individuals who maintained the mainframes and were employed by the organization for years. These trusted, seasoned veterans could almost feel system inconsistencies and were the first to report suspicious activities. Today, many parts of the IT department, such as development work and credit card processing, are outsourced to third parties. Large portions of the IT department may be temporary or on short-term employment contracts. As a result, many employees do not feel responsible for the information security of the enterprise. However, it is important for employees to protect sensitive information from unauthorized access, modification, destruction, and disclosures. If your enterprise cannot do this, then you can expect a loss of customer confidence and competitive advantage.

The number of real-world frauds perpetrated each year is unknown. Financial crimes are often discovered long after the event. The same situation exists for computer crimes: Victims may detect them quickly or never at all. Consumers frequently ask customer service and sales representatives about the safety of the web-based business. These individuals want to know the identity of those who are attacking your organization, the frequency of attacks, and the methods intruders are likely to use. Many organizations do not have this information. According to the *2001 CSI/FBI Survey*, of 538 respondents, 31 percent do not track this information.

When a company does detect a crime, it is often unwilling to report it to law enforcement agencies, its customers, or organizations like the National Infrastructure Protection Center (NIPC) located at FBI headquarters [http://www.nipc.gov]. Therefore, there are many inherent problems in acquiring statistics on computer crime and in understanding the latest methods used by criminals. To sum up, there are no national databases, like those used in the insurance industry, for deter-

Survey Results: Which source poses the greatest
security threat to your organization?

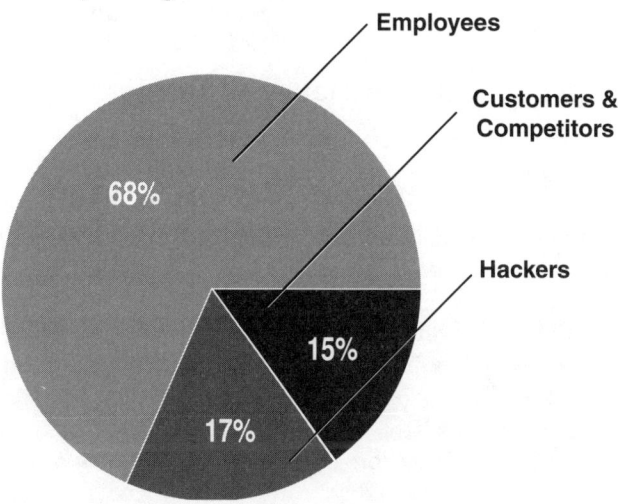

Figure 8.1   Insiders pose the biggest information security threat

mining the risk and performance level of a web business. However, the
current data do point to some conclusions.

➤ Who Are the Attackers?

Several books and articles are available that profile attackers. However,
no one knows for certain if these publications fairly represent the
hacker population at large. Figure 8.1 illustrates the results of a recent
survey of industry professionals by TechRepublic [http://www.tech-
republic.com]. Results indicate that insiders are likely to be responsible
for 68 percent of the organization's security breaches, compared to 17
percent by hackers and 15 percent by customers and competitors.

➤ Who Is Likely to Get Attacked?

There are no statistics about which market sectors are attacked the
most. Many attack organizations target their victims on the basis of not
who they are but of their vulnerabilities. If your organization has a great
deal of vulnerability, then you are a bigger target. One security issue is
complacency. Over and over again, web-based security firms note that

attacks stem from very well-known vulnerabilities that could have been easily prevented. Other appealing targets of attack organizations are web-based businesses with plenty of credit card numbers.

➤ What Kinds of Data Are Being Stolen?

All types of data are subject to theft, tampering, and disclosure. Accordingly, it is wise to be concerned about all types of information that could have monetary value to another individual, entity, or competitor. As a general rule, credit card theft receives the most media attention. Industrial espionage (the sale of proprietary data to competitors) also receives generous amounts of publicity.

Richard Power, editorial director of the Computer Security Institute (2001), subdivides insider theft into the categories of industrial espionage and information-age espionage. Conventional industrial espionage requires coercion or the subterfuge of an insider to attain the required information. Information-age espionage consists of a hack perpetrated by an insider *or an outsider* into the information system in order for competitors to gain the same proprietary information. It is important to note that government agencies, web-based businesses, and all types of organizations are subject to this type of information warfare.

The 2001 CSI/FBI report indicates that insider attacks are the most serious threat to an organziation's information security. Table 8.1 shows the total insider attacks as a percentage of the total number of attacks reported by study respondents. Study interviewees indicated that 59 percent of all incidents originated with insiders. What is more alarming is that 4 percent of these inside attackers attempted security breaches more than 61 times in a one-year period. This type of bombardment illustrates how important it is to clearly understand insider information security threats.

■ THE DEVIL YOU KNOW: INTERNAL THREATS

Web-based businesses usually have so many mobile employees, contract employees, outsourcers, affiliates, and business partners that it is difficult to determine who is an *insider* (a disgruntled employee or paid informant) and who is an *outsider* (a malicious intruder). For the most part, insiders already know the systems and the ways things work within the enterprise. Additionally, insiders have access to the organi-

Table 8.1 How Many Incidents from Inside?

Year	Percentage Experiencing Insider Incidents, by Number of Incidents					Total Percentage Experiencing Insider Incidents
	1 to 5	6 to 10	11 to 30	31 to 60	61 or More	
2001 (484)	40%	12%	3%	0%	4%	59%
2000 (583)	38%	16%	5%	1%	3%	63%
1999 (460)	37%	16%	9%	1%	2%	65%

Note: Number of survey respondents in parentheses.

zation's physical assets and the network. Outsiders must spend the time and effort to discover the same weaknesses. For example, in 1997 George Parente, a part-time computer contractor for Forbes, Inc., was charged with causing five of eight network servers to crash on the day that his employment was terminated. FBI agents found internal Forbes documents and literature on hacking on Parente's home computer. This apparently vengeful act erased all of the data on the attacked servers, making restoration impossible. The insider server attack resulted in a two-day shutdown of the publishing company's New York operations and in monetary losses of over $1,000,000.

Discovering insiders before they damage the system is difficult, if not impossible. Insiders have attacked even security-conscious organizations such as the FBI and the CIA. (Remember the CIA's Aldrich Ames and the FBI's Robert Hanssen?) Consequently, an unknown number of crimes go undetected. There are hard statistics for financial frauds, insurance scams, and other types of deceptions. However, the victims of information security crimes may not be able to detect the crime. Consequently, industry professionals believe that only one-tenth of all crimes against computer systems are detected.

Lewis Koch, a writer for *Inter@ctive Week* (2000), points out several recent examples of insider crimes. In the first instance, a systems administrator at a hospital, upon hearing a rumor that she might be fired, encrypted all patient records. Next, she blackmailed management into providing a comfortable severance package with no prosecution. Upon receipt of her ill-gotten gains, she decrypted the patient records. The second example is the case of a praise-starved systems administrator. On a regular basis the administrator created computer outages that stumped others and could only be fixed by his purported brilliance.

There are many reasons that an insider may commit information crimes. Paul Proctor (2001) provides an overview of malicious insiders and their possible motivations:

➤ Disgruntled employees: individuals who believe they are underpaid, underappreciated, and discriminated against. Possibly they have also been overlooked for promotions or feel they have been mistreated in some fashion. Their motivation is revenge.

➤ Paid informants: information brokers, criminal organizations, or spies that steal data, corporate secrets, and processes. Their motivation is financial gain.

➤ Compromised or coerced employees: employees that are induced by past experiences or personal connections to act as agents for criminal or terrorist organizations seeking information. Their motivation is fear.

➤ Former employees, who often maintain their relationships with their colleagues. These individuals may still have access to the system and understand the security of the organization. This can lead to additional insights about where and when to attack. Their motivation may be revenge or financial gain.

➤ Pseudo-employees or temporary employees, who are generally the first hired and the first fired. These individuals usually have the same privileges and access as full-time employees but do not undergo the same type of scrutiny. These individuals may be motivated by financial gain or fear.

➤ Business associates, whose partnership relationships with many web-based businesses provide them with a competitive edge. Business associates may be motivated to take advantage of this insider knowledge to expand their networks into areas like supply chain management.

■ MISSING THE CLICK: ACCIDENTAL LOSSES

Security for a web-based business is a multifaceted subject. There are a variety of risks to take into consideration, different levels of security to determine, and different approaches to achieving the level of security you require. Hardware and software can assist you, but employees are often the most important part of your organization's security. You need to hire not only trustworthy employees, but trustworthy partners, contractors, and janitorial service personnel as well.

In the business world, it is not unusual to receive the wrong file. An e-mail attachment may be thought to be the latest version, but an earlier version of the file could have been sent by mistake. The latest version of the file may be in a different location in the file system. Usually this type of error causes some confusion until the correct file is located and the older file is deleted. However, accidental mistakes can range from a simple miscommunication to the kiss of death if proprietary information is released from the internal network. For example, sensitive information may be included in documents and contracts that have revision histories. A new contractor can track the revision history of a contract and discover the rates of pay for previous contractors.

➤ Unauthorized Employee Access and Modifications and Erasures of Data

Another type of accidental loss is unauthorized access to or modifications or erasures of data by employees. Employees typically log onto the system by entering a user identification name or number and a password. The user identification can provide the appropriate level of access for the user. However, for the sake of convenience or perceived efficiency, some employees may share passwords, or a system administrator may give elevated privileges to an unauthorized individual or contractor to perform a specific task. In this situation, data can be altered, forms or formats changed, and defaults or application program modifications implemented. If the organization suffers a loss due to these changes (because of the breakdown in the organization's security policy), the perpetrator will be difficult to locate and identify, or an employee may be accused of wrongs that he or she did not commit. Examples of abuses of unauthorized employee access include the following:

- ➤ Changing one's work performance evaluation
- ➤ Changing the pricing for products or services on the company's web site
- ➤ Gaining proprietary competitive bidding information
- ➤ Stealing or modifying patient medical records
- ➤ Erasing of hacking activities by altering server logs

➤ Employees Downloading Forbidden Data and Removing Software

Accidental losses can include the downloading of data and the copying or removal of the web-based organization's software. Probably the most important incident of this type was the February 2000 revelation that ex-CIA Director John Deutch violated agency security procedures (and possibly federal law) by downloading and storing classified data on a home computer. This instance indicates that many individuals do not believe that copying data or a software program, then using it on their home computer, can cause a loss to the business. However, many software application programs have licensing agreements that limit the number of times they can be downloaded.

Koch (2000) provides a variation on this issue. Suppose an employee downloads pornographic material using his office desktop computer and then uses the company's equipment to make duplicate CDs, later selling the bootlegged disks at a computer show. This activity would bring sexually explicit material into the workplace. If another employee saw this material, the enterprise might be held liable. If the downloads are considered to be illegal by local law, the company might have to face criminal charges. What if the employee downloaded the pornographic material during off-hours? The activity would still affect the company's image. (Remember that webmasters can easily track frequent visitors.) Additionally, off-hours usage would not lessen the legal implications of sexual harassment, misrepresentation, and other related issues.

➤ Employees Downloading or Loading Unlicensed Software on the System

Employees can unintentionally be subject to copyright infringement laws when they download software programs, photographs, or proprietary documents that are available on the Internet. Free access does not equal cost-free.

Accidental losses can be incurred when employees load unlicensed or pirated software into the web-based business's system. Without the knowledge of system administrators, these rogue programs may cause changes in the configuration of the system and provide security holes for attack organizations to exploit.

■ SOCIAL ENGINEERING LOSSES

Social engineering is often a more effective hacking tool than some technological solutions. Social engineering can be defined as the practice of tricking, misleading, or misdirecting corporate insiders into giving information to outsiders through social interaction. Many skilled social engineers have the ability to obtain the information they want without raising suspicions. Social engineers often seek the following:

➤ Information that violates an individual's privacy
➤ Information about business activities that affect share prices (e.g., pending mergers, acquisitions)
➤ Financial, accounting, and inventory information that can be used to perpetrate a theft or fraud
➤ Information about the location and security of valuable assets
➤ Marketing plans and sales information that may be useful to competitors
➤ Results of research and development initiatives, scientific and engineering plans and progress
➤ Information about production and process data

According to a February 2001 interview with Kevin Mitnick (who was the first person on the FBI's Most Wanted List for computer crimes and the first to be prosecuted under the tougher federal computer crime laws enacted in the 1980s), his most damaging attacks were achieved through people, rather than machines. Mitnick goes on to state that security is only as strong as its weakest link, which is usually the human element. A good example of social engineering occurred when Kevin Mitnick wanted to gain access to the schematics for the latest Motorola cellular telephone. Mitnick convinced Motorola employees that he was on the team and entitled to the information. Over a two year period using this method and similar social engineering methods, Kevin Mitnick cost companies like NEC USA, Nokia, and Sun at least $290 million.

Social engineering is a social, political, and cultural problem for the enterprise. Keep in mind that a lack of respect for sensitive data can assist intruders in achieving security break-ins through social engineering. That is, simple human interaction can assist in the theft of proprietary information such as passwords. For example, an experienced attacker can go to an employee's office, ask a few general questions, make a few observations about the décor, and walk out with a list of probable passwords. The employee's password is frequently listed somewhere in the office: the name of a loved one, spouse, pet, or sports team.

To sum up, there are many ways in which a so-called social engineer can inveigle sensitive information from individuals in your web-based enterprise. On one occasion, Kevin Mitnick, posing as a headquarters employee, asked that information be faxed to him. The corporate employee was happy to oblige. To gain insider information, Mitnick also visited targets where physical security was not an obstacle. Social engineering can include using the telephone or face-to-face communications to con proprietary information from unsuspecting employees, e-mail correspondence that is spoofed so that it appears to originate within the organization, and facsimiles used to send sensitive information to another location. These examples show how sensitive information can be exposed, either voluntarily or involuntarily.

■ INCIDENT READINESS AND INADEQUATE TRAINING

External security measures are generally the main focus of information security. However, the internal environment must also be secured. Here, biometric technology may be helpful. Biometric technologies use individual physical characteristics, such as fingerprint, face, or iris recognition, to build security applications. For example, Siemens (www.siemans.com/biometrics) offers the ID Mouse Professional, a plug-and-play solution for users seeking to protect corporate proprietary information and confidential intellectual capital. The Siemens ID mouse utilizes a fingerprint sensor placed on the side of a standard-sized mouse. Only the person with the authorized fingerprint has access. However, using biometrics can be costly and time consuming. Moreover, administrative issues, such as enrolling a new finger in the system if a user injures his or her authentication finger may cause unforeseen security problems. To sum it up, biometrics cannot replace incident readiness and adequate training.

Many employees fax sensitive information in clear text or discuss trade secrets over cellular or wireless phones. When this happens, the information is considered to be part of the public domain and not confidential. This lapse shows how good information security consists of much more than just hardware and technological solutions. It includes social, political, and cultural issues that go well beyond the IT department. Add the need to keep up-to-date on the security of new operating systems (which may have undiscovered security holes), laptops used for telecommuting, and wireless PDAs (personal digital assistants), and the security problems for a web-based business may seem overwhelming.

Disclosing sensitive information is often made possible by a failure to train staff and management in the appropriate way to make social engineering more difficult. This type of training minimizes the gullibility of potential victims. Donn B. Parker (2001) suggests the following helpful list for determining when information should be kept private and when trusted individuals should feel secure in disclosing the requested information.

➤ Is the information generally known?
➤ Will the information violate the privacy of others?

If the information meets the first two criteria, then the following questions should be asked.

➤ Do you gain something by revealing the requested information?
➤ Can the source of the information remain anonymous?
➤ Is it possible to obtain authorization to disclose the information?

■ DEVELOPING AND IMPLEMENTING SECURITY AWARENESS CAMPAIGNS

The first step in developing and implementing security awareness is to teach employees to recognize security incidents and hazards. Loraine Lawson (2000) reports that Chris Zoladz, vice president of information protection for Marriott International, Inc., suggests that managers ask themselves the following questions to determine whether they have a culture of security:

➤ If one of your employees sees another employee doing something wrong, what do you think would happen?
➤ Would the employee know if the action was right or wrong?
➤ Would the employee report the action to another employee or a supervisor?
➤ Would the employee know how to correctly report the action?

You can also look at actual occurrences in your web-based business to assist you in your answers. Do not be surprised if your organization does not have a culture of security. Many organizations do not have a culture of security because information security was considered to be within the boundaries of the IT department and not an enterprise-wide objective.

Donn B. Parker (2000) states that your employees should be "spoof proofed." For example, it is acceptable to state to outsiders that the web-based business uses security measures such as passwords, user IDs, and other security protocols for logons. However, it is never appropriate to reveal the numbers and characters used in passwords, or the guidelines for passwords, logon attempt limits, timeouts, and so on. Employees should receive detailed written directions concerning these matters. Information about the organization's security *controls* for protecting sensitive information should be protected as much as the sensitive data.

Overall, the difference between skilled and unskilled attack organizations may be that sophisticated attack organizations attack people and amateurs attack systems. Scanning a network and running through a password string is tedious and time consuming. One telephone call to the Human Resource Department requesting a password to verify some payment records is more effective. Therefore, targets for social engineering often include

➤ Passwords and user identification
➤ Personal identification numbers (PINs)
➤ Computer logon protocols
➤ Operational commands
➤ Utility functions
➤ Instructions for computer applications
➤ Names of data files
➤ Dial-in telephone numbers to computers
➤ Information about security controls
➤ Information about other users' practices

In developing security awareness, you need to involve every area of the enterprise. Management must ensure that all divisions and employees appreciate and understand the need for security. The next step toward a culture of security is to integrate security practices into the everyday lives of all employees. This often means shifting the corporate culture and getting all levels of management to provide overwhelming support of the firm's security policy. In this situation, workers will need upper management to set the example by rigorously following security procedures such as wearing name tags, shutting down computers before leaving the office, and choosing difficult-to-guess passwords.

■ WRITING AND STATING GUIDELINES FOR EMPLOYEE PRACTICES

A recent nationwide network security survey by Camelot IT, Ltd. [http://www.camelot.com] and *eWeek* magazine [http://www.eweek.com] indicates that respondents are very concerned about outsider security breaches. However, 57 percent of the security breaches they experienced were caused by insiders' accessing unauthorized resources, 43 percent of the security violations were due to accounts that were not closed after an employee left the company, and 21 percent of the attempted or successful attacks were the work of angry employees. Overall, the survey points out that management tends to underestimate the likelihood of security breaches by insiders such as employees, contractors, and consultants. The report points out that as web-based companies downsize, merge, or acquire other companies, the internal risk to proprietary information increases. Add the risk of expanding the network while protecting customer privacy, and you start to grasp the need for clearly defined internal security guidelines.

John O'Leary, of the Computer Security Institute (www.csi.com), states in a seminar titled "How to Create and Sustain a Quality Security Awareness Program" that large investments in state-of-the-art security technology cannot by themselves protect the organization's sensitive information. Employees need to know what makes information security important so they can voluntarily change their behavior.

Clever, persistent employees can always find ways to circumvent the rules, regardless of what controls are written into the internal security guidelines. It is easy to install a security patch on the server but almost impossible to predict the behavior of even one employee. Additionally, the culture of some enterprises encourages the sharing of information. This can result in distributing passwords, sharing proprietary information over the telephone, and even holding the security door open for someone. (For more on developing a successful security policy, see Chapter 14.)

Often companies hire individuals who preach about security programs rather than teach employees about the importance of information security. Debra Donston (2001) reports that Aetna, a company with 43,000 employees, uses its web-based Aetna InfoSec Awareness program to enforce its internal security policy. Before beginning the exam, the employee must sign off on Aetna's security policy, then take the exam within the first 30 days of hire and annually thereafter.

The Aetna exam is broken into six modules and takes about 30 minutes to complete. One of the areas covered is a code of conduct, which dictates the use of technology and information resources and the handling of information. Managers are required to enforce Aetna's security awareness training policy. Compliance with the interactive program was 85 percent the first year and 100 percent last year. Individuals who complete the exam receive a certificate (which they often display in their work areas). According to Aetna officials, the cost of designing and implementing the program was between $70,000 and $100,000.

The success of the Aetna program and O'Leary (2000) point to the three necessary ingredients of an effective internal security plan: management must support the necessary measures, make security relevant to employees, and establish the importance of security to the organization.

> ➤ Good internal security starts with the overwhelming support of management. The security goals determined by management must be aligned with the company's business goals to be relevant. Items such as confidentiality, integrity, and availability are directly linked to the mission of the web-based business.
>
> ➤ Employees do not need lectures on the importance of security. Instead, it is essential for employees to understand why they need to change their behavior and how this can assist the company in meeting its security goals. In other words, management must understand what makes security relevant to each employee. Messages should be tailored to the audience. Additionally, the enterprise needs its employees to "buy into the program." Some organizations achieve this by asking employees for their help. This is a great way to get cooperation, and it is often more effective than telling employees what to do.
>
> ➤ From day one, show employees that security is important. Security training should be part of the employee orientation pro-

cess. Provide new employees with the organization's general security rules. Detail how to identify and report security violations. Provide the names and contact information for employees to use if they suspect any security violation.

■ YOUR INSIDER SECURITY CHECKLIST

Attacks on your web-based business are a people problem, not a computer problem. Granted, there can be accidental losses due to carelessness, poor configuration, and faulty software, but these elements only make the job easier for intruders. For every security breach, there is a human being entering the command. The following checklist can assist you in reducing the likelihood of insider attacks.

✓ Social engineering is often used to gain access to confidential data, user names, and passwords. Train employees to use a callback procedure to verify callers before distributing any sensitive information over the telephone.

✓ Frequently, password systems come with vendor-installed user names and passwords, which inside and outside attackers can use to gain unauthorized access. Therefore, all vendor-installed user names and passwords should be changed.

✓ Easy-to-remember passwords can be quickly guessed by attackers. Require passwords with at least six characters that are a mix of number and letters.

✓ Provide employees with examples of proprietary and sensitive information classifications as well as guidelines for disclosure.

✓ Establish an internal written security policy. This policy must include tools that can check for passwords, logon information, and a way to detect changes in system files.

✓ Provide employees with contact information with which to report violations and vendor numbers for emergencies.

✓ Place restrictions on some types of information. Install strong password authentication procedures and technological solutions. Perform daily back-ups and store the data off-site.

✓ Initiate an ongoing security awareness training and education program. Gain the support of all levels of management, and enlist the help of employees to make the security program relevant.

■ REFERENCES

Andress, Mandy. 2001. Test Center: Biometrics at work? 28 May. Available at [http://ask.elibrary.com]. 5 December 2001.

Bertin, Michael. 2001. The new security threats: Three out of four businesses are wide open to attack. Is your company next? The top new Internet security threats and how to protect your company. *Ziff Davis Smart Business for the New Economy,* 15 January. Available at [http://www.zdnet.com.au]. 4 December 2001.

Developing an Internet access policy: A guide to developing your company's Internet access policy (IAP). 2000. *Surfcontrol* white paper, February. Available at [http://www.surfcontrol.com]. 4 December 2001.

Donston, Debra. 2001. A healthy security attitude. *eWeek,* 10 June. Available at [http://www.zdnet.com]. 4 December 2001.

Edwards, Bob. 2001. Profile: Social engineering as an effective hacker tool. *Morning Edition* [National Public Radio (NPR) interview], 23 February. Available at [http://ask.elibrary.com]. 4 December 2001.

Fisher, Dennis. 2001. Insiders are main computer security threat. *eWeek,* 20 June. Available at [http://www.zdnet.com]. 4 December 2001.

Freeh, Louis J. 2000. Cyber attack investigations: Louis J. Freeh. *Congressional Testimony,* 28 March. Available at [http://ask.elibrary.com]. 5 December 2001.

Howard, John D. 1997. An analysis of security incidents on the Internet 1989–1995. Ph.D. diss., Carnegie Mellon University, 7 April. Available at [http://www.cert.org/research/JHThesis/Chapter6.html]. 20 May 2001. No longer available online.

Huey, Hanna. 1999. Intelligence and software: Fear thyself. *Telephony,* 21 June. Available online at [http://ask.elibrary.com]. 4 December 2001.

Kabay, M.D. 1998. *ICSA white paper on Computer Crime Statistics.* Available at [http://www.itpapers.com]. 20 May 2001.

Koch, Lewis Z. 2000. The devil you know. *Inter@active Week,* 13 July. Available at [http://www.zdnet.com]. 4 December 2001.

Lawson, Loraine. 2001. A new approach to the old problem of enterprise security. *TechRepublic,* 7 June. Available at [http://www.techrepublic.com]. 4 December 2001.

——. 2001. Three basic steps to help you create a culture of security. *TechRepublic,* 27 September. Available at [http://www.techrepublic.com]. 4 December 2001.

Parker, Donn B. 1998. *Fighting computer crime.* New York: Wiley.

Power, Richard. 2001. Computer security issues and trends. *Computer Security Institute,* 15 March. Available at [http://www.csi.com)].

Proctor, Paul E. 2001. *The practical intrusion detection handbook.* Upper Saddle River, New Jersey: Prentice Hall.

Ryder, Josh. 2000. Preventing Information Loss: Strengthening a Weak Link. *Security Portal,* 22 August. Available at [http://www.security-portal.com]. 20 May 2001.

Steadman, Bob. 1997. Fighting the enemies within. *Computing Canada,* 5 August. Available at [http://cma.zdnet.com]. 4 December 2001.

Steel Scharbach Associates. 2001. *Computer security: Protecting against what?* L.L.C. white paper, 15 June. Available at [http://www.itpapers.com]. 20 May 2001.

Chapter

9

Handling Public Relations After a Cyber-Attack

In this chapter

➤ Preparing and Planning for Crisis Communications
➤ Determining General Procedures for Disaster Communications
➤ Identifying Information Security Assaults
➤ Exercising Your Crisis Communication Plan
➤ Potential Launch Events for Your Communication Plan
➤ Handling Media Relations
➤ Issuing a Press Release
➤ Inspiring Confidence After an Attack
➤ To Report a Cyber-Crime, or Not?
➤ Checklist: After the Hack Attack

If your web-based business suffers a security breach, you will probably lose sensitive information, experience expensive downtime, and have to rebuild damaged files and servers. In addition to confronting these concerns, you must effectively handle media and customer relations. In many situations, the way you manage your firm's public relations after a cyber-attack will affect the future profitability of your enterprise. Being prepared with an effective communications plan can save you time, embarrassment, and liability. For example, in September 2000, an attack organization stole 16,000 credit card numbers from Western Union customers. Western Union handled the situation in a

responsible way, with a crisis communication plan that almost automatically went into effect: Each customer was contacted and told about
the theft. A few weeks after the incident, customer levels were back to
normal. Today, Western Union customers barely remember the incident. Situations like this one prove that investing the time and money
to prepare in advance of an attack is often invaluable. This chapter
shows how you can develop a communication plan that is geared to the
needs and requirements of your web-based business. You will discover
who should be on your crisis team and how to make an effective points
of contact (POC) list for specific types of disasters. You will gain an understanding of what security information events need management attention and when you should launch your communication plan. This
chapter includes step-by-step instructions on how to create and conduct crisis communication simulations. You will discover exactly what
should be in your press statement and how to inspire customer confidence after an attack. The chapter concludes with a discussion of reporting cyber-crimes.

■ PREPARING AND PLANNING FOR CRISIS COMMUNICATION

Even the most expensive and sophisticated security measures may not
be enough to stop a security breach. Therefore, it is wise to be prepared
with a way to communicate the bad news to customers, investors, and
others in a positive way. The first step in developing your crisis communications plan is to establish a crisis team. Then the crisis team will
determine the type of attacks the firm might experience and who
should be contacted if the undesirable event does occur. According to
Barbara Eiler (1999) of *TechRepublic,* crisis teams often include the top
management for each of the enterprise's functional areas and a representative from the firm's public relations firm. Team members will
know who to call and what general procedures to follow if an attack organization calls and threatens the web-based business. These procedures include contacting each member of the crisis team and setting up
a contact center or a telephone conference to coordinate the next step
in the crisis communication plan. The question of who gets contacted
and when is important in a crisis. Contacting too many people in a
short amount of time may lead to adverse publicity, whereas calling too
few people can lead to consumer liability lawsuits.

A POC list should be developed for each type of security breach before it occurs. Figure 9.1 is an example of a POC list. The list starts with the category of the computer incident or type of attack (for details on classifying attacks, see "Identifying Information Security Attacks," later in this chapter). Next listed is the name of the department, agency, or subcontractor to be contacted. Sometimes the direct contact information for your vendor or service representative is also helpful. Critical information about resources (such as the availability of a second server, off-site storage of backup data, etc.) is included. Do not forget to include the location of back-up equipment and software. You may want to note the *minimum* requirements based on whatever mission-critical applications that you expect to be hit (e.g., e-mail servers, telephone system, database applications). List the equipment and software needed that is not currently on hand and the contact information of local vendors who can quickly supply the needed materials. Without special arrangements large companies such as Dell and IBM will likely take weeks to make a delivery. Therefore, it is wise to contact local vendors in advance of a disaster to determine how quickly they can respond. This section is followed by a list of the names, positions, home telephone numbers, work telephone numbers, pager numbers, 24-hour contact numbers, cellular telephone numbers, and e-mail addresses of the key corporate personnel to be contacted. These key individuals have a detailed knowledge of the system, are authorized to make purchases, and will likely direct operations during an emergency. Widely disseminate the POC list so that if an event does occur, employees are familiar with what to do.

When creating the POC list, take into consideration realistic time-distance considerations. Individuals who live closest to the site should be contacted first for the most urgent tasks during nonworking hours. Make certain that all employees understand why certain actions are being taken and how they are expected to behave. Tell employees what they can say (and cannot say) to customers and others outside the corporation. If you provide employees with a written statement, such as "Sorry, our systems are unavailable at this time; they are being upgraded to serve you better," you may avoid customer service representatives' saying something like "Sorry, I can't process your order right now; the system's down due to a computer virus. We are trying to contain the problem and clean things up."

Name of Security Event _____

Security Event Point-of-Contact list

Name of Department, Agency, or Subcontractor _____
Address _____

Resources Available, Including Locations:
1. _____
2. _____
3. _____
Note: Minimum resources required are marked with an asterisk (*).

Contact Information for Acquiring Required Equipment:

1. Company Name _____
Name, Title _____
Home Phone _____ **Work Phone** _____
Pager _____ **24-Hr. Contact Phone** _____
Cellular Phone _____ **E-Mail** _____

2. Company Name _____
Name, Title _____
Home Phone _____ **Work Phone** _____
Pager _____ **24-Hr. Contact Phone** _____
Cellular Phone _____ **E-Mail** _____

Key Contact Personnel:

1. Name _____
Home Phone _____ **Work Phone** _____
Pager _____ **24-Hr. Contact Phone** _____
Cellular Phone _____ **E-Mail** _____

2. Name _____
Home Phone _____ **Work Phone** _____
Pager _____ **24-Hr. Contact Phone** _____
Cellular Phone _____ **E-Mail** _____

3. Name _____
Home Phone _____ **Work Phone** _____
Pager _____ **24-Hr. Contact Phone** _____
Cellular Phone _____ **E-Mail** _____

4. Name _____
Home Phone _____ **Work Phone** _____
Pager _____ **24-Hr. Contact Phone** _____
Cellular Phone _____ **E-Mail** _____

Figure 9.1   Example of a computer incident contact form

■ DETERMINING GENERAL PROCEDURES FOR DISASTER COMMUNICATIONS

The first step in your communication with customers and partners is not to panic. Make certain you have your facts straight. You do not want to overlook anything, so make a checklist (similar to the one at the end of this chapter) of items you will need to cover with management, staff, customers, and others. In an attack, web-based companies are often hit hard and fast. Management will not have the leisure to contemplate an appropriate response. It is useful to spend the time now to develop the general procedures for a communication crisis. If a security event does materialize, you will just add a few details that accord with the specific type of attack.

For the planning session include upper management, high-level managers from each functional area of the enterprise, and representatives from your marketing department and public relations firm. When hammering out your crisis communication plan, keep these four key points in mind:

➤ Tell the truth: Public information is a vital component of your crisis communication plan. You may even want to consider including a representative from the local press in the planning process in order to reduce misunderstandings during an incident. Planning can include establishing a telephone hotline for breaking news and educating the public through articles so they have a clear understanding of the specific type of security breach that has occurred. It not wise to lie about security breaches. If a reporter discovers that your media representative lied, expect a public relations nightmare that will affect the profitability of your web-based business.

➤ Respond quickly and accurately: Accurate information should be made available to the public as soon as possible. Media sources need to know where they can obtain information or receive briefings. You may want to set up an off-site public information office/media assembly and briefing area. Do not allow the media time to speculate on the source and depth of the attack. Let customers, investors, and the public know what you are doing to restore order. Let the public know that every effort is being made to track the intruders. You may want to mention that your organization has filed complaints with the appropriate authorities.

➤ Keep communication lines open: Determine who will be the lead spokesperson. Select someone with public relations experience. Issue a press release, but keep in mind that one press release is not enough. Be cooperative but careful when speaking with the media. Media relations are important for communicating vital information to the public. Avoid using qualifying phrases such as "I believe" or "I think," and be certain of your facts. You will need to keep customers, investors, and the public informed about how you are managing the situation and the progress you have made.

➤ Have one consistent response: Compose written responses for common questions and provide this list to all employees, board members, and executives. This will help to ensure consistency and make the web-based business appear to be in control of the situation. Provide one telephone number for "data-driven" individuals who demand more information. Never provide details of how the intruder gained access to your system; this might add to any adverse publicity.

■ IDENTIFYING INFORMATION SECURITY ASSAULTS

Systems administrators perform many tests on the system, and security companies are sometimes hired to test the system for vulnerabilities. Employees may not be informed of these activities and may interpret the anomalies as system intrusions. This can cause confusion when trying to identify an incident. When trying to identify a security breach, another consideration is that some information security incidents cause a chain of events to occur. Consequently, investigators have to follow this trail back to its source to determine the type of incident. For example, is this a cyber-terrorism incident? Keep in mind the difference between attackers and cyber-terrorists. Extremists with a single focus or political cause may want to cause property damage or physical harm to individuals. The goals of cyber-terrorists often surpass spraying cyber-graffiti on a web page. Therefore, it is wise for your organization to identify extremist organizations that may have the resources and wherewithal to complete the deliberate destruction of the information infrastructure of your web-based business.

➤ Defining an Information System Attack

Some industry professionals differentiate between an information system attack and a computer incident. An *attack* can be defined as one attempt (which may or may not be successful) at unauthorized access. Dorothy and Peter Denning (1998) group attacks into eight categories.

1. Eavesdropping: An attack organization frequently reads unencrypted corporate communications and exploits design flaws in an effort to gather sensitive information.

2. Snooping into databases: An attack organization monitors mass storage devices, such as disk and tape drives, to derive information about the best way to strike your enterprise.

3. Tampering: Corrupting information in the information system is often the goal of an attack organization. Tampering refers to making unauthorized alterations to databases, modifying or deleting files, reconfiguring the system, and so on.

4. Spoofing: The attack organization hides its identity by using various methods. This makes it difficult, if not impossible, for the enterprise to track down perpetrators of cyber-crimes.

5. Jamming: Jamming can include buffer overflows (flooding) and the consumption of bandwidth (resource starvation). Attack organizations sometimes jam organizations with thousands of useless requests, thus denying legitimate service to employees, customers, users, suppliers, and others.

6. Injecting code: A sophisticated attacker can use Common Gateway Interface (CGI) scripts to install malicious programs in unsuspecting servers and hosts.

7. Exploiting flaws: New software or the misconfiguration of software applications can provide an intruder with an opportunity to attack the web-based business.

8. Cracking: The aim of a cracker is to break into a secure system. In contrast, a hacker is more interested in knowing about the entire security system of the enterprise.

➤ Spotting the Difference between Attacks and Incidents

An incident may involve a group of attacks united by timing, similar attack methods, and other characteristics. Consequently, the analysis of incidents is useful in classifying attacks. The following are a few guidelines for the classification of *incidents*.

- ➤ False alarm: An anomaly is reported but proves to be a false alarm and not a security incident.
- ➤ Unauthorized access incident: Unauthorized access at the root level or account level. A root-level break-in grants the privileges of system administrators to an intruder. An account level break-in is achieved through at least one attack during the incident. An access attempt indicates that access was attempted at least once but was not successful.
- ➤ Unauthorized use incident: An unauthorized use can be further classified into three categories. The first category concerns instances when a computer is turned into a zombie to launch a denial of service attack. The second category of unauthorized use incidents is the corruption of information, for example, the spoofing of an e-mail return address to disguise the sender's true identity. The third unauthorized use category is the disclosure of information, for example, depositing and transferring pirated software or proprietary information.

■ EXERCISING YOUR CRISIS COMMUNICATION PLAN

Conduct a real-life crisis simulation and evaluate the results and weaknesses. Remember, these exercises are not tests, but ways to understand weaknesses and to determine the best approach for confronting what could destroy years of customer loyalty and goodwill. The goal of a simulation is to clarify responsibilities, identify roles for key personnel, and acquire and enhance skills. Plus, a simulation builds teamwork and assesses capabilities for successfully implementing the communication crisis plan. You will evaluate mistakes or omissions in the communication crisis plan for each type of hack attack. Crisis communication team members will assess performance, measure resources, and provide management feedback.

Simulations can range from friendly orientation sessions to full-scale organization-wide events. The following list shows four types of exercises and describes when each type is appropriate.

➤ Orientation briefing: An introduction to the enterprise's crisis communication plan. Communication crisis team members are familiarized with roles, responsibilities, and expectations.

➤ Tabletop simulations: A limited simulation of a communications crisis plan for a certain type of hack attack. Plans, procedures, coordination of equipment and personnel, and the assignment of resources are evaluated.

➤ Functional simulations: Limited involvement by enterprise personnel to test preparedness, availability, and deployment of necessary equipment or personnel to support the crisis communication plan.

➤ Full-scale simulations: Includes the entire web-based business to simulate a real-life attack and communications response.

Do not be disappointed that your simulation does not turn out as expected. It is better to learn about mistakes now than during an actual event. Simulations should be realistic but not complicated. You will often be compressing a real situation that can last several days into a simulation that lasts two or three hours. Exercises should be relatively simple but complex enough to hold the interest of participants. For each exercise, you may want to focus on just one or two key threats (e.g., eavesdropping or jamming by an attack organization). Start with a tabletop exercise and determine the frequency of planned simulations. You many want to consider limiting the number of simulations, because too many drills may make employees less alert to a real disaster.

Jones, Kowalk, and Miller provide an excellent overview in *Critical Incident Protocol: A Public and Private Partnership* (2000) of how to conduct a tabletop exercise. The following list shows some of the key points to consider when designing simulations for crisis communication.

➤ Tabletop exercises can last from 1 to 2 hours, but the design of the exercise may take 40 hours of preparation.

➤ Clearly state the goals of the tabletop exercise. In this way, participants can see and understand their roles and the roles of their department within the organization.

➤ The scenario should stimulate participation by all participants of the tabletop exercise. If the scenario does not directly affect a participant, that participant should not be involved in the tabletop exercise.

➤ The tabletop exercise should be realistic and follow organizational policies, protocols, and procedures that are currently in place. Participants should not have to break the rules to be successful.

➤ Information used in the tabletop scenario should be consistent to avoid participant frustration. Select a situation that is plausible so it does not receive an "It can't happen here" response.

➤ Allow interaction between participants. Dialogue and discussions can assist participants in learning about how the communications plan affects others in the organization.

➤ Consider bringing participants in later to discuss what changes were made in their departments as a result of the tabletop exercise.

➤ Tabletop simulation evaluators can be outside consultants or individuals knowledgeable in communications and public relations. The evaluators should provide constructive critiques to the participants and make the simulation a learning experience.

■ POTENTIAL LAUNCH EVENTS FOR YOUR COMMUNICATION PLAN

Not all computer security events require management's instant attention. Sometimes a change in the enterprise's database or the theft of sensitive information (such as credit card numbers) is not immediately discovered. Therefore, some computer incidents may be in real-time, and others may require taking responsibility for events that happened several years ago. Regardless of when the event happened, management must be informed of the following thirteen types of incidents. The occurrence of any one of these events may trigger the need for management to put its crisis communication plan into effect.

1. System crashes, usually defined as a serious computer system failure that signifies either a hardware failure or a serious software problem.
2. High activity in a previously low usage account or the inexplicable creation of a new account. Systems administrators are

responsible for tracking information and reporting this type of activity immediately.

3. The appearance of new files with strange names in the directory (data.ss or k or .xx). Most systems administrators are familiar with the names of files in certain locations of the system. Any strange names should be reported immediately.

4. Accounting discrepancies. For example, copies of server log files may be bigger than files that are currently on the system.

5. Changes in file lengths or dates. A comparison of current to backup server logs activity dates may indicate that intruders are attempting to cover or erase the audit trail of their malicious activities.

6. Attempts to write to the system. Intruders may attempt to inject code into the system using tainted CGI scripts.

7. Data modification or deletion (files start to disappear).

8. Distributed denial of service (DDoS) to system administrators and others. In other words, legitimate users cannot use system resources due to an attack by intruders.

9. Slower operation of system resources than is usual. Slowed system resources may indicate the beginning of a DDoS attack and should be investigated immediately.

10. Frequent beeps and other anomalies. This may indicate the presence of a Trojan horse program in your system.

11. A large number of unsuccessful logon attempts or probes. This may indicate an automatic port scanning of your web site.

12. Suspicious browsing. Someone is reading files on different user accounts.

13. The inability of a user to log in due to the modification of his or her user account.

■ HANDLING MEDIA RELATIONS

It is impossible to foresee each and every type of disaster. However, a survey of the types of attacks on competitors and similar companies can point you in the right direction to determine likely categories of disasters (such as industrial espionage, DDoS threats, or employee misconduct). Develop a communication action plan for each category of disaster. This can save you valuable time if the undesirable event materializes. Complete a series of key messages and detailed questions and answers. Do not let the media push you into stating something that is unplanned or shows anger. The way your company reacts to a security breach should be based on a set of predetermined procedures.

Collect facts before releasing a statement to the public. It is important to be able to answer the following questions:

> Exactly what happened to your security and information system? (Keep in mind that someone in the organization ought to maintain a master time stamp. Use of a master time stamp ensures a documentation record if hackers have changed computer records.)

> How can your organization immediately avoid further exploitation of the same vulnerability? Do you need to strip the server of all information, or will a security patch solve the problem?

> How can your enterprise steer clear of further incidents or an escalation of the current attack? For example, if the weak link in your security is your ISP, can you quickly change to another provider?

> Did attackers gain access to sensitive customer information, or were they limited to public information on your web site? Assess the impact and damage of the attack.

> What must you do to recover from the incident? How long will it take to repair or replace damaged files and servers?

> How soon can your enterprise update security policies and procedures as needed? (The security policy of any web-based business is a "living document" that changes with newly created methodologies and technologies.)

> Who attacked your web-based business? (If possible, find out. You do not want the attack organization to successfully infiltrate your security a second time.)

Use this information to create fact sheets, statistics, and backgrounds for crisis team members. You may also want to use this information to post a message geared to customers on your home page or to redirect customers to an emergency web site that can be switched on externally.

■ ISSUING A PRESS RELEASE

Before an incident, determine the one person who will interact with the media (a representative from your public relations firm, a member

For example, at the end of a news article, there may be a quote by a security professional stating that his company always believed that security at your web-based business was lax (or outdated or understaffed). Negative reports like this need to be countered immediately.

According to McCormick (2001) to counter adverse reports, you and your organization need to become aware of what people are saying in real time and have a planned response. It is useful to assign an individual from the marketing department to this task. This individual should search paper-based media, Usenet newsgroups, and message boards, such as Google [http://groups.google.com/advanced_group_searchwww.google.com] and Yahoo! Finance Forums[http://dir.yahoo.com/business_and_economy/finance_and_investment/chats_and_forums]. Additionally, companies like eNow [http://www.enow.com] are valuable in locating information about your web-based business on broadcast television and radio, newswires, web pages, message boards, and additional media sources. The content collected by eNow is delivered in real time via an easy-to-use web interface.

A major hack attack may call for a strong response using the web, print, and broadcast media. Exactly how you respond can build your company's reputation or tear down years of customer confidence in a matter of hours. Face the situation head-on and act immediately to counter adverse publicity. It is useless to hide or ignore negative reports. Assemble your team, put your crisis communication plan into effect, and decide (from your predetermined responses) what actions to take.

■ TO REPORT A CYBER-CRIME, OR NOT?

Many web-based businesses do not report computer incidents, intrusion rates, or credit card frauds. These organizations are afraid of losing customer confidence. After all, they are not required to report these crimes and risk being subjected to adverse media attention should they do so. Additionally, there are no universal standards for reporting credit card fraud (use of counterfeit, stolen, or even disputed cards). According to the *2001 CSI/FBI Computer Crime and Security Survey,* when 151 interviewees were asked why they did not report computer crime to law enforcement agencies, most respondents (90 percent) stated that they wanted to sidestep the negative publicity. While the number of respondents is low in terms of statistical accuracy, the raw data collected can be used as a pointer toward a general trend. The 2001 CSI/FBI Computer Crime and Security Survey continues by noting that about 75 percent of the interviewees said they viewed reporting cyber-crimes as giving away competitive advantage, and 54 percent stated that they were unaware they could report a cyber-crime. The majority (64 percent) said they would take care of the situation themselves. (Taking into consideration that the majority of attacks are from insiders, this is not an unreasonable approach.)

There is no doubt that the defacement of your web site is a public relations problem. There are many organizations that collect and archive Web site defacements. One such organization is the Norway-based Alldas [http://www.alldas.org], shown in Figure 9.2. Alldas copies and archives all types of web site defacements from around the world. No one wants a copy of his or her defaced web site hung in a so-called hall of shame.

One of the issues to consider is how you will proceed if you decide

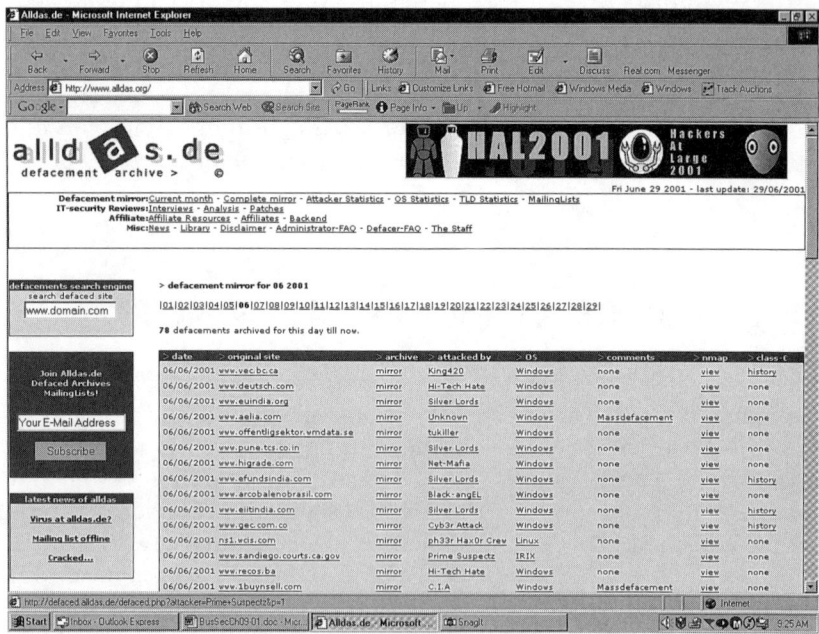

Figure 9.2 Alldas is just one of the many organizations that collects and displays defaced web sites

to report internal attackers or an outside attack organization. The type of damage your web-based business has sustained from the attack is likely to play a large role in this decision. Do you want to make the perpetrator an example, or do you just want to stop further criminal activity? If you do decide to prosecute the attacker, be prepared to provide evidence of the corporate crime and documentation of the entire investigation.

Cyber-crime does not follow the normal investigative course. Most cyber-crimes are discovered well after the event. Incriminating electronic information is often archived, deleted, or scattered throughout the organization. When someone does discover the interference with sensitive information, the compromise in the database, or the theft of code, it is often difficult to determine exactly what happened. (For more information on this issue, see Chapter 14.)

Keep in mind that evidence is direct proof of a fact. It can also be an inference-based fact based on experience and logic (known as circumstantial evidence). Breaking into a system without authorization is a crime. Stealing and destroying electronic information from your web-based business is a crime. Abusing a position of authority and trust is also a crime. Many professionals believe there are three types of cyber-criminals: tool makers, tool users, and script followers. This population can be divided into two groups: benign "white hat hackers" and malicious "black hat hackers." Each group frequently shares information about tools, knowledge, and targets, as well as what portions of the hacker community consist of hardened cyber-criminals. Many white hat hackers believe that they are doing you a favor by hacking into your web-based business because you will become aware of the intrusion and improve your security. Consequently, these hackers believe that hacking (without making any changes to the invaded site) is not criminal if it is done as a hobby.

■ CHECKLIST: AFTER THE HACK ATTACK

If your enterprise is successfully attacked, you will experience downtime, unexpected costs, and the necessity of restoring corrupted files and damaged servers. In addition to these concerns, you must effectively handle any adverse or negative publicity and manage customer relations. How you handle your web-based enterprise's public relations after an attack can affect future profits and, in some situations, the vi-

ability of your web-based business. The following list, while not comprehensive, can provide you with an overview of the types of actions
needed for your communication plan.

✓ Determine who should be on your communication crisis team.
   Select representatives from all functional areas in addition to
   legal counsel and a representative from your pubic relations firm.
   You may also want to include a member of the local media.

✓ Research the types of attacks comparable companies have suffered. List the types of attacks you have received in the past.
   Develop a series of realistic crisis situations on the basis of this
   information and similar research.

✓ Have the crisis team develop key messages and detailed questions and answers with which to respond to likely questions if
   any of the potential crisis situations materializes.

✓ Create an effective POC list of the individuals, vendors, and
   back-up software and equipment available for each disaster
   scenario.

✓ Select a crisis communication representative who has media
   experience. Make certain this person can effectively deliver
   your company's message.

✓ It may be wise to create an off-site media center to facilitate
   communications with the reporters.

✓ Press releases should tell the truth but should not be too technical. Never feel pressured into making a statement before you
   are prepared, and never release a statement that is not part of
   the predetermined communication plan.

✓ Create a series of simulations to determine if the crisis communication plan works. This drill can take a few hours or a few
   days. If there is a weakness in the communications plan, it is
   better to know in advance of the actual event.

✓ Show customers you care by contacting each customer by e-
   mail and U.S. mail. Apologize for any inconvenience and reas-
   sure customers that attackers did not gain access to sensitive
   information.

✓ Consider including a message on the home page of your web
   site or redirecting customers to an emergency web site.

■ REFERENCES

Atanasov, Maria. 2001. The truth about Internet fraud. *Smart Business,* 12 March. Available at [http://cma.zdnet.com]. 6 December 2001.

Bolar, Suman. 2001. You've been hacked . . . now what? *Workz.com,* 9 February. Available at [http://www.workz.com/content/2096.asp]. 6 December 2001.

Denning, Dorothy E., and Peter J. Denning. 1998. *Internet besieged: Countering cyberspace scofflaws.* New York: ACM Press, a division of Addison-Wesley.

The electronic frontier: The challenge of unlawful conduct involving the use of the Internet. 2000. A report of the President's Working Group on Unlawful Conduct on the Internet. United States Department of Justice, March. Available at [http://www.usdoj.gov/criminal/cybercrime/unlawful.htm]. 6 December 2001.

Fisher, Dennis. 2001. Experts study vulnerability reporting practices. *Securing the Enterprise,* a Ziff Davis e-mail newsletter. 26 June 2001. No longer available online.

Fitzpatrick, Kathy R. 1995. Ten guidelines for reducing legal risks in crisis management. *Public Relations Quarterly* 40 (2), 33–38.

Jones, Radford W., Margaret A. Kowalk, and Patricia P. Miller. 2000. Critical incident protocol: A public and private partnership. Michigan State University, State and Local Domestic Preparedness Support. Available at [http://www.ojp.usdoj.gov/odp/docs/cip.pdf]. 6 December 2001.

Lynch, Ian. 2000. HSBC reassures customers after hack attack. Available at [http://www.vnunet.com/News/1111233]. 6 December 2001.

McCormick, John. 2001. Are you protecting your company from destructive rumors? *TechRepublic,* 7 September. Available at [http://www.techrepublic.com]. 6 December 2001.

Mendell, Ronald L. 2001. Cyber-Terrorism. An online publication of *Security Portal,* 28 June. Available at [http://www.securityportal.com]. 28 June. Not available online. 28 June 2001.

Nitzberg, Sam. 1998. Conflict and the computer: Information warfare and related ethical issues. Presentation for the *National Information Systems Security Conference 1998.* Available at [http://www.iamsam.com/papers/holland/holland.htm]. 6 December 2001.

Osborn, Mathew. 1999. Managing a public relations crisis. *TechRepublic,* 16 September. Available at [http://www.techrepublic.com]. 6 December 2001.

Parmar, S. K. 1999. Information resource guide: Computer, Internet and network systems security: An Introduction to Security: Security Manual. An online publication of *Security Focus*. Available at [http://www.securityfocus.com/data/library]. 26 June 2001. No longer available online.

Schultz, E. Eugene, Jr., David S. Brown, and Thomas A. Longstaff. 1990. Responding to computer security incidents: Guidelines for incident handling. A 67-page joint effort of the Federal government and the University of California, Lawrence Livermore Laboratory, 23 July.

Chapter

10

Protecting Your Web-Based Business from Invisible Cyber-Crimes and Frauds

In this chapter:

➤ Invisible Infringement: Protecting Your Innovations
➤ Taking Stock of Your Intellectual Assets
➤ What's in a Domain Name? Just About Everything . . .
➤ Pilfering Your Trademark with Meta Tags
➤ Filching Your Web Site Design
➤ Pocketing Your Content by Linking It to Another Site
➤ Using Technology to Protect Your Intellectual Property
➤ Restricting Access with Digital Rights Management
➤ How Digital Watermarks Work
➤ Signing on the Digital Line and Fraudulent Customers
➤ Your Invisible Cyber-Crimes and Frauds Checklist

A wide variety of e-pirates and bootleggers pose new challenges for web-based businesses. Web-based enterprises are designed for public access, but this does not mean that the public is free to pirate, counterfeit, or defraud your business. The controversial 1998 Digital Millennium Copyright Act (DMCA) is designed to bridge the gap between traditional copyright laws and the need to copyright digital content. While the DMCA has defined what is legal or "fair use" on the Internet, in some situations lawsuits are still being tried on a case-by-case basis. This chapter shows how web-based enterprises need to proactively protect their content and resources. The chapter begins with a detailed look at the different types of "invisible" cyber-crimes organizations are subject to and how these cyber-crimes are ranked by seriousness. You'll gain an understanding of when another web-based entity cannot use your domain name, trademark, meta tags keywords, or web site design without your permission. This chapter also explores how to avoid financial losses by managing digital signatures (another source of invisible cyber-crime). The chapter concludes with information about the different kinds of digital rights management (DRM) tools your web-based enterprise can use to maintain its uniqueness and competitive advantage.

■ INVISIBLE INFRINGEMENT: PROTECTING YOUR INNOVATIONS

Resources on the Internet are designed for public access. By default this material is protected by copyright laws, but copies of documents have to be transmitted to the user's browser and stored in the user's computer in order to be viewed. Strictly speaking, this can be considered an infringement of the copyright. Likewise, the Internet user may be considered to be breaking copyright laws if he or she reproduces the document by printing it. To shed some light on this situation, the enactment of the 1998 DMCA seeks to update traditional copyright laws for today's digital age. The UCLA Online Institute for Cyberspace Law and Policy (2001) provides an excellent summary of the 1998 DMCA, which

> ➤ Exempts some not-for-profit institutions such as libraries, archives, and educational institutions from DMCA legislation
> ➤ Makes it a crime to skirt the antipiracy measures built into most commercial software applications
> ➤ Outlaws the creation, manufacture, sale, or distribution of code-cracking devices used to illegally copy software
> ➤ Limits the liability of Internet service providers for transmitting information over the Internet
> ➤ Requires webcasters to pay recording companies licensing fees for broadcasting over the Internet
> ➤ Requires the Register of Copyrights to submit to Congress rec-

ommendations regarding how to promote distance education while "maintaining an appropriate balance between the rights of copyright holders and the needs of users"

➤ States that "nothing in this section shall affect rights, remedies, limitations, or defense to copyright infringement, including fair use"

For details about the DMCA, see [http://www.loc.gov/copyright/legislation/hr2281.pdf].

■ TAKING STOCK OF YOUR INTELLECTUAL ASSETS

Today there are new online communication opportunities and tools for creating innovative products and services for your web-based company. These new creations, processes, and innovations require the attention of management and the implementation of intellectual property protection. This type of intellectual property (IP) security is frequently call digital rights management (DRM). DRM became prominent when the recording industry clashed with companies like Napster about the distribution of music files. However, the issue of digital rights is widespread and pervades many more industries than music alone. For example, an auto parts dealership may spend thousands of dollars to create an online graphic catalog. If another firm copies the images for their own use, the raided company loses its competitive advantage.

Enterprises need to actively pursue their intellectual property claims and protect themselves from invisible cyber-crimes, or they will lose customers and possibly their claims to the ownership of their own business materials and innovations. According to the authors of a *U.S. News and World Report* (2000) in an article titled "The Web's Dark Side," the Grateful Dead rock group budgets an extra $5,000 to $7,000 per month to monitor the web in pursuit of individuals and organizations that are selling pirated concert videos, knockoff dancing bear T-shirts, and studio albums. By performing such monitoring, Grateful Dead lawyers recently located 19 illegal auctions of Grateful Dead music.

Online businesses need to constantly pursue Internet pirates to protect their enterprises. Forrester Research (September 2000) notes that digital security and lawsuits will not stop the theft of your web site resources such as content, expensive graphics, and web site design.

Forrester estimates that by the year 2005 the music industry will lose $3.1 billion and book publishers will be cheated out of $1.5 billion due to counterfeiting.

To protect their assets, many web-based businesses have sent "cease and desist" letters to companies that have used unauthorized material. However, in cyberspace there are no hard and fast rules about trademark infringement, copyright violation, and unfair competition. Intellectual property crimes vary by type and by the seriousness of the offense. Federal prosecutors often avoid technical or inconsequential cases in order to focus their limited resources on more serious crimes. The U.S. Department of Justice (2001) tends to rank the seriousness of intellectual property crimes using the following criteria:

1. The potential health or safety threat posed by the counterfeit goods or services (for example, counterfeit antibiotic medicine or jet airplane parts)
2. The scope of the infringing or counterfeiting activities, as well as the volume of infringing items manufactured or distributed (for example, worldwide operations or hundreds of thousands of counterfeit copies)
3. The scale of the infringing or counterfeiting activities compared to the size of the intellectual property holder (for example, the total amount of ill-gotten gains or the total amount of illegitimate revenue received by the counterfeiter compared to the intellectual property holder)
4. The number of individuals in the illicit operation and the degree of involvement with organized crime
5. The scale of the victim's loss or potential loss, including the value of the infringed items, the size of the market for the infringed item, and the impact of the infringed item on that market
6. The presence of any precautions on the part of the intellectual property victim to prevent this type of theft (for example, does the intellectual property holder have a registered trademark?)
7. The extent to which purchasers of the counterfeit items were victims of fraudulent schemes, or the reasonable likelihood of consumer mistake as a result of the subject's actions (for example, did the counterfeiter claim a special relationship to, or sponsorship or endorsement of, the intellectual property holder?)

Intellectual property crimes have clear and direct victims. What makes intellectual property theft so insidious is that it can be perpetrated without direct contact with the two victims (the intellectual property holder and the recipient of the counterfeit goods or pirated work). There are many ways in which your resources can be pilfered; the following are a few examples of this type of invisible infringement.

■ WHAT'S IN A DOMAIN NAME? JUST ABOUT EVERYTHING . . .

The domain name system (DNS) links a numerical address to a domain name so that Internet users can quickly find the web sites they are seeking. Companies register for domain names using firms like Network Solutions (networksolutions.com) and ICANN (icann.com). There are millions of web pages on the Internet, and new web sites are added and deleted each day. Consequently, there is no comprehensive directory, so Internet users often try to guess the domain names that coincide with the products, trademarks, or brands of the company they want to find.

In some cases, a competing company may register the name of your company, product, or service as an Internet domain name to prevent your firm from using it. This tactic is often used in elections so that one candidate can disparage another. Sometimes, however, two firms have a legitimate claim to the same domain name. For example, United Airlines, a commercial airline company, and United Van Lines, a moving company, can with equal justice claim the name united.com. (For your information, the domain name for United Airlines is ual.com, and the domain name for United Van Lines is unitedvanline.com.) Other types of online trademark disputes involve the following:

➤ Cyber-squatting. Cyber-squatters are individuals or companies that register thousands of trademarked names (or even common surnames) as domain names. These domain names are then sold at hefty prices to the trademark holders. Lisa T. Oratz of Perkins Cole provides this example of a firm that purchased many surnames to sell to individuals who could use them in their e-mail addresses. Two of the names were Avery and Dennison. In a trademark infringement lawsuit, the names were deemed to be famous, so they fell under the 1996 Anti-Dilution Act. (The Anti-Dilution Act provides the owner of a famous trademark an injunction against another person's commercial use of the trademark if the use begins after the trademark becomes famous and causes dilution of the distinctive quality of the mark.) Therefore, the court ordered the domain name holders to sell the names of Avery and Dennison for $300 each to Avery Dennison.

➤ Typosquatting. Typosquatters are individuals or companies that cash in on Internet user typing errors. Recent examples include using the misspelling of amazon.com (as amazom.com) and of microsoft.msn.com (as microsfot.msn.com). The misspelling of cbssportsline.com as cbssportline.com and budweiser.com as budwesier.com results in visitors' being transported to casino44.com.

➤ Taking your name in vain. According to Ben Charny (2000), the entertainer Madonna wants her name back. There are about 87 web sites on the Internet that feature the word "madonna" in their address. While some of these web sites are for hospitals and not-for-profit organizations, like madonna.net and madonna.org, others are erotic in content and, in Madonna's opinion, tarnish her name. Yahoo! presented a similar complaint to the World Intellectual Property Organization (wipo.org) and was successful in forcing 40 Internet web sites containing the word Yahoo! to cease and desist. (The World Intellectual Property Organization is one of 16 agencies of the United Nations system of organizations. WIPO administers 21 international treaties that deal with the different aspects of IP protection.)

■ PILFERING YOUR TRADEMARK WITH META TAGS

Meta tags are HTML tags with site descriptions and keywords that indicate the web site's content but are not visible to the Internet user. If another company uses your trademark in its meta tags, it will appear to match an Internet user's search for your trademark on a search engine. At first glance, this may not appear to be important: After all, meta tags are invisible to Internet users. However, web search engines use these meta tags to position web sites using the terms entered by the searcher. Advertisers often pay web site owners for the number of hits to their web sites. Therefore, search engine placement can affect the revenue of a web site. If a competitor uses your trademark in its meta tags, this can be considered Internet trademark infringement and can negatively affect the advertising revenue your web-based business expects to receive.

The issue of using a trademark name in a meta tag was the source of a recent lawsuit between 1981 Playmate Terri Welles and Playboy Enterprises, Inc. To promote her career, Terri Welles created a Web site (terriwelles.com), in which she repeatedly referred to her status as a former Playboy model in the web site's meta tags. However, the web pages included disclaimers stating that the web site was not part of Playboy Entertainment. The court ruled in favor of Terri Welles and determined that her use of the Playboy trademark was fair use because it was used to accurately describe her identity and was not designed to confuse Internet users into believing that the web site was endorsed or sponsored by Playboy.

■ FILCHING YOUR WEB SITE DESIGN

If you are an experienced Internet user, you are probably familiar with the copying ability of your Internet browser. Click on *View* and then select *Source* from your browser's menu. Next you will see the source code for that specific page. This allows you to quickly copy the particular layout of the selected page. If the design of the page is strikingly creative, others may use this method to hijack your page layout. Susan Stellin (1997) points out one case of design snatching. The disputed layout was creative HTML virtual doors that, when pulled apart (using the visitors cursor), revealed text underneath. The design was used in *Fray* magazine (fray.com) for a story called "Meeting Peter" and later in *Salon* magazine (salon.com) for a column titled "Sizing it Up." Figure 10.1 shows a conceptual diagram of the disputed layout.

Figure 10.2 is a conceptual diagram showing the virtual doors opened to reveal the text underneath. Visitors are invited to click on the text for more information. The web page layout dispute was settled out of court when *Salon* added a caption to its column acknowledging HTML coding inspired by Alexis Massid and Derek Powazek of the *Fray*. This type of activity may be categorized as copyright infringement or a violation of trade dress (the design or packaging of a company's product or service).

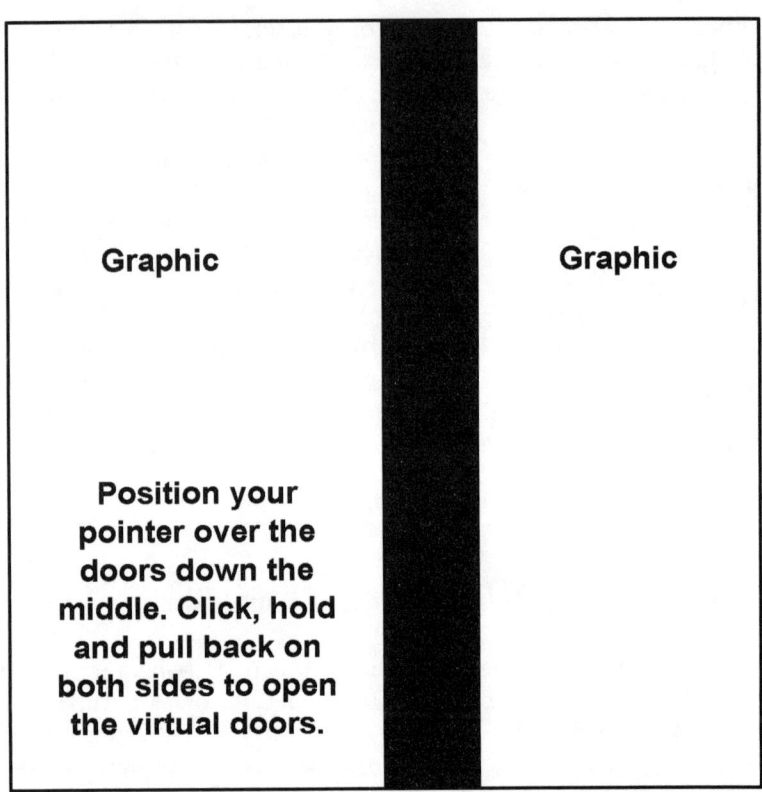

Figure 10.1 This rendering shows how *Fray* magazine's innovative web page design presents virtual doors for users to open

■ POCKETING YOUR CONTENT BY LINKING IT TO ANOTHER WEB SITE

Linking permits Internet users to automatically move from one web site or page to another just by clicking on text or on an icon that is hyperlinked. These hyperlinks make the Internet a quick and convenient way to locate information. Some web sites, like Yahoo! (yahoo.com), are completely comprised of links to other web sites. Many web sites have discovered that resource pages and external links to other web-based businesses provide their customers with added value and can in-

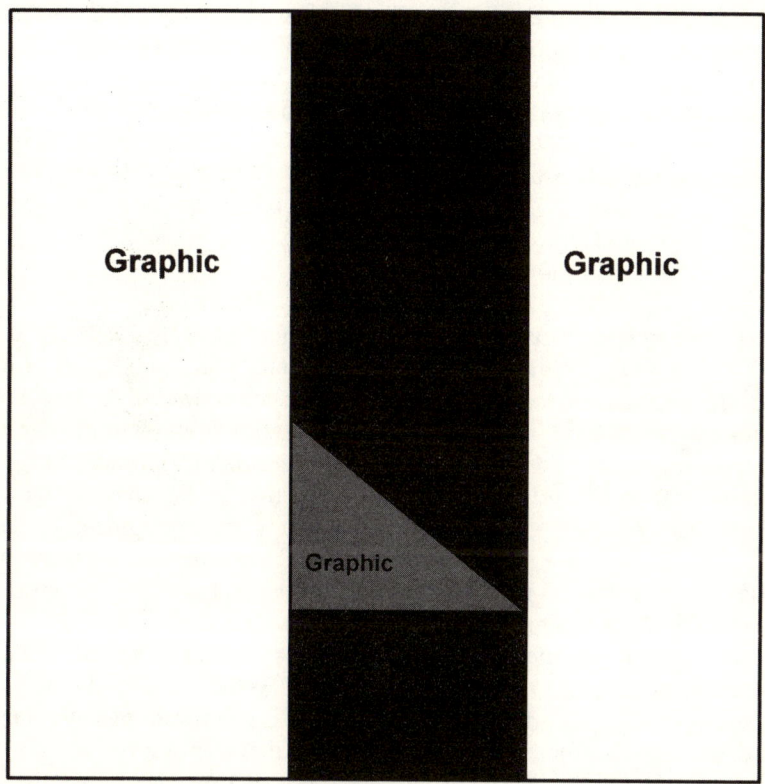

Figure 10.2   This rendering shows the completed design

crease the popularity and loyalty of users. However, there are both legal and illegal ways in which external links may be used.

Buford (2001) provides some insights about the four primary types of links, starting with local and remote links. First, local links are links in one web page that refer to another web page that resides at the same physical site. Second, a remote link on a web page sends the user to another physical site. The next two types of links are invoke-to-load and auto-load. Invoke-to-load links require the user to select or click on the link before the link's target is located. The Internet user's browser invokes the auto-load links automatically when the parent web page containing the link is shown. Auto-load links are often used to display images "in-line" with the selected web page: That is, when a web page presents text, the accompanying image is often an auto-load link with an in-line image (as often seen in online magazines and newspapers). This means that others can link to your web site in four ways:

1. Local invoke-to-load
2. Local auto-load
3. Remote invoke-to-load
4. Remote auto-load

Other web sites can use any of these methods to link to your web site. In general, others do not need to contact your web-based enterprise for permission to mention the name of your company and its URL as long as they do not misrepresent their relationship to your organization. Moreover, another web site can link to your web site without permission if it completely sends visitors to your web site. In other words, when visitors click an icon or hyperlink, they are transported to your web site and can view your URL address in their Internet browsers. Additionally, permission is not required if a new Internet browser window is "spawned" when the link to your web site is clicked.

In contrast, another web site cannot link your images (works of art, company logos, cartoons, and so on) to their web site without your permission. In this situation, the other web site has not copied your artwork, but is using the *exact image* by means of one (or more) of the linking methods described earlier. Furthermore, without your permission other web sites cannot link your web site to theirs using a "frame" that cuts off some of your content and prevents users from seeing your URL. Additionally, in some cases, linking to web pages deep within your web site (so users avoid seeing paid advertisements) can also be a source of litigation.

■ USING TECHNOLOGY TO PROTECT YOUR INTELLECTUAL PROPERTY

A number of technological solutions can assist you in reducing the likelihood of unauthorized use of your web-based enterprise's intellectual property. Web server logs track the activities of each web site visitor. Server logs show which web pages are the most popular, and referrer logs show which web site visitors just came from. By using server log analysis software, you can comb referrer log files to determine if competitors or potential hackers have just browsed your web site. Use of these tools can help you pinpoint which web pages need to have tighter security. Moreover, log information can help you draw other useful conclusions that can prevent or reduce the likelihood of copyright problems and theft of your intellectual property. The web offers a few free log analyzer software programs (Analog at www.analog.com is a good example). Log analyzers such as Wusage (www.boutell.com/Wusage), WebTrends (www.webtrends.com), and Sane Solutions (www.sane.com) range in price from $100 to $800.

As with all security for web-based businesses, these solutions are not a silver bullet that can prevent fraudsters who are intent on counterfeiting or litigation over the ownership of and rights to works. In other words, the best that technology can do is help you stay ahead of those who want to reap the rewards of your hard work and creativity. Generally, the more far-reaching the digital rights management (DRM) solution, the higher the cost and inconvenience. Ideally, the perfect DRM system will allow your web-based enterprise to keep track of the following:

➤ Operations: The number of times the content is viewed, printed, copied, or passed along

➤ Transactions: Setting the conditions for accessing your content and accepting payment

➤ Extent of use: Setting the number of times that your content can be viewed or printed or the length of time that the customer has access.

According to the Committee on Intellectual Property Rights and the Emerging Information Infrastructure (2000), there are five ways technology can assist you in keeping what's yours:

1. Restricting and enforcing access privileges to files. This is the traditional security approach to problems with theft, tampering, or copying. Unauthorized users are prevented access to files containing, for example, financial documents or original audio and video files.
2. Use of rights management languages, which are readable using special programs that detail the responsibilities of owners, dis-

tributors, users, and so on. This may also allow IP holders to determine if use falls within the permitted range—for example, in how many times a file can be downloaded from the Internet.

3. Watermarking, which embeds information about ownership into a digital work. Often intellectual property can include a watermark, so if it is copied the watermark can assist owners in tracking down the pirated work.
4. Encryption that allows users to be legitimately identified, for example, by requiring digital or electronic signatures to authorize access.
5. Persistent encryption that allows consumers to use information while the system maintains it in encrypted form.

■ RESTRICTING ACCESS WITH DIGITAL RIGHTS MANAGEMENT

E-pirates and bootleggers pose new challenges to innovative web-based businesses. Ensuring that only authorized users can access your network is the first step in preventing the theft of creative artwork, innovative programs, and sensitive information. For details about traditional approaches to access to control see Chapter 4. In addition to the traditional approaches to access control, there are many new DRM products that provide security for digital content. These technological solutions make digital content much less susceptible to unauthorized copying.

The importance of DRM technology is illustrated by a CNET (2000) article that cites an International Data Corporation report which states that the retail market for downloading software purchases over the Internet will increase to $14.9 billion in two years. This is remarkable, considering that revenue for this retail market was estimated to be only $351 million in 1998. Statistics like this highlight the importance of DRM and show the need for new technology that will promote the legal use of copyrighted material over the Internet, as well as providing the ability to follow sales for marketing purposes and charging royalty fees.

Additionally, one of the key tools of digital rights management is persistent security. Persistent security allows copyright holders to track the movement of IP, such as offline music recordings that are downloaded to portable music players and PC computers. Persistent encryption controls access privileges to decryption keys, so access privileges can be instantly canceled at any time, leaving the file unreadable for the unauthorized user. The following are a few examples of DRM technological solutions for different business models, including subscription-based delivery, rental, and video-on-demand.

➤ Blue Spike (bluespike.com) offers digital watermark copyright protection designed for those who create, produce, distribute, promote, and package digital artwork and music. Blue Spike uses a cryptographic system that *removes* selected bits or tones in a very narrow band to protect digital content.

➤ Verance (verance.com) provides audio watermarking technology solutions for broadcast monitoring and copyright management. Verance audio watermarking technologies are the foundation for ConfirMedia, a broadcast airplay verification service. ConfirMedia is the music industry standard for DVD audio copy control and the standard for the Secure Digital Music Initiative (SDMI). Licensees include Matsushita Electronics, Sanyo, Sony, and RioPort. The digital watermark is created by *adding* signals that are just out of the human perceptual range.

➤ Macrovision (macrovision.com) supplies video, audio, and software copy protection and digital rights management using encryption. Safeaudio is Macrovision's software-based audio copy protection solution for music CDs. Safeaudio is designed to prevent unauthorized copying or ripping of songs with a minimum of problems to sound quality and is applied to CDs as they are manufactured.

➤ InterTrust (intertrust.com) has a digital rights management architecture called the Rights|System, which aims to accommodate any kinds of content for any type of business model, by using all kinds of distributions methods on all types of devices. For example, the flexibility of the Rights|System suite allows service providers to deliver secured content to a broad range of devices, such as PCs, set top boxes, video recorders, mobile communicators, game stations, and so on. InterTrust's licensees and partners include Adobe, AOL/TimeWarner, Block-Buster, BMG Entertainment, Cirrus, Compaq, Digital World Services, Enron, Magex, Mercurix, Mitsubishi, Nokia, Philips, Samsung, Texas Instruments, and Universal Music Group.

➤ Digimarc (digimarc.com) applies a digital watermark to traditional and digital content, including movies, artwork, photographs, and documents (financial instruments, passports, tickets, and so on). Additionally, the firm provides the DigimarcSpider image tracker, which searches the Internet for watermarked images and reports details about when and where they can be found.

■ HOW DIGITAL WATERMARKS WORK

One method of sharing copyrighted material over the Internet employs digital watermarks. Digital watermarks are patterns of bits inserted into digital images and audio and video files that identify the IP holder. The digital watermarks are scattered throughout the file and designed to be invisible to users. To view the watermark, copyright holders use a special program that knows how to extract the watermarked data. Digital watermarks can often survive image rotating, cropping, cutting, pasting, and color separating. Additionally, the watermark can often survive data compression and reproduction over the Internet and other kinds of electronic and print media. If all works as planned, the digital watermark will remain even if the content is printed or faxed. Many dedicated e-pirates use compression programs to shrink music files in an attempt to exclude the unwanted information of the watermark. In some cases, the extra tones are stripped out, making the file free of the watermark (and available for copying) because the algorithm concludes that they are not likely to be heard by human ears.

■ SIGNING ON THE DIGITAL LINE AND FRAUDULENT CUSTOMERS

Invisible cyber-crimes include customer impersonation, which occurs when one person or entity poses as someone else in an effort to defraud the web-based business. False electronic identification can result in major financial losses. The only protection for the web-based business using long-lived digitally or electronically signed documents is to maintain an unspoofable audit trail. When we analyze a purchase transaction, we find several approval points that can be falsified by both insiders and outsiders. Moreover, there is a difference between electronic signatures and digital signatures.

According to Tom Melling, a writer for the *e-Business Advisor* (2000), an electronic signature, which is designed to replace a hand-written signature, can be an electronic mark. This electronic mark can be a process attached to or logically associated with an electronic file or adopted by a person with the intent to sign the file. Some legal authorities conclude that an electronic signature could even include an electronic sound. Thus, the definition of an electronic signature is broad enough to cover several different types of technologies. Electronic signatures can include the following:

➤ Clickwrap signatures: A customer clicks on a button that states "I Accept" (or a similar message) before proceeding to the next step. This approach is frequently used for software agreements, agreements to web site privacy statements, and web access agreements.

➤ Interactive clickwrap signatures: A customer types in his or her signature, then clicks on an acceptance button.

➤ Passwords or personal identification numbers: The web site uses an assigned password or shared secret password to authenticate the document signer.

➤ Biometric signatures: This type of electronic signature includes some type of physical measurement of the customer (retinal scan, fingerprint, voiceprint, etc.).

Digital signatures include encrypted messaging, as discussed in Chapter 6. Digital signatures use public key cryptology, which contains a key generator, signing function, and verification function. The user activates the key generator to create a public key and a secret key, as shown in Figure 10.3. The secret key and public key are used to create a digital object that becomes part of the signing function. This becomes the customer's digital signature, which is a unique and complex encrypted number or set of bits. The critical element of the digital signature is that it requires access to both the digital object and the secret key. The web-based business verifies the digital signature by using the public key, the digital object, and the signature. The verification function can also compare the user's public key to determine whether the signature was produced by the signing function from the object and the secret key. If this process confirms the customer's digital signature, the web-based enterprise knows that the signature authorizing the contract or purchase order has not been altered, and the order is confirmed. If the digital signature is not confirmed, the web-based organization

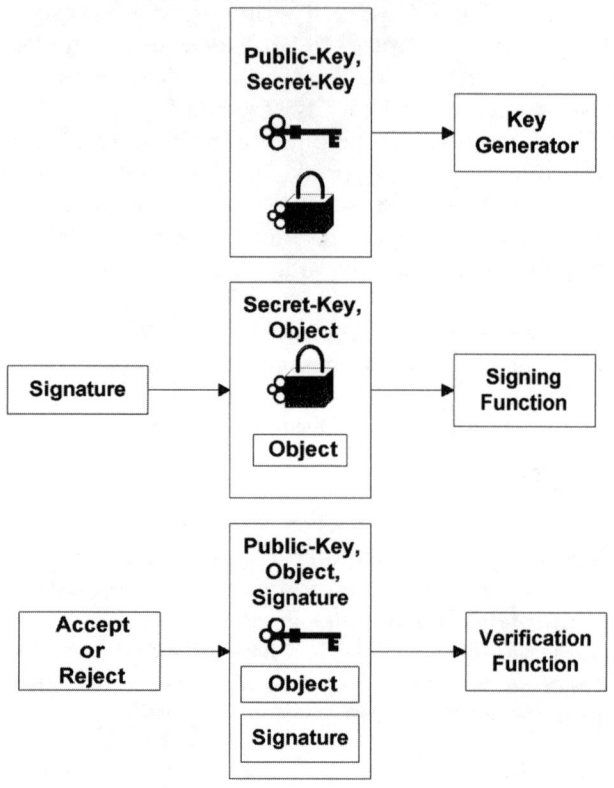

Figure 10.3 Diagram of the digital signature process

knows that someone who was not the original customer has tampered with the order.

Digital signatures are useful for converting paper contracts to electronic contracts, thus saving web-based enterprises time and money. The digital signature provides evidence of the signer's identity and ties the consumer to a certain contract or purchase order because the digital signature changes each time it is used. In the paper-based world, the signature is based only on the person doing the signing. For the virtual world, the 2000 Digital Signature Act details how a digital signature is a function of an individual's personal signature. The Center for the Study of Democracy (http://www.csd.bg/law/draftCSDrevE.htm#_Toc476468480) provides an easy-to-understand summary of this relatively new law.

Not all business interactions require contracts or signatures. In the United States, some contracts *must* have a handwritten signature. A signature may be a required legal formality to be used as evidence of the customer's identity and the customer's intent to be bound to the terms of the contract and of the actual agreement. One of the biggest problems with electronic signatures is retention. How can you microfilm and archive an electronic click for 5 or 10 years? How can your organization prove when the customer clicked the "I Accept" button? For short-term purchases this may not be a problem. However, in the future this issue may become of prime importance for medical records and financial documents that may need to be retrieved after the death of the signer.

■ YOUR INVISIBLE CYBER-CRIMES AND FRAUDS CHECKLIST

Web-based enterprises need to cover their bases online and offline by searching for and protecting the company from invisible infringement. The following is a checklist to help you get started on a program to protect your web-based business from invisible cyber-crimes and frauds.

✓ Conduct a trademark search to determine if your company name infringes on another organization's existing trademark. Your trademark may be locally known but still unsafe to use on the Internet.

✓ The security of your intellectual property is as important as the security of your network. Identify your intellectual assets and determine what you need to do to protect your rights.

✓ Select the appropriate digital rights management approach for your web site. Determine who will be responsible for tracking royalty fees, authorizing re-uses, and managing copyright permission requests.

✓ Consider including a Rules of Use page that details whether visitors must seek your permission to download, distribute, or publish in hard copy content obtained from your web site.

✓ Protect your intellectual property with a copyright statement on each web page. Include a "©," the notation that "all rights are reserved," the year, and your company name.

✓ Use Internet search engines to discover if another web-based enterprise, without your permission, has linked to your web site using your company logo, icon, or illustrations.
✓ Use an Internet search engine to verify that your trademark is not being used as a meta tag for another web-based enterprise.
✓ Determine whether another web-based business has linked to web pages deep within your web site or framed your digital content on its web page.
✓ Investigate your company's need for electronic or digital signatures to avoid customer impersonation and financial losses.

■ REFERENCES

Book industry continues to ponder security of digital content delivery. 2000. *Book Publishing Report,* 25 September. Available at [http://ask.elibrary.com]. 7 December 2001.

Buford, Tiger. 2001. Rules for linking to other sites. *Webtomorrow,* July. Available at [http://www.webtomorrow.com]. Available at [http://webtomorrow.com/linkrule.htm]. 7 December 2001.

Cavazos, Edward A., and Coe F. Miles. 1997. Copyright on the WWW: Linking and liability. *The Richmond Journal of Law and Technology* 4 (2). Available at [http://www.Richmond.ed./jolt/v412/cavazos.html]. 7 December 2001.

Charny, Ben. 2000. Madonna wants her name back. *ZDNetNews,* 19 August. Available at [http://cma.zdnet.com]. 7 December 2001.

Committee on Intellectual Property Rights and the Emerging Information Infrastructure. 2000. *The digital dilemma: Intellectual property in the information age.* National Academy Press, February. Available at [http://books.nap.edu/catalog/9601.html?onpi_newsdoc110399]. 7 December 2001.

The Digital Millennium Copyright Act. 2001. *The UCLA Online Institute for Cyberspace Law and Policy,* 8 February. Available at [http://www.gseis.ucla.edu/iclp/dmca1.htm]. 7 December 2001.

Hansen, Evan. 2000. Start-ups lead push to manage digital rights. *CNET News.com,* 17 February. Available at [http://news.cnet.com]. 7 December 2001.

Hunter, R., and W. Malik. 2000. Your data or your life. *Gartner Interactive,* 7 December. Available at [http://gartner3.gartnerweb.com/public/static/hotc/hc00094480.html]. 7 December 2001.

Hurst, Ray. 2001. What tools can I use to measure the performance of my web site? Available at [http://www.bcentral.co.uk/marketing/web/WebsitePerformance.asp]. 7 December 2001.

Melling, Tom. 2000. Digital signatures vs. electronic signatures. *E-Business Advisor,* 1 April. Available at [http://cma.zdnet.com]. 7 December 2001.

Moskowitz, Robert. 2000. Tracking digital signatures. *Network Computing,* 21 August. Available at [http://networkcomputing.com/1116/1116colmoskowitz.html]. 7 December 2001.

Oratz, Lisa T. 1999. Trademarks and the Internet. *ITPapers.com,* June. Available at [http://www.itpapers.com]. 5 July 2001.

Stellin, Susan. 1997. Law and the web: What you don't know can hurt you. *CNet Builder,* 17 July. Available at [http://builder.cnet.com/webbuilding/pages/Business/Law/]. 7 December 2001.

Vigneaux, Stevan. 1999. Securing data requires more than access control. *Computing Canada* 25 (35): 29.

Chapter

11

Firewalls and Protecting Your Distributed Office

In this chapter:

➤ What You Can Expect from a Firewall
➤ Firewall Insecurity
➤ Management Decisions for Firewalls
➤ Determining the Network Connection Policy
➤ Selecting the Firewall That Is Best for You
➤ Network-Level Firewalls
➤ Application-Level Firewalls
➤ Circuit-Level Firewalls
➤ Poking a Hole in the Firewall with a Virtual Private Network
➤ Firewalls and Your Distributed Office Checklist

Opening your web-based enterprise to the Internet or to remote users who dial in can increase sales, boost productivity, and leverage your current infrastructure. On the other hand, letting telecommuters, business partners, and employees access your private network or use your private network to access the Internet can make your system vulnerable to unwanted intruders. In this chapter you will discover how firewalls can limit access and verify the authenticity of users before allowing them access to sensitive information, confidential data, and internal resources. You will see how developing an effective network connection policy can assist you in selecting the firewall that works best for your web-based enterprise. You will gain a good understanding of the different types of firewalls and the advantages and limitations of each type.

This chapter can help you learn how a firewall can assist you in automatically policing security policies, monitoring employee access to the Internet from the company's local area network (LAN), and regulating dial-in-access to the LAN from remote locations. You will become aware of how a firewall system operates as a choke point that exercises control over all inbound and outbound network traffic. The chapter includes a discussion of how some companies avoid using the Internet because they do not want intruders to eavesdrop on their proprietary communications. This chapter shows how these firms can poke a hole in their firewalls and avoid leasing expensive line connections for this type of security. This chapter explores how virtual private network (VPN) technological solutions with advanced tunneling, encryption, and firewall technologies can help render communications between remote locations and users accessible, affordable, and secure.

■ WHAT YOU CAN EXPECT FROM A FIREWALL

In the past a *firewall* was defined as a barrier used in construction to prevent the spread of fire from one section of a building to another. In the field of technology, firewalls are frequently defined as gatekeepers that check the password and identification of anyone attempting to gain access to the network from the outside. In other words, firewalls can keep unwanted visitors out and escort privileged users to predetermined areas of the network where they are allowed access. For example, the firewall may allow an employee using his or her laptop computer and dial-up modem to download marketing reports and sales materials, while preventing the same employee from downloading salary records and performance reports, data that employees are not privileged to access.

As shown in Figure 11.1, a firewall is part of the overall security system of the web-based enterprise and creates a perimeter defense to protect the organziation's data. The usefulness of this defense is dependent upon the selection of the right type of firewall and development of effective security guidelines that detail network connection policies. Over the last several years, as Internet use has become more widespread, enterprises have been upgrading their firewalls. Many companies have deployed several types of firewalls within their organ-

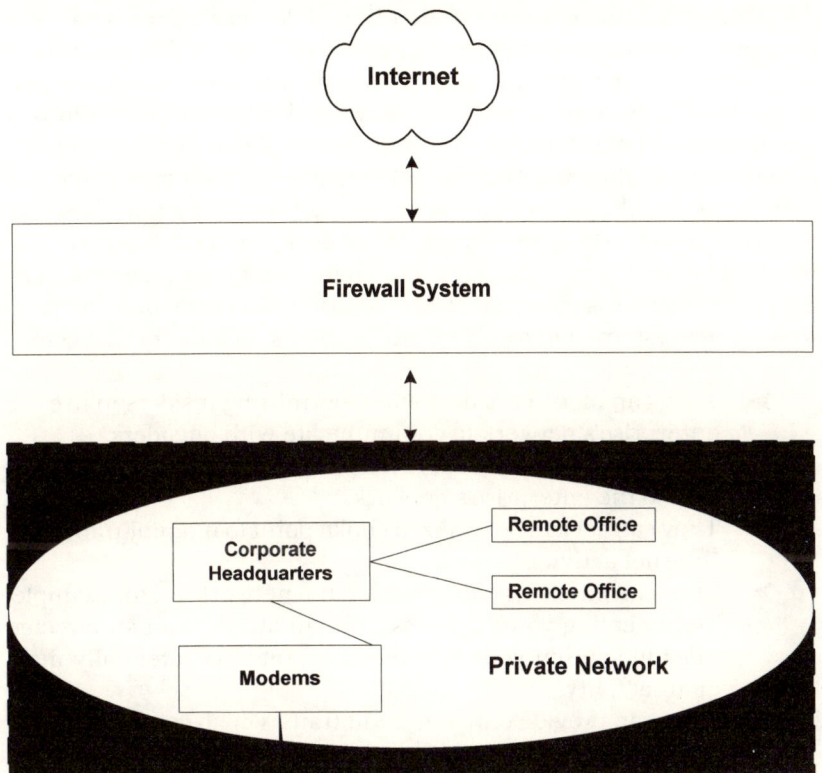

Figure 11.1 Conceptual diagram of how a firewall protects your private network

izations to improve security, availability, and the throughput of their intranets (internal Internets) and extranets (intranets that are available to authorized outsiders).

Ideally, a firewall between the network and the Internet is a system or group of systems designed to enforce access control from one network to another. Typically, one network is a trusted network and the other an untrusted network. Firewalls systems may be required to perform the following functions:

➤ Control access from remote users
➤ Provide external connections to business partners
➤ Prevent the exchange of sensitive information between departments or corporate divisions

A firewall is the enterprise's first line of defense against attackers. Frequently firewalls are a system or group of systems that control the access of traffic between two networks. How the firewall actually performs that operation varies. For example, the firewall may redirect e-mail traffic to a different server to protect the network from attacks by outsiders, so that incoming e-mail messages do not come in contact with the rest of the network because a packet-screening filter has redirected all mail to a selected server. At the designated e-mail server, the incoming e-mail messages are examined for malicious code or damaging subliminal messages (such as the addition of a new name and password to the system). Other benefits of firewalls include the following:

➤ They can block outsiders while permitting insiders to use the enterprise's network to communicate with outsiders.

➤ They can prevent intruders from using the Internet to gain access to the enterprise's network.

➤ They can act as a centralized choke point to monitor traffic and Internet activity.

➤ They can enforce security within the network, as, for example, by protecting your business from an attack from an infected machine within your network that contains potentially malicious activity.

➤ They can provide effective audit trails, which can assist the IT department and law enforcement in analyzing an incident and possibly locating an attack organization.

➤ They can partition one section of the organization off from another so that employees do not see performance reviews, sales data, corporate secrets, and the like.

➤ They can restrict public access to specific files, documents, downloads, software upgrades, and so on. (Many web-based businesses provide information on the Internet for public access, which allows the Internet to become the "ambassador" for the web-based business.)

■ FIREWALL INSECURITY

Although administrators may keep their systems up to date with the latest alerts and rigorously follow security policies, firewalls sometimes do not address all the vulnerabilities of the web-based business.

Firewalls are not intrusion detection systems and do not provide the same benefits because they are designed to block unwanted traffic instead of analyzing and identifying suspicious activity and launching automatic responses or notifying IT personnel. (For details about intrusion detection systems [IDS], see Chapter 4.)

To make matters worse, web-based businesses sometimes use a firewall that is comparable to the steel door of a bank vault but forget that the security level of the rest of the enterprise is the equivalent of a screen door. For example, many unwanted intruders have discovered that the easiest way to enter the protected network of a large web-based business is through the trusted networks of smaller businesses and individual users. This form of entry provides intruders with easier access points and results in the waste of the organization's investment of time, money, and effort in the firewall. Other firewall limitations include the following:

➤ Firewalls are not designed to ensure data integrity. For example, they do not screen for viruses and Trojan horses.

➤ Firewalls cannot prevent the physical destruction of your data.

➤ Firewalls are often susceptible to spoofing by attack organizations masquerading as legitimate users. (Often the sources of these attacks cannot be traced.)

➤ Firewalls do not guard the confidentiality of data on the internal network.

➤ Firewalls cannot protect the organization from completely new attacks.

➤ Firewalls cannot prevent the web-based business from malicious insiders who are intent on causing the organization harm.

➤ Firewalls cannot protect the enterprise from attacks that circumvent the firewall. For example, the ISP connection shown in Figure 11.2 illustrates a security breach of the firewall.

■ MANAGEMENT DECISIONS FOR FIREWALLS

Your web-based business may feature security measures analogous to a special key card for the front door and a video camera that records all activity, but the lack of a network connection policy leaves your web-based business open to potential intruders intent on stealing the information that is vital to your business. There are about 600 vendors who

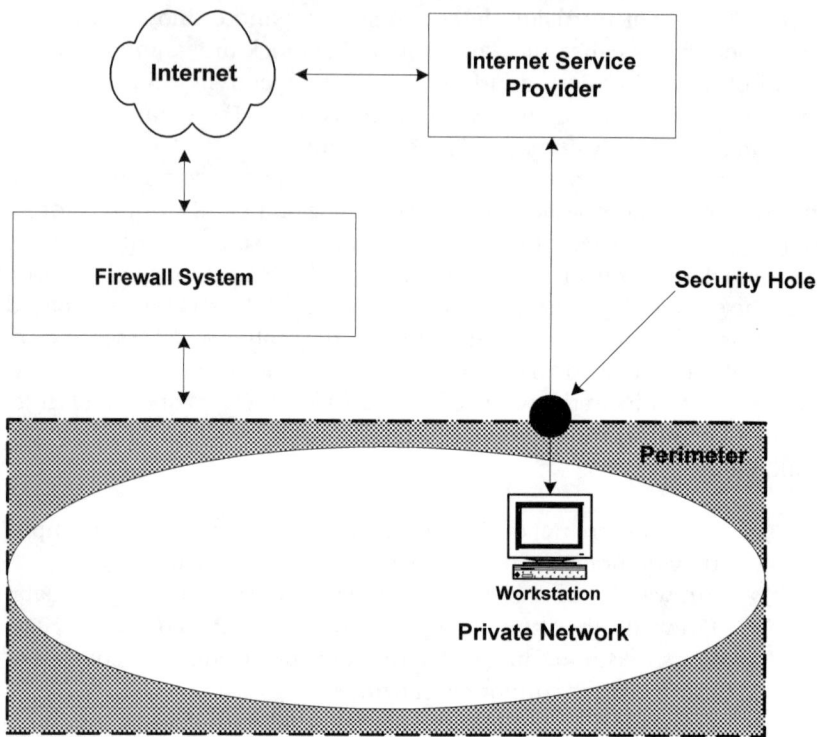

Figure 11.2 Conceptual diagram of how attackers can circumvent the firewall

provide firewall security solutions for companies of all sizes, home offices, and remote workplaces. According to Alex Salkever (2000), a writer for *BusinessWeek,* firewall security has been "commoditized." This has driven the average $20,000 price down to less than $50 for personal software and around $200 for home office products. On the other hand, the sales of small-business security products and services are expected to skyrocket from $994 million in 1999 to $7.9 billion by 2004. The cost of the firewall is also a management issue. Firewalls can vary in cost from nothing to over $30,000. For example, if the organization connects to the Internet, it needs a router. As shown later in Figure 11.3, routers often have packet screening capabilities and can be used as firewalls. Therefore, there is no extra cost for the firewall. Commercial firewalls vary in price from $4,000 to $30,000 depending on the complexity of the software and hardware, the number of systems to be protected, and personnel costs. Hidden costs of firewalls are the continuing personnel support for the installation of upgrades and security patches.

Firewall vendors make a variety of claims about their products. According to Lincoln Stein (1998), there are seven major areas that decision makers should be aware of as they consider a firewall:

1. The firewall operating system: You can mix and match the operating systems of your network and your firewall system. For example, a Windows NT system can have a Unix-based firewall.
2. The firewall protocol: Check the types of protocols handled by the firewall system to find one that is appropriate for the services you use. For example, if you need video conferencing, make certain the firewall you select can handle the required protocol.
3. The firewall filter: There are a wide variety of filter types. Application-level proxies provide high-level security but are slower than other types of filters. Circuit-level gateways are faster than application gateways but cannot read the contents of packets (which may be carrying malicious codes sent by attack organizations).
4. The firewall login features: Extensive login and analysis capabilities are valuable. The better the log analysis, the better the firewall is at detecting unusual activity.
5. The firewall administration capabilities: Firewalls with easy-to-understand graphical user interfaces can provide managers with more information than command-line programs that look like lines of computer code. In addition to remote administration capabilities, with the proper authentication, can provide managers with additional control over inbound and outbound traffic.
6. The simplicity of the firewall: Often the simplest firewalls are the best firewalls. Proxy firewalls are frequently simple servers that isolate traffic and can be easily verified by administrators.
7. The availability of the firewall for additional services: Some firewalls allow organizations to poke a hole in the firewall for a virtual private network (VPN). If you require a VPN for propriety communications, make certain that the firewall you have selected has this capability.

■ DETERMINING THE NETWORK CONNECTION POLICY

Some firewalls are designed to block out all traffic from the network, unless access is specifically granted for the service requested. Each service or application can be treated on a case-by-case basis. Unfortunately, this type of policy places security ahead of the convenience of the user community and can cause a decrease in productivity and profitability. In contrast, a policy that allows users access to all resources that are not specifically denied is more flexible. This policy also has its drawbacks, because it makes administrators react to security incidents by placing ease of use first. These two approaches show how the organization has to deal with firewall security in order to integrate it with the organization's overall security policy (see Chapter 14). The network connection policy should designate the kinds of devices that can be connected to the network—laptop computers, hand-held devices, home desktop computers, smart telephones, and so on. Once the network connection policy is determined, the information must be distributed to users so that they know what is being protected and how connecting to the network fits into the overall security policy of the organization.

The following questions from Lars Klander (1997) and Terry Ogletree (2000) can help you gain an understanding of your network requirements. Keep in mind that once you have determined the network connection policy for the organization, this information can be used to design the ideal architecture for your firewall system.

> ➤ Will you require all employees to exchange data via a floppy disk or other removable storage device?
> ➤ Will you allow devices from remote locations to be connected to network? What types of devices will you allow?
> ➤ Will you allow employee access to the Internet? Will you deny access to the network for certain users?
> ➤ Will you allow employees' laptop computers to be connected to other networks (such as the network of a customer when the employee is traveling)?
> ➤ What type of virus protection software will you install, and how will you make certain it is regularly updated?
> ➤ How can your user community open new user accounts, and how will you deactivate user accounts?

➤ What security procedures will you require for additional hardware and software components?

➤ How will you handle employees and others who are probing the network (attempting to gain access to data that are not relevant to their user privileges)?

■ NETWORK POLICY AND TELECOMMUTING

Companies and telecommuters use more and more laptop computers. In 1999, more than 300,000 laptop computers were reported stolen, according to an article by Anne Chen of *eWeek* (2001). Even the security-conscious FBI recently reported "misplacing" 180 laptop computers. A recent study of 273 companies by CSI and the FBI shows that laptop theft resulted in losses of $10.4 million last year. As the use of personal digital assistants (PDAs), hand-held devices, cell telephones, and other wireless devices becomes more prevalent this problem will likely increase. Therefore, your network connection policy must cover what will happen to lost, stolen, or misplaced electronic devices that use broadband or dial-up modems to access your network.

Keep in mind that although your web-based enterprise may fret over the loss of a $3,000 piece of hardware, the data on the laptop are often far more valuable than the hardware itself. If the information on these computers or electronic devices gets into the hands of the wrong individuals, it can be devastating. The FBI reports that 57 percent of computer crime is linked to stolen laptop computers. Luckily, there are software developers that provide a type of firewall solution for laptops. Some of the features include the ability to encrypt any portion of the hard disk you choose and to install a so-called phone home feature, which calls a central monitoring location if the machine is stolen and subsequently used by the thief. The following are a few examples of such systems:

➤ Black Ice Defender (networkice.com) calls home by connecting to the corporate network when a thief goes online.

➤ CyberAngel (sentryinc.com) places a call to a laptop manufacturer when it is stolen, updating owners about the telephone numbers the laptop is using.

➤ CompuTrace (computrace.com) places a call to a laptop manufacturer when it is stolen, updating owners about telephone numbers the laptop is using.

■ SELECTING THE FIREWALL THAT IS BEST FOR YOU

The simplest firewall is a router with screening capabilities. The screening filter can be programmed to meet your network connection and security policy requirements, but it only looks at the addresses of the data packets. In other words, the contents of the data packets are never examined. The inflexibility of packet filtering routers has spurred the development of several types of firewalls. Firewall systems for web-based enterprises can include one, a few, or several different types of firewalls. Firewalls can be divided into three types:

1. Network-level firewalls evaluate only the source, destination, priority, and privilege of requests and permits those that pass muster. They do not consider the type of application that is being used—only the sender and receiver. Calls that conform to well-known attack signatures (addresses) or indicate a potential for misbehavior are blocked.
2. Application-level firewalls use proxy servers that intercept messages entering or leaving the network and substitute the real sending/receiving addresses with proxies or temporary addresses. The actual addresses of the sender and receiver do not pass through the firewall. The proxy server acts on behalf of your organization and hides your enterprise's true network address so that attackers can't use this information to spoof their way into your network. Frequently, different proxies are used for different applications or services (e-mail, File Transfer Protocol [FTP], etc.).
3. Circuit gateways are mechanisms for making a secure but separate connection between networks. Once the gateway is connected, data packets can flow between the sender and host without further investigation.

■ NETWORK-LEVEL FIREWALLS

Network-level firewalls are usually the organization's first line of defense. A network-level firewall is generally a screening filter, which filters data packets that are routed to the network. This screening prevents access to machines or ports inside your network in addition to preventing a network machine from directly accessing the Internet (something that is very important for military organizations with classified data). Today, firewalls are so important that Microsoft's XP includes a firewall and the ability to block or disconnect a dial-up connection remotely in its operating system. That is, broadband (DSL or cable modem) and dial-up users can easily set up firewall protection by selecting the type of connection they desire and its corresponding IP address. Once in place, the Windows XP operating system blocks everything else.

➤ Static Packet-Filtering Firewalls

Before the Internet revolution, placing a firewall between two networks was standard operating procedure. The firewall mediates and monitors the connection between any two networks. For example, the firewall can prevent one department from having access to the data in another department within the enterprise. Today most corporations provide employees access to the Internet (outbound) and provide remote access to their internal corporate networks (inbound). Figure 11.3

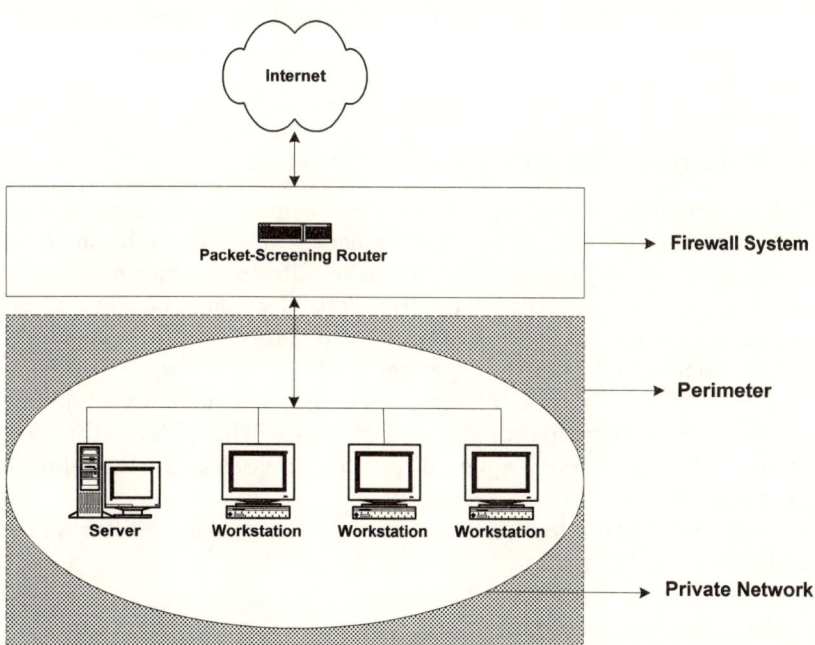

Figure 11.3 Conceptual diagram of how a screening router protects a network

shows how traffic passes through a static filter to the network. Packet-screening routers are fast and transparent to the user community. This type of filtering is often considered a low- to medium-cost firewall solution, because all connections from the network to the Internet require a router, and routers usually include packet-filtering capabilities. However, most web-based businesses require a higher level of security.

Static packet filters screen traffic coming in and out of the network and check each IP packet for source and destination IP address, protocol, service types, and so on. This information is compared to the predetermined guest list. These rules can specify actions for certain source or destination IP addresses or port numbers. If all goes as planned, the static router will discard data packets that contain certain destination ports, packets with spoofed IP addresses, and malicious packets designed to bypass security measures. A primary weakness of packet filtering is the direct connection between source (outside) and destination (inside) computers. If the firewall approves the source computer's address as one that is trusted, a connection is made to the destination computer. This can expose other computers inside your network. Additionally, static packet filters have little or no logging capabilities, may be difficult to configure, and can require a highly skilled administrator. Any one of these weaknesses can allow a tainted data packet to gain access to the network.

➤ Dynamic/Stateful Packet Filtering

Dynamic/stateful screening filters are a supercharged advance in static traffic screening. With stateless packet filtering each packet is evaluated on its own merits. Stateful packet filtering (sometimes called *stateful inspection*) performs all the functions of stateless packet screening and examines the context of packets to determine the state of the communication by keeping in memory the state of the current session. In other words, dynamic/stateful inspections match each client request with its corresponding server response. This reduces the likelihood of intruders' using spoofed return addresses as a way to break into your system.

Some of the best features of dynamic/stateful packet filtering include the ability to

➤ Check each IP packet and follow filtering rules based on that information
➤ Identify data packets that have a spoofed source IP address

➤ Analyze an IP packet in the context of its previous communications

➤ Verify the state of an IP packet based on its application information

Although stateful packet-screening filters are an improvement over stateless screening filters, they still have some disadvantages. Packet-screening filters are not very flexible. As a general rule, screening routers cannot be customized to meet the specifications of large corporations with diverse needs. The screening router does not authenticate users and does not include the capacity to audit. Additionally, if the screening router is improperly configured, it may become a trapdoor for unscrupulous users.

■ APPLICATION-LEVEL FIREWALLS

Both application-level gateways and circuit-level gateways include proxy servers (a server that acts on behalf of another). These proxy servers are an alternative to filtering because they prevent traffic from passing directly between networks. Packet filters inspect the IP address and other header information but do not change them. In contrast, proxy servers substitute temporary addresses (which cannot be spoofed since they change over time), provide more services, and ensure that the real source and destination addresses of IP packets are never directly connected. The proxy server in its role as middleman talks to both sides of the connection (internal and external) but assures that they will never connect. As confusing as this sounds, the proxy server does not route any traffic (it leaves that to the router) and never attempts to make any connections.

Figure 11.4 shows an application-level firewall. Application-level firewalls offer more flexibility than screening filters because they allow administrators to control what's happening on the application layer of the system. The application proxy firewall, acting as a server, accepts packets and checks the data portion of the packet to see if it is allowed into the network. In other words, the internal network is not directly connected to the external Internet, and traffic on your network never directly interacts with traffic from another network. If the connection is allowed, the firewall *re-creates* the packets and resends them, acting as a client. The application proxy firewall then returns the results to the

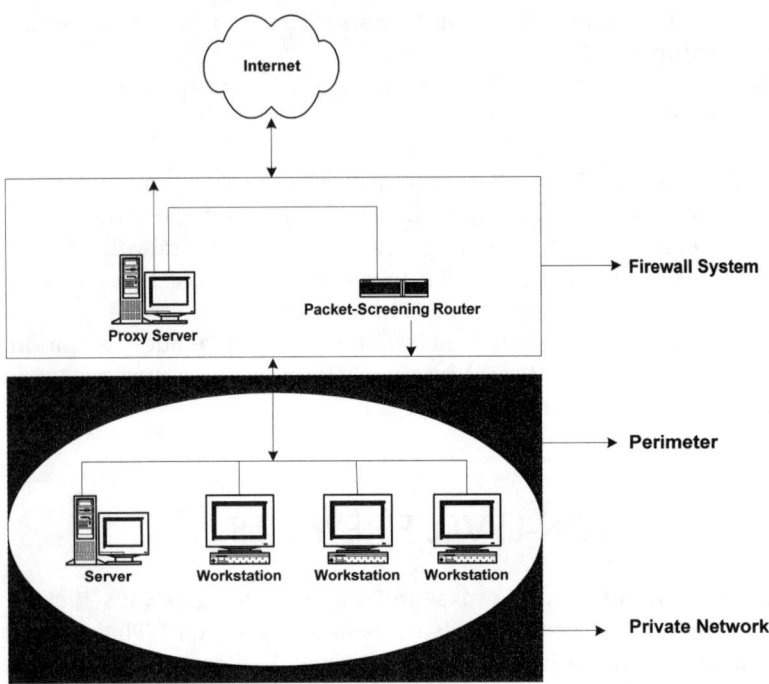

Figure 11.4 Conceptual diagram of how proxies are used in an application level firewall

sender (acting like the middleman). Overall, proxy servers provide an excellent single point in the network to control access. However, if the proxy server fails, so does the security for the entire system. The following is a step-by-step example of how an application-level gateway firewall works in an outbound example:

1. An employee uses his or her workstation to request a web page from the external web server on the Internet.
2. The proxy server receives the request on its internal network adapter, which is connected to the internal LAN.
3. The proxy server compares the request to the predetermined network connection policy to decide if the request should be granted or denied.
4. If the employee is allowed access to the external Internet, the request is approved. Next, the proxy server replaces the

real internal source address with a fictitious (or proxy) address and forwards the request for a web page to the external Internet.

5. The proxy server receives the requested web page from the external web server. The proxy server then checks the incoming packets, which now show the source's proxy address as the destination, since this is a reply to the original request based on a set of predetermined criteria.

6. Finally, the proxy server replaces the fictitious (now destination) address of the internal workstation to its original value and returns the web page to the employee.

7. Throughout this exchange, the external web server (or anyone snooping on the web) never sees the real internal address of the requesting workstation. This is the goal of the proxy server — to hide all internal addresses from outside intruders.

One of the best features of application gateway firewalls is their ability to check the content and type of data being requested and returned. This can be very useful for enterprises that are worried about employees' wasting time at work by aimlessly surfing the Internet. Additionally, some application-level firewalls allow one type of traffic across the gateway but prevent other types of traffic. For example, you can enforce rules concerning such issues as the stripping-out of macros in Microsoft Word documents and the removal of active content from web pages. Application-based firewalls often require less maintenance and fewer upgrades than network-level firewalls. The downside is slower performance, which may cause serious bottlenecks.

■ CIRCUIT-LEVEL FIREWALLS

Internet firewalls are often called secure Internet gateways. The gateways let in wanted traffic according to predetermined access rules. Circuit-level gateways create a circuit between the network and the proxy server. Two popular types of circuit level architectures are dual-homed gateways and screened-host gateways. Bastion host firewalls appear to be circuit gateways and provide a third circuit level firewall approach. Traffic goes through a circuit to the proxy server, which delivers it to the Internet after changing the IP address. Responses are sent to the proxy server and sent back through the circuit to the network. This means that external users only see the IP address of the proxy server. Additionally, circuit-level gateways give the enterprise control over connections and the ability to log all connections. This makes circuit-level gateways much safer than packet-screening filters. One disadvantage of circuit-level gateways is that they cannot prevent application-level attacks that use malicious code hidden in IP packets.

➤ Dual-Homed Host Architecture

Figure 11.5 shows the dual-homed host architecture for an enterprise's firewall system. The dual-homed host architecture includes firewall software and a host computer with two network cards that act as gateway connectors. The gateway connectors are internal and external interfaces. The firewall acts like a software router that provides secure

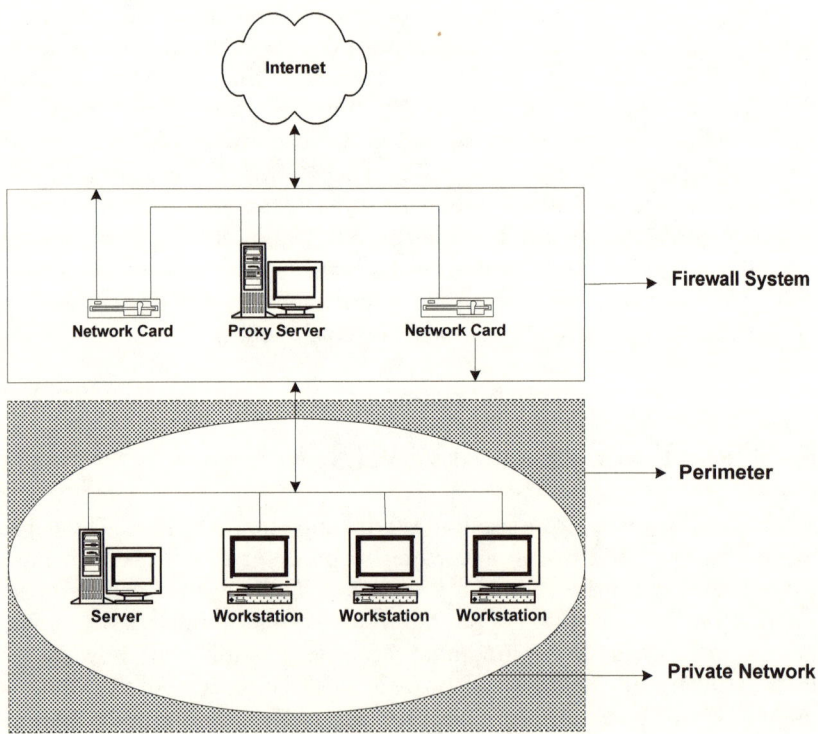

Figure 11.5   Conceptual diagram of dual-homed host firewall architecture

connectivity through packet filtering. For example, if an employee makes a request for a web page, the request goes out of the LAN but does not directly reach the Internet. The request instead goes to the internal interface (one network card) that is controlled by the software of the application proxy server running on the host. The request is then checked against a set of predetermined standards. If the request is granted, the proxy server recreates the employee's request by sending out packets (which mask the sender's true IP address) on the external interface, a second network card. Each network card or interface "talks" to its side of the transaction and there is no connection between the interfaces. Dual-homed host firewalls are not recommended for web-based enterprises that need high-level security due to software vulnerabilities. A major weakness of the dual-home host architecture is its reliance on one host machine and the operating system of that machine. If intruders are successful in breaking into the host, then the firewall is useless.

➤ Screened-Host Firewall Architecture

Figure 11.6 shows a conceptual diagram of a screened-host firewall. A screen host includes a packet-screening router deployed in front of an application proxy server that is hosted on a private network. The proxy server allows traffic into the private network via the packet-screening router. This type of architecture can support many hosts, such as multiple proxy servers or web servers. One advantage of the screened-host firewall is that it makes the rest of your network invisible to outsiders. In other words, screened-host firewalls do not allow outsiders to determine how many or what types of machines are on the private network.

Many industry professionals believe that screened-host firewalls are more secure than dual-homed host firewalls because the proxy server, which acts as a host, is effectively isolated from the private network. A weakness of this approach is the packet-screening router. If the packet-screening router fails, then there is a loss of security. Screened-host firewall architecture is recommended for small- to medium-sized businesses that require simple but effective firewall solutions.

➤ Bastion Hosts: Creating Interior Firewalls

The dual-homed gateway and the screened-host gateway appear to outsiders like a single bastion host machine. The term *bastion host* is based on a medieval term describing the thick walls within a castle that are

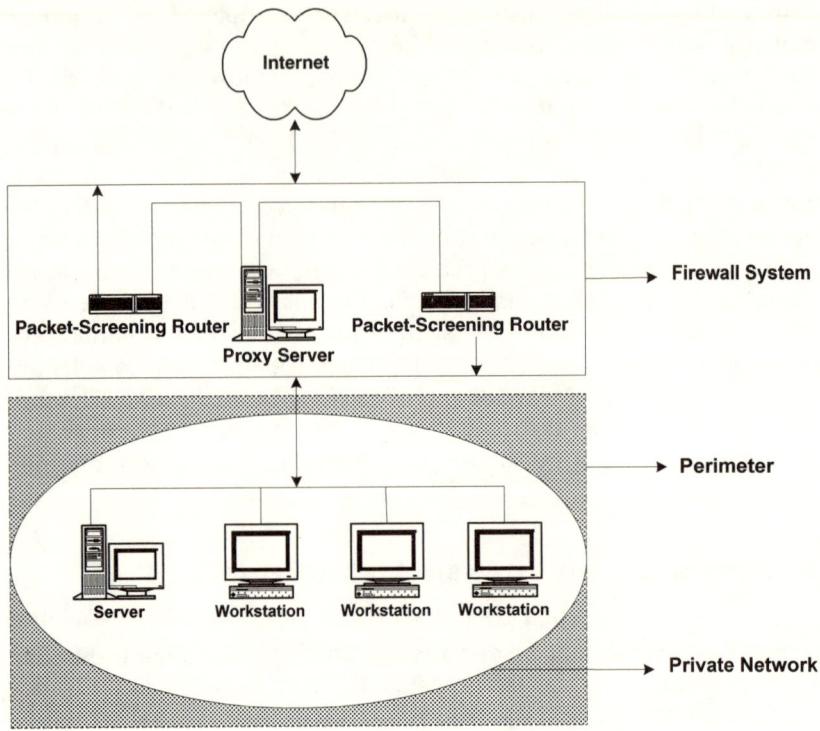

Figure 11.6 Conceptual diagram of a screened-host firewall

used to repel attacks. Some firms use an actual bastion-host firewall, as shown in Figure 11.7. The bastion host is a computer dedicated to preventing unauthorized access to the network.

The bastion host can eliminate the need for sophisticated packet-screening routers, which can cost $18,000 or more. For Unix- and Linux-based environments, a bastion host can be as simple as a workstation. Bastion hosts are usually placed between the trusted and non-trusted network where the IP forwarding is broken. This is a choke point for all inbound and outbound traffic. All Internet traffic is centralized at the bastion host, and only the bastion host is connected to the Internet. The only place that both networks can be accessed is at the bastion host. The bastion host requires double identification (once for the bastion host and once for the remote host). One drawback of the

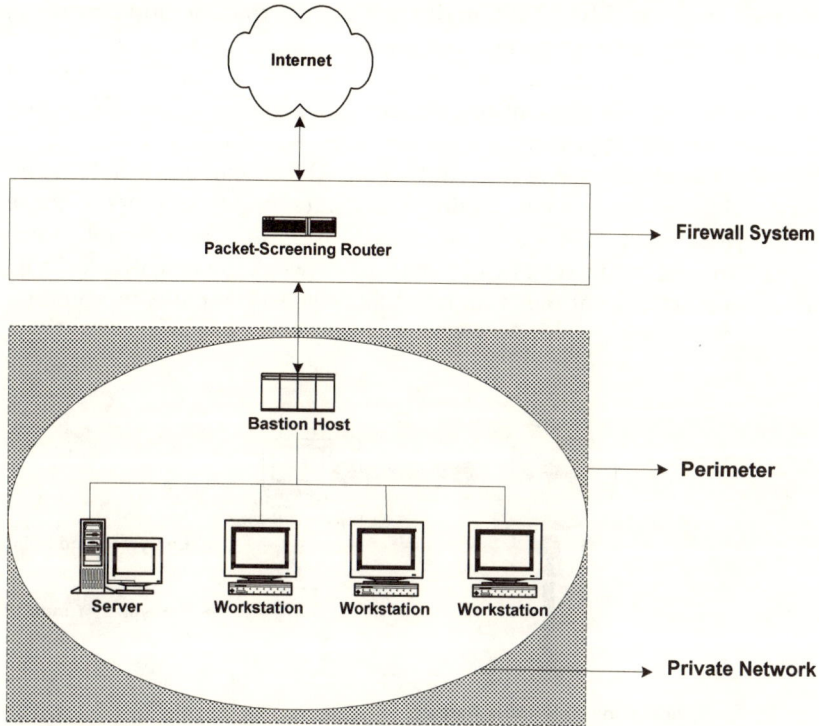

Figure 11.7 Conceptual diagram of a firewall with a bastion host

bastion host is its reliance on one machine. If attackers are successful in breaching the security of the bastion host, then the firewall is worthless. One alternative is using a packet-screening filter as a redundant firewall. While this is not a ideal firewall, it may fend off intruders while the bastion host is replaced or repaired.

■ POKING A HOLE IN THE FIREWALL WITH A VIRTUAL PRIVATE NETWORK

Many web-based companies are surprised to learn that information such as medical records, e-mail messages between executives, movie scripts transmitted by FTP, e-mail attachments that include contracts, and personnel files from law corporations, medical centers, and accounting firms are available to unwanted intruders. Installing a virtual private network (VPN) can often solve this problem of electronically and safely sending proprietary information over the Internet.

Web-based businesses are often scattered throughout the nation and the world. The employees, business partners, and customers of these enterprises need access to corporate information from remote locations. This access must be available from network-to-network, desktop-to-desktop, and client-to-server connections. Additionally, remote and

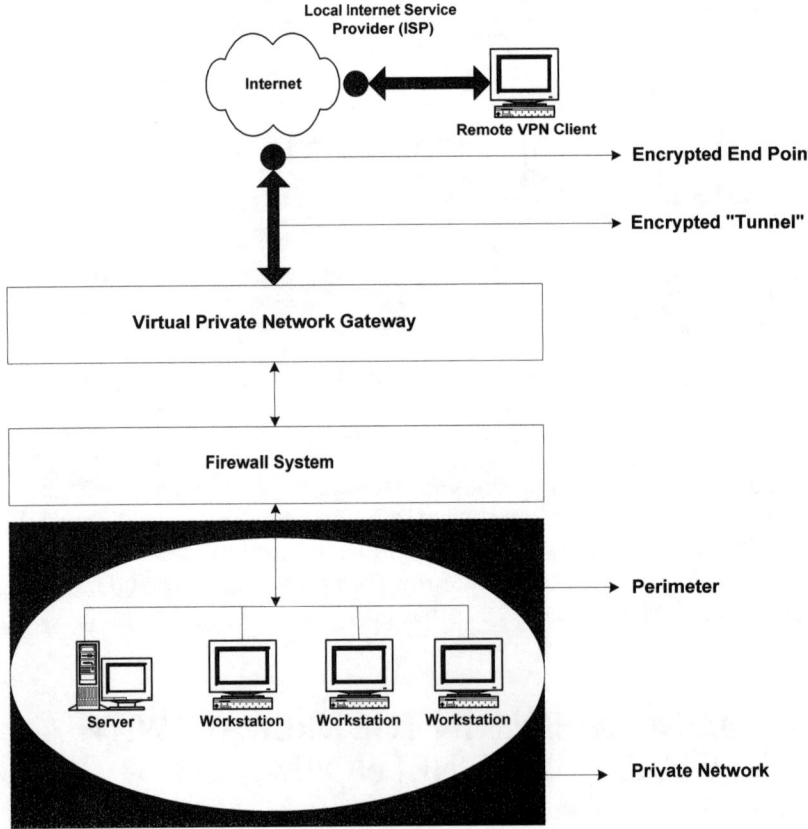

Figure 11.8 Conceptual diagram of a virtual private network (VPN)

mobile users will need to access network resources at different hours during the day and night.

Figure 11.8 shows how VPN technology allows companies to create so-called tunnel connections between sites on the network via the Internet. Once connected, employees at remote sites can receive the same computing services as employees at the home office. Company data published on internal web servers at any site can be shared with employees at other sites. Like expensive leased line connections, these tunnels encrypt the data so that Internet service providers (ISPs) and hackers cannot eavesdrop. In the past, companies paid hefty prices to lease line connections in order for the organization to have a VPN. Today, VPN technology can establish low-cost secure private networks to other computers, hand-held devices, and smart telephones via the Internet. Therefore, you may want to consider a VPN if you want to reduce the high costs of remote access and site-to-site communications, improve performance for distributed access, and have the ability to create a consistent network connection and security policy throughout the organization.

As shown in Figure 11.8, a VPN is a network tunnel for communications between two or more authenticated users. A secure VPN encrypts data before passing them through the network tunnel. This ensures user privacy and data integrity and authenticity. VPNs often include circuit-level firewalls that protect your organization's internal network by monitoring and controlling incoming and outgoing connections. There are four primary benefits of VPNs:

➤ They allow your web-based business to establish a secure extranet environment that is transparent to users. Users can communicate with your organization using dial-in modems or desktop computers with fixed IP addresses.

➤ They include a circuit-level firewall that can assist your firm in tracking and controlling the state of all traffic connections. Additionally, they provide detailed auditing and logging capabilities that can assist you in implementing and enforcing the firm's security policy.

➤ They allow you to optimize your intranet. You have the option of encrypting all communications or encrypting some of your interactions based upon their source, destination, IP address, application port, and protocol.

■ FIREWALLS AND YOUR DISTRIBUTED OFFICE CHECKLIST

The following firewall security checklist can assist you in protecting your network and data. There are several books that detail each firewall type and the method for configuring and installing the selected firewall. The items listed below are simple defensive measures. If management makes certain these procedures are followed, then the odds of evading an attack on the network are much higher.

✓ Install a firewall before you have connected your web-based business to the Internet.

✓ Develop rigorous access rules for connecting to the network.

✓ Stay informed about the latest security upgrades, patches, and threats. Firewalls will not solve all of your information security problems, but they are your first line of defense.

✓ Determine your network connection policy before you select your firewall solution. Make certain your network connection policy is consistent with the firm's detailed security policy.

✓ Because firewalls are generally firewall systems, keep in mind that you may want to use several firewall components or a VPN for the transmission of sensitive information.

✓ Remember that your user community will rely on the availability of information from your databases and corporate headquarters. The solution you select will have to provide access 24 hours a day, 7 days a week, 365 days a year.

✓ Look for scalability in your firewall selection. It is likely that you will quickly outgrow your firewall hardware, software, and bandwidth.

✓ Expect to see changes in the years ahead as firewall vendors change due to mergers and acquisitions.

✓ The firewall software you select may include many features you will not use, install only the firewall features you need.

✓ Be wary of vendors who promise plug-and-play solutions. Firewalls are configured to meet the individual needs of your web-based business.

✓ Be aware that the firewall you installed several years ago may not be the best solution today. If you decide to change your firewall system, proceed carefully and be prepared for a significant effort.

■ REFERENCES

Anderson, Ross. 2001. *Security engineering: A guide to building dependable distributed systems.* New York: Wiley.

Ashan, Muninder P. 2000. Firewalls: A perspective. CNet Enterprise (enterprise.cnet.com), a Dataquest Perspective, 8 March. Available at [http://home-internal.cnet.com/enterprise/0-9567-7-2481743.html]. 7 December 2001.

Curtin, Matt, and Marcus J. Ranum. 2000. Internet firewall: Frequently asked questions. *Interhack,* 1 December. Available at [http://www.faqs.org/faqs/firewalls-faq/]. 7 December 2001.

Chen, Anne. 2001. If the FBI can't protect laptops, who can? *eWeek,* 20 July. Available at [http://cma.zdnet.com]. 7 December 2001.

Denning, Dorothy E., and Peter J. Denning. 1998. *Internet besieged: Countering cyberspace scofflaws.* Reading, Mass.: Addison-Wesley.

Ghosh, Anup. 1998. *E-commerce security: Weak links, best defenses.* New York: Wiley.

Klander, Lars. 1997. *Hacker proof: The ultimate guide to network security.* Houston: Jamsa Press.

Ogletree, Terry William. 2000. *Practical firewalls.* Indianapolis, Ind.: Que.

Salkever, Alex. 2000. Firewalls any outfit can afford. *Business Week Online,* 3 October. Available at [http://www.businessweek.com/bwdaily/dnflash/oct2000/nf2000103_462.htm]. 7 December 2001.

Semeria, Chuck. 1996. Internet firewalls and security. *3Com,* 30 July. Available at [http://www.3com.de/produkte/datenbletter/pdf/50061901.pdf]. 1 August 2001. No longer available online.

Stein, Lincoln D. 1998. *Web security: A step-by-step reference guide.* Boston: Addison-Wesley.

What is a firewall? 2000. *IT Security Newsletter,* December. Available at [http://www.itsecurity.gov.in/fr_files/fh_firewalls1.htm]. 7 December 2001.

Zwicky, Elizabeth D., Simon Cooper, and D. Brent Chapman. 2000. *Building Internet firewalls.* 2d ed. San Francisco: O'Reilly.

Chapter

Safeguarding Your Customers' Privacy and Personal Information

In this chapter:

- ➤ Cookie Basics for Web-Based Businesses
- ➤ Looking at the Dark Side of Cookies
- ➤ Some Cookies Leave Consumers with a Bad Taste
- ➤ Establishing a Policy for Better-Tasting Cookies
- ➤ Cookie Piracy and Protecting Customer Information
- ➤ Protecting Customer Information Checklist

Most online customers prefer privacy and anonymity when they are shopping or planning to make a purchase. How many times have you told a salesperson that you are "just browsing" when you visit a department store? You would probably be offended if the same salesperson took out a notebook and wrote down your name or noted what items caught your attention. Cookies can be used in a similar manner. When used correctly, cookies can make online purchasing quick and convenient. However, cookies have the potential to be abused. That is, they provide the ability to spy on customers by following their Internet click trails without customer approval or awareness. Additionally, there are many ways cookies can be intercepted by interlopers. Therefore, your web-based business needs to encourage customer trust by only using cookies when necessary and by incorporating strong cookie policies in privacy statements so that customers know how the web-based business is protecting their privacy and confidential information.

■ COOKIE BASICS FOR WEB-BASED BUSINESSES

Web-based enterprises often use cookies to track the navigation path of users through their web sites. Previous to the use of cookies, interacting with the web site was similar to watching television or listening to the radio. Internet user interactions, such as requesting information, were anonymous client-side transactions. In other words, a user's browser connected to a web server, fetched a URL, and shut down the connection. If the user wanted to continue using the Internet, the transaction started from scratch and was repeated using an entirely new connection. Each request, even clicking on a link within the first requested web page, was considered a new transaction. This approach made an ongoing conversation impossible. With cookie-enabled browsers, this one-way relationship ended. Cookies require less use of storage space for Internet actions, so a customer can now place a dozen items or more in a shopping cart and then check out. Each time the customer clicks, the web server can remember who the customer is and what items have already been selected.

Cookies are not programs and are not executable on the client's machine. Rather, they are small text files that are stored on a user's hard drive after a client contacts the web server and requests a document. When the connection is made, the web server sends the requested document and a cookie to the client. Different Internet browsers store cookies in different ways on the hard disk of the client's computer. Here are some things that normal cookies cannot do:

> Read or write a file to the user's machine. As a general rule, cookies do not include programs that allow them to read or write to existing files.

> Steal passwords that are stored on the user's machine. Cookies are not programmed to find passwords on the user's computer.

> Re-format the user's hard disk. Cookies reside on the user's hard disk but do not have an executable program that can re-format the user's hard disk. Additionally, cookies are generally

so small that they do not make a significant difference in the storage capacity of the user's hard disk.

➤ Send e-mail from the user's machine. Cookies do not include executable programs that can take over the e-mail function of the user's computer.

➤ Transmit a virus from the user's machine to another machine. Usually cookies are too small to include a virus.

➤ Cookies Come in Different Flavors

Cookies are usually small text files that are around 50 to 150 bytes and always less than 4kb. As a general rule, a web server can only accommodate 20 cookies per individual, and users only accommodate up to 300 cookies on their computers. In general, there are two types of cookies:

➤ Session cookies, which exist only as long as your Internet session. A session cookie may remember the information about your current shopping trip. Session cookies are downloaded by web servers to the hard disk drives of Internet users and are deleted when users close their browsers.

➤ Persistent cookies, which reside on the user's hard drive. These are used by web site owners to remember the preferences of users and by advertisers to track the online behavior of users in order to target ads that match their interests. A persistent cookie recognizes users when they return the next day for a second shopping trip. Persistent cookies can remain for months or even years.

➤ How Cookies are Good for Web-Based Enterprises

Persistent cookies allow users to find content that interests them (based on previous web site visits), help users personalize web pages, and can automatically fill in the content for new forms or questionnaires. If persistent cookies are used correctly, each shopping trip allows the web server to gather more information about the shopping preferences of the user. Thus, cookies save users time because they remember information that users enter. However, this information is not associated with an individual, but tracks as the online buying behavior of an un-specified "someone." If the user never submits any personal information, the cookie only knows that someone with the same cookie has re-turned to the web site.

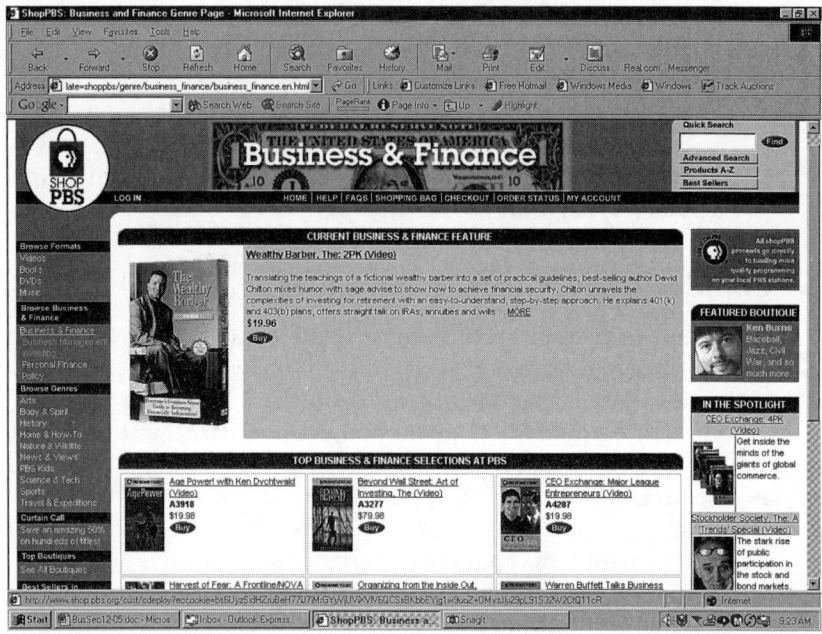

Figure 12.1 E-commerce web sites like the online PBS store use cookies

Web-based businesses almost always use cookies. As an example of this cookie use, Figure 12.1 shows the Public Broadcasting Service (PBS) Store (pbs.org) for Business and Finance. PBS uses cookies to remember what items users have selected for their shopping carts. Customers search for the products they want, then add the items to their shopping carts by clicking on a web page. The information is recorded on a cookie that is active for the session. When customers check out, they view the contents of their shopping carts. That is, the web server reads the information from the cookie and displays it for the customer. The customer completes the order by adding a credit card number and billing and shipping addresses.

Many web-based businesses, such as amazon.com, let customers reuse the information they have provided by writing it on another cookie, which is stored on the web-based enterprises' secured web servers. This approach is often called *one-click shopping*. To use one-click shopping, the customer enters a customer identification number (often an e-mail address) and a password. Then the credit card information and billing and shipping addresses already provided by the customer can be accessed to quickly complete a transaction.

■ LOOKING AT THE DARK SIDE OF COOKIES

When Internet users visit your web site, their visit is tracked in a log file that is hosted by your internet service provider (ISP) or resides on the web server. These server logs provide information about the date and time of each user's visit, the web pages visited, and the path the visitor navigated through the web site. The type of Internet browsers used, the route through which the visitors came (such as search engine referrals or other web sites), the cities or countries in which visitors are located, and even the keywords used at the search engines will be recorded in the server logs. However, all these data do not indicate exactly who a user is.

The cookie file may be identified as "UserID" and have a number such as 423. The web server can now distinguish the activities of this user from those of others. Suppose the user decides to register for a sweepstakes or for additional online resources at the web site. The user may provide just his or her e-mail address, but this can be leveraged to increase the web-based organization's level of user knowledge. In this example, combining the user's e-mail address and syndicated data available from a number of providers could build a personal profile that includes the Internet user's real name and address, phone number, and other demographic data.

If your web-based enterprise uses cookies, you can also see if the user is visiting your web site for the first time or if the user is a frequent visitor. You can determine whether the user has ever purchased any-thing (or the number of past purchases), as well as where the customer went when he or she left your web site. This type of activity can only be measured with cookies. For web-based businesses, this type of in-formation is vital in providing customers with the products and services that meet their needs and desires.

Tracking cookies stalk Internet users because these cookies are not exclusive to the original web site the user visits. For example, ads containing cookies can be downloaded from separate (called *third-party*) web servers at the time the web page is requested. If the user right-clicks on the ad, then clicks on *Properties* in his or her browser, he or she can see that the ad was downloaded from a third-party web server such as those owned by media network companies like DoubleClick, Focalink, Globaltrack, and ADSmart. However, many users are unaware of extremely small or transparent images in ads hosted by third-party web servers. Consequently, they are not warned that they are accepting cookies by default.

Media Network companies, such as DoubleClick, use tracking cookies on all their client web sites. The tracking cookies report back to headquarters each time someone visits a client's web site. This information is added to the customer's profile when he or she visits another DoubleClick client's web site. Over time, the customer profile, the aggregated contents of which are unknown to the user, indicates the user's Internet behavior. This information is then used for advertising and marketing. Many customers consider this aggregation of information an invasion of privacy.

Users can decide if they want to accept or reject cookies. Crumbling all cookies is one way for customers to keep their privacy, but it is not very practical. Users can always set their Internet browser to "Always confirm before setting a cookie." Unfortunately, many web pages include two or three cookies. If someone uses the Internet for several hours per day, it is almost impossible (and highly annoying) to confirm the use of each cookie. Therefore frequent Internet users can limit their cookies by opting out at media network web sites such as DoubleClick (doubleclick.com) using cookie management software applications, such as Cookie Cruncher, or manually deleting specific cookies files from their hard disks.

■ SOME COOKIES LEAVE CONSUMERS WITH A BAD TASTE

According to DoubleClick, some web sites use clear Graphic Interchange Format (GIF) images or very small pixel tags (sometimes called *web beacons*). Each item is a line of code that web businesses place on their web sites to help marketers analyze customer behaviors. These tracking cookies are sometimes called *web bugs*. This is how web bugs work: A user is at web site A and clicks on an ad. The user is then transported to the advertiser's web page B. The advertiser's web page will contain the web bug, which can collect certain anonymous information about the user's visit. When the user revisits web page A, due to the cookie the advertisement presented will be a brand new banner ad with an updated cookie.

For many companies, any association with web bugs has the potential to undermine customer trust. Additionally, small web-based businesses that link to third parties, such as large community sites, may not be aware that web bugs are embedded in the links, allowing large media networks to collect information about their customers.

In June 2001, the Privacy Foundation (privacyfoundation.org) released a free downloadable program called Bugnosis (bugnosis.org). The Bugnosis program lets consumers know if a web page or e-mail message contains a tracking cookie. At this time, the Bugnosis program only works with the Internet Explorer browser, but developers are working on an e-mail version for Microsoft Outlook and Outlook Express. When Bugnosis finds a tracking cookie on a web site, it launches a blinking bug on the page and makes a cute "uh-oh" sound. A box at the bottom of the browser screen pops up, listing the types of web bugs that may be embedded in the web page.

Web bugs are objects (images, frames, tracking cookies, etc.) that are embedded in a web site and cause part of the web page to be retrieved by a different web server than the one originally used for the web page. For example, if you use Bugnosis or a similar program, such as Cookie-Pal (kburra.com) or Cookie Cop (cookiecop.com), you will be notified that an image has a different Internet address from the URL listed at the top of the browser. For example, the image URL could be something like [http://m.doubleclick.net/viewed/378385_600off_Aug25.gif]. This could mean that the image comes from a different domain than the document and manipulates a cookie (that is, from a third-party web sever). Figure 12.2 shows how the Bugnosis software analyzed the PBS Business and Finance Store. As you can see at the bottom of the browser, according to the Bugnosis analysis, "no suspicious images were found."

Companies like Security Space (securityspace.com) provide monthly reports about the use of web bugs on the Internet. According to Security Space, the most common web bugs are banner ads. Security Space's Web Bug Site Count Report has sampled about 1.5 million pages, retrieved from over 200,000 web sites. Each month, Security Space reports the top 100 domains using web bugs and provides a free web bug traffic count report. According to this report, some of the top domains doing the bugging are doubleclick.net, marketsource.com, hitbox.com, AOL.com, goto.com, USAToday.com, and yahoo.com.

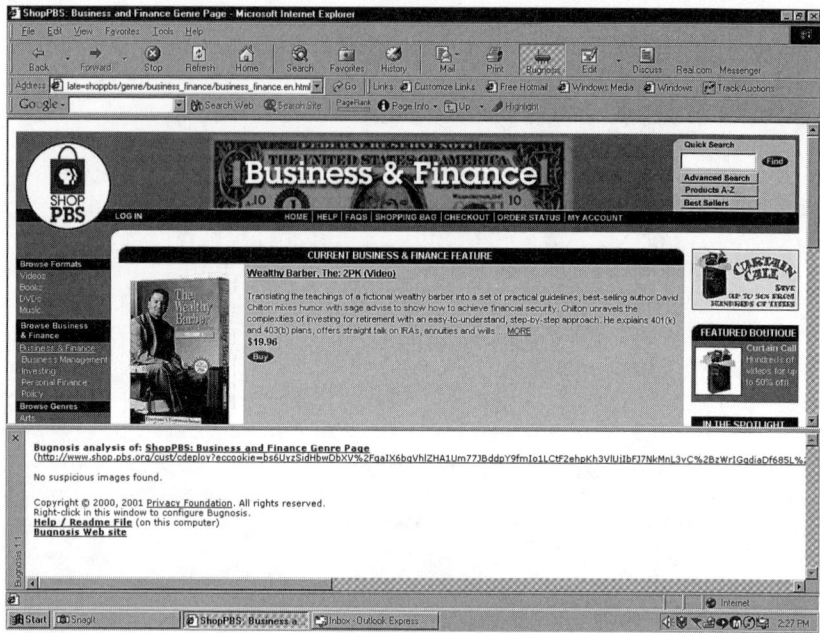

Figure 12.2   Free software from the Privacy Foundation can check for web bugs

■ ESTABLISHING A POLICY FOR BETTER-TASTING COOKIES

The first rule of cookies is to use them only when necessary. The IT department should be aware of the security dangers of cookies' being intercepted and the potential problems of using cookies for authentication. The primary rule of cookies is that they should contain as little private information as possible.

Potentially sensitive customer information can be tampered with, copied, or stolen via cookies. Therefore, when determining what information you want to store on a cookie, try not to store credit card information, social security number, mother's maiden name, or similarly personal information. If personal information must be included in the cookie, it should be encrypted. According to Lincoln Stein (1998), cookie information should, if possible, only include the following:

➤ The session ID or authorization information
➤ The time and date the cookie was issued
➤ The expiration date, which limits the potential damage a high-jack can do before it becomes invalid
➤ A message authenticity code (MAC), which ensures that none of the fields of the cookie have been corrupted or tampered with

➤ Creating an Effective Cookie Policy

Cookies can assist web-based enterprises in allowing their users to have continuity from visit to visit. Cookies allow users to quickly access the areas of the web sites that interest them the most and can present personalized information in a way that is meaningful to the user. Users can receive geographically specific data, such as interest rates for their local area, or information about services that are within reach. However, the first rule of using cookies is to ask first and explain the benefits of cookies. According to Scott Martin (2001) of the Personalization Consortium (personalization.org), a successful cookie policy includes a statement detailing the following:

1. What type of customer data are collected
2. How client information is collected
3. How long records are held
4. If and how data are shared
5. How personal customer information is used

The cookie policy statement lets users know where they can find your cookies on their hard drive. Martin (2001) goes on to state that effective cookie policies include six principles: relevance, security, choice, sensitive information, access and accuracy, and communication. A more detailed exploration of these principles follows below.

Relevance. Provide customers with clear and conspicuous notice of the firm's information collection practices. Let customers know that your organization will only collect the amount of individual and household information necessary to perform a specified set of tasks. List the situations that require the user to provide some personal information (such as registering to enter secured areas of the web site, making online purchases, and making inquiries that require an e-mail response).

Security. Explain how web server logs and cookies are used. Let users know your policy for retaining personal information. Include a statement about the type of cookies the web site uses (session or persistent), and what types of information are collected on the server logs. For example, if personal information is retained, is it in a statistical (anonymized) form? What about e-mail addresses and mailing information?

Clearly specify how your organization controls personal information. What security methods and technologies are in place to safeguard customer information? Clarify what internal measures your organization takes to prevent others from spying on their sensitive information (such as limiting access to employees or contractors who need access to personally identifiable information to do their jobs, or not keeping personal information in plain text cookies). Explain how your organization encrypts all sensitive information to prevent interception and decoding by interlopers. Assure customers that your organization has high standards for securing personal information from unauthorized access, misuse, tampering, loss, or destruction.

Choice. In advance, ask customers if they want a cookie before sending one to their hard disk drives. Next, notify customers about how the enterprise collects, holds, uses, or shares individual or household information, and seek the consent of users through notices and opportunities to "opt out."

Single out third-party web servers to clearly distinguish your internal web site and external links to third-party web servers (which may provide online resources, reports, new articles, and so on). Check the privacy policy of your linked web sites. What are their privacy policies? Do they conflict with your stated guidelines? For example, are there any third-party advertisements on linked web pages?

Sensitive Information. Make a statement that your organization does not share, trade, sell, or otherwise disclose personal information. It is important to note that information is used for technical support, affiliate programs, deliveries, credit verifications, and follow-up on job applications or resumes. State that disclosure occurs only with the customer's consent. Specify what would cause an exception to this policy. For example, your organization may disclose customer data if the information is required for credit verification; through subpoena; by federal, state, or local law; or for similar lawful purposes.

Access and Accuracy. Let users know how to get a copy of their personal profile, if one exists, so that corrections and updates can be made to previously submitted personal information (subject to legal, technological, and security constraints). You may want to contact users one year after they first visit your web site. Offer users an anniversary gift of a discount or some other incentive to encourage them to delete, update, or edit their personal profiles. Make it clear that users will have to offer proof of identity to avoid fraud or mischief.

Communication. Explain how changes in the organization's cookie policy will be communicated. Let users know how you plan to contact them about any changes. For example, you may want to notify users of significant changes by posting notices at the web site not less than two weeks before a planned change. Additionally, discuss what will happen to each customer's personal information if your firm is acquired by another company or merges with another enterprise. Do not forget to include information about how to contact the organization about the cookie policy. Let users and customers know that you welcome their inquiries and comments about their privacy and personal information.

■ COOKIE PIRACY AND PROTECTING CUSTOMER INFORMATION

Basically, cookies cannot harm your customers' computers. This does not mean that cookies do not pose any security problems. The problem is not what cookies do to machines, but rather what information cookies can store and pass on to others. Cookie piracy can take many forms, including the theft of confidential customer information from the databases of web-based organizations by insiders. Cookies can be pirated for unlimited access to high-priced subscription web sites, seized by hijackers to take over an Internet session, or intercepted by eavesdroppers seeking confidential information. The following are descriptions of a few cookie piracy security breaches your web-based enterprise may experience. (For more about intercepting and hijacking Internet sessions, see Chapter 5.)

➤ Getting a Free Ride: Web Server-to-Client Piracy

Cookie piracy can lead to authentication and access control problems. One of the disadvantages of using unsecured session ID cookies for access control is that they are vulnerable to interlopers. Suppose a web-based business provides high-priced industry reports. Cookies can be sniffed in transit during the subscriber's Internet session: That is, eavesdroppers could use packet sniffers to intercept cookies from the browsers of legitimate customers when they interact with the web site server. The intercepted passwords could be used (or sold on the black market) as free admission tickets to industry reports.

➤ Hijacking Cookies to Gain Access to Your Secured Internet Session

There is a vulnerability (and a security patch that eliminates this vulnerability) in web servers that use Microsoft's Internet Information Server (IIS) Software 4.0 and 5.0. This vulnerability allows an interloper to hijack another user's secured Internet session if the intruder has control of the user's communications with the web site. The IIS application supports session cookies to track the user's current session. However, the software does not support Active Server Pages (ASP). Consequently, both secured and nonsecured pages on the web site use the same session ID cookie.

Consider the following scenario as an example. An eavesdropper was monitoring the user's web sessions by using a packet sniffer and accessing your network. The user goes to a secured socket layer (SSL) secured page. The intruder can see the data moving between the web server and the browser but cannot read the encrypted text. If the user goes to a nonsecured web page at the same web site, the same session cookie will be exchanged, but this time in *plain text*. Using this session ID cookie information, the eavesdropper can go back to the secured page. At this point, the interloper has hijacked the secured session and can take any action on the secured page that the legitimate user could take.

➤ Pirating Someone Else's Cookies

Cookies appear to be more secure than they really are. For example, many individuals share their computers with others at the workplace, in cyber-cafes, or when traveling. Additionally, computers generally do not follow people. If someone moves to another office or location, all of the cookies are left on the computer in his or her old office. This lets others snoop around the cookie file or use preset cookies that were left behind on the hard drive. Imagine that a user subscribes to the Wall Street Journal Interactive Edition. If the subscriber requests that his or her user ID and password be saved on the computer, then others with access to this computer can use the preset cookie containing this information to access the online publication.

➤ Stealing the Cookies on Your Wireless Device

Cookies make it easy to access Internet sites via wireless devices because users do not have to enter the same information again and again. Unfortunately, there is a black market for mobile cookie information. For example, second-party audit companies may be hired to verify e-commerce purchases. Additionally, if the device is stolen while the user is in the middle of a transaction, such as an online trade, then all of the user's information is decrypted. This allows the thief to have access to all secured information on the web site.

Usually, wireless users cannot directly access their cookies. The cookies are hosted on the operator's network and can move with the users as they upgrade to newer or faster wireless devices. A security problem is created when someone loses his or her PDA. However, there are companies like Mobileum (mobileum.com) that offer cookie control capabilities, which allow individuals to use their cellular telephones to turn off the cookies on the lost PDA.

■ PROTECTING CUSTOMER INFORMATION CHECKLIST

Securing customer information must be a high priority for all web-based businesses. The next priority is developing an effective customer privacy policy, for the simple reason that: you can have security without a privacy policy, but you cannot have a privacy policy without some form of security. The following checklist can assist you in increasing customer confidence in your firm's abilities to safeguard sensitive customer information, and provides insights into how to set high standards for securing customer information from unauthorized access.

- ✓ Determine if your organization will use cookies and, if so, what kind: Will your organization use session ID cookies, persistent cookies, or a combination of both?
- ✓ Restrict the use of cookies, as they can lead to security problems. Cookie pirates can intercept customer cookies to hijack Internet sessions, gaining free admission to the enterprise's web site.
- ✓ Determine how you can manage with the least amount of cus-

tomer information as possible. The best way to keep customer information confidential is to not collect it.

✓ Find out if you use all the log information you collect. For example, are you collecting referral information but never analyzing the data?

✓ Limit access to customer records as necessary. (Do all employees and contractors need access to customer information?)

✓ Establish an effective cookie policy that lets customers know when and why you use cookies. Publish this cookie privacy policy. Notify customers in advance of any changes.

✓ Do you hire media networks that aggregate information about Internet user behaviors? If so, inform your customers about your data collection policies and give them the opportunity to opt out.

✓ Many online enterprises have advertisements, links, and other ties to third-party web servers. Make certain that the privacy policies on these other web sites are consistent with your organization's privacy policy. Notify customers that third-party web servers owned by large media networks may track online behavior.

■ REFERENCES

Castagna, Rich. 2001. Make cookies more appetizing. *Computer Shopper,* 12 February. Available at [http://cma.zdnet.com]. 7 December 2001.

Cookie monsters. 2000. *Developer,* 11 August. Available at [http://cma.zdnet.com]. 7 December 2001.

Glass, Brett. 2001. Cookies: The good, the bad, and the sneaky. *PC Magazine,* 19 May. Available at [http://www.zdnet.com]. 7 December 2001.

Larson, Eric, and Brian Stephens. 2000. *Administrating web servers, security, and maintenance.* Upper Saddle River, Ill.: Prentice Hall.

Martin, Scott. 2001. Personalization consortium privacy principles abbreviated. Personal communication, 11 August.

Olsen, Stephanie. 2001. Web bug swarm grows 500 percent. *CNET News.com,* 14 August. Available at [http://cma.zdnet.com]. 7 December 2001.

Rockhold, John. 2001. How the cookies crumble. *Wireless Review,* 15 June. Available at [http://cma.zdnet.com]. 7 December 2001.

Session ID Cookie Marking Vulnerability (Patch Available). 2001. *Securi-Team.com,* 24 October. Available at [http://www.securiteam.com/windowsntfocus/6J00M1500I.html]. 7 December 2001.

Stein, Lincoln D. 1998. *Web security: A step-by-step reference guide.* Boston: Addison-Wesley.

Sweiger, Mark. 2001. Cookies: The perfect user ID snack. *Enterprise Systems Journal,* 1 March. Available at [http://cma.zdnet.com]. 7 December 2001.

Chapter

13

Antivirus Technology and Your Online Business

In this chapter:

- ➤ Catching a Computer Virus
- ➤ Understanding Different Classes of Viruses
- ➤ Hoaxes and Urban Legends about Computer Viruses
- ➤ Developing a User Antivirus Policy
- ➤ Anti-Virus Technologies and Your Web-Based Business
- ➤ Establishing Post-Virus Attack Procedures
- ➤ Law Enforcement's Role in Your Cyber-Crime Investigation
- ➤ Hiring Consultants to Investigate a Virus Attack
- ➤ Antivirus Technology and Your Online Business Checklist

Computer viruses attach themselves to other programs and repli-cate themselves. As a general rule, they do not infect the same program or disk twice and target specific program types (.exe, .com, .sys, and so on). Some viruses are quick to act, while others are slow, in which case users do not see obvious signs of the infection. This chapter explores the three primary classifications of viruses. You'll discover how pure viruses need executable programs and humans to infect others. You'll find out how worms work without human help in order to spread more rapidly than viruses. You'll see how Trojan horse programs can mas-querade as benign programs but carry deadly infections. This chapter discusses the common symptoms of viruses. You'll discover how to determine if a virus warning is genuine and how to develop an effective user antivirus policy for your web-based enterprise. This chapter provides an overview of the latest in antivirus technology and offers suggestions for establishing security procedures to assist you if your firm suffers a virus attack. This chapter concludes with a discussion about the advantages and disadvantages of reporting a virus attack to a law enforcement agency.

■ CATCHING A COMPUTER VIRUS

According to Donn B. Parker (1998), author of *Fighting Computer Crime,* distributing a computer virus and installing a Trojan horse may be considered trespassing, destruction, fraud, violation of privacy, and harassment, or other misuse of electronic information. Today there are thousands of different types of viruses, and more sophisticated and deadly viruses are created each day. Some viruses are spread because victims are unaware that they are spreading the infection by downloading documents from the Internet or opening documents on diskettes or in e-mail attachments. Other employees may visit shady web sites or play infected games on their home computers, then connect to the enterprise's network and spread the virus to the web-based business. Consequently, web-based businesses need clear user guidelines and policies for employee Internet and e-mail usage.

Viruses can be destructive to hardware, software, and productivity. Every virus causes some degradation of system resources and wasted time for computer users. Consequently, no computer virus can be considered a good or benign virus. According to the *2001 CSI/FBI Computer Crime and Security Survey* (2001), interviewees reported $29.2 million in losses due to viruses in the year 2000. In 2001 this number jumped 65 percent to an estimated $45.3 million in losses due to viruses. However, the actual amount of losses may be greater than the figures reported, because 37 percent of respondents could not quantify their losses. The following is a list of the malicious activities that viruses, worms, and Trojan horses can inflict on a web-based business:

➤ Network-aware infections infect all the detected file servers and files within those servers. A network-aware virus can start replicating at maximum speed and lock the network.

➤ Mass mailings send e-mail messages to users with malicious code embedded within the messages.

➤ File destruction corrupts or removes various files from the system.

➤ Data export locates personal information such as passwords, social security numbers, or credit card numbers and sends the information via e-mail or to a predetermined Internet location.

➤ System interception allows the monitoring, altering, or disabling of system components. It may be used to launch a malicious program.

➤ Hardware damage may attempt to erase the CMOS memory (settings for date, time, and system setup parameters) or flash the BIOS software (the code required to control the keyboard, display screen, disk drives, serial communications, etc.).

➤ Visual payload displays messages or graphics (such as by adding the phrase "is a jerk" to the name of the registered user).

➤ Backdoor/remote control listens for commands coming from other unauthorized computers and executes them.

➤ Social engineering deceives users into opening files that contain malicious code.

■ UNDERSTANDING DIFFERENT CLASSES OF VIRUSES

There are numerous ways in which individuals can attack a web-based business. Some attacks are designed to gain access to your network, while others target critical operations in an effort to prevent legitimate customers from using your services. Still other attackers just want to annoy or embarrass the web-based enterprise or to destroy its data. Viruses exist in software and can be designed to be anything from a petty annoyance to a catastrophe. In order for viruses to be effective, they must go undetected long enough to replicate and spread to new hosts. Many computer users are surprised by the length of time a virus takes after the original infection before it manifests itself. This delay makes tracking the cyber-criminals who wrote or infected the host computer difficult. Attack organizations rely on the time between infection and manifestation to cover their tracks. A virus may be designed to deliver its payload on a certain date (for example, March 6 for the Michelangelo virus), at a certain time of day or night, or whenever the user selects a particular sequence of keystrokes.

➤ The Classic or Pure Virus

Viruses are designed to spread themselves from one file to another on a single computer. The virus can quickly infect the entire target computer's application files or slowly infect documents. A pure virus relies on humans to spread the infection to other computers. Typically, the size of a virus is 1,000 to 3,000 bytes. As technology matures and grows smarter, so do virus programs. As virus programs become more complex, web-based enterprises are finding it harder to keep current with antiviral issues and technologies. According to Chris Lee, a writer for *ZDNET* (2001), the Love Letter virus alone cost businesses worldwide an estimated $7 billion.

Viruses are composed of a malicious code that has the ability to insert itself into a program, file, or diskette, or into a portion of the hard disk from which it can replicate itself into an executable program. Executable programs may include programs that end with .com, .exe, .sys, or .dll. Viruses are appropriately named because they propagate themselves just as biological viruses do. Computer viruses are just like a human infection, such as a common cold, which can start with a sniffle and end with a serious case of pneumonia. A computer virus has two tasks:

1. To complete its mission, by doing whatever it was designed to do (reformat your hard drive, corrupt Microsoft Word files, etc.). This includes the automated capacity to replicate or propagate itself.
2. To achieve a method of transfer, by attaching itself to other programs and infecting them with the same virus. Viruses can be transported via diskettes, e-mail attachments, file sharing on a network, and the Internet.

Figure 13.1 shows how a file infector virus is transferred. When the user runs an infected program, the computer copies the virus and stores it in the RAM section of the machine until it can be executed. The malicious code copies itself in a part of the RAM that is separate from the program so that it can continue its destructive work after the user starts to run other software programs. Once the infection is in place, the virus passes control back to the infected program. When the

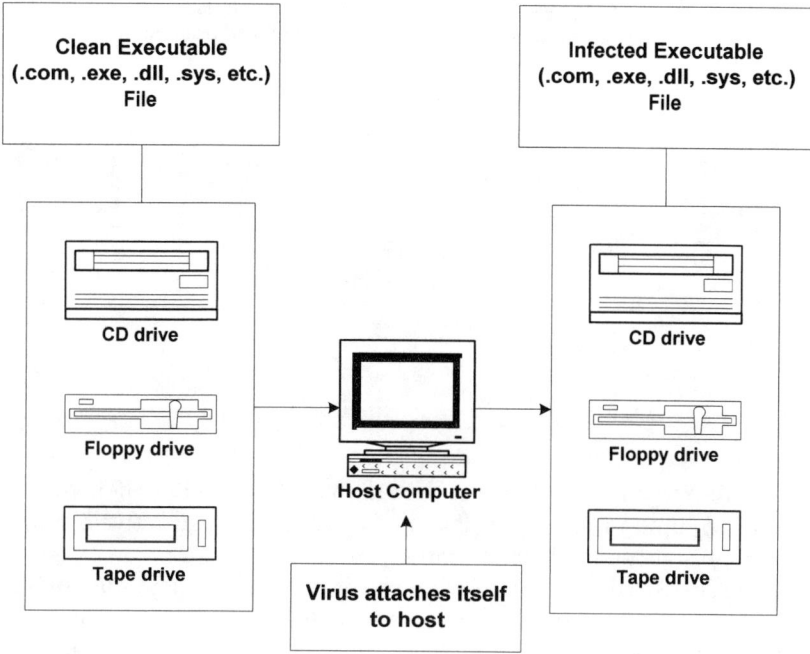

Figure 13.1 How a pure virus is transported

user runs a different program, the dormant virus begins to run again. The virus inserts a copy of itself into the previously uninfected software so that the cycle, with the help of human users, can repeat itself.

A Macrovirus: The Most Popular Virus in the World

A macrovirus is a type of virus that is embedded in a document that used the macro programming language. If you send or receive spreadsheets or documents, it is likely that you have already received or will be infected with a macrovirus. Macroviruses were first discovered in 1995, and today they are considered the most prevalent type of virus. Infected files, such as Microsoft Word documents and Excel spreadsheets are sent as e-mail attachments via the Internet. When the attachment is opened, the macrovirus infects the new user's machine. Many macroviruses are not destructive and only include irritating visual payloads that are designed to humiliate or embarrass the user by

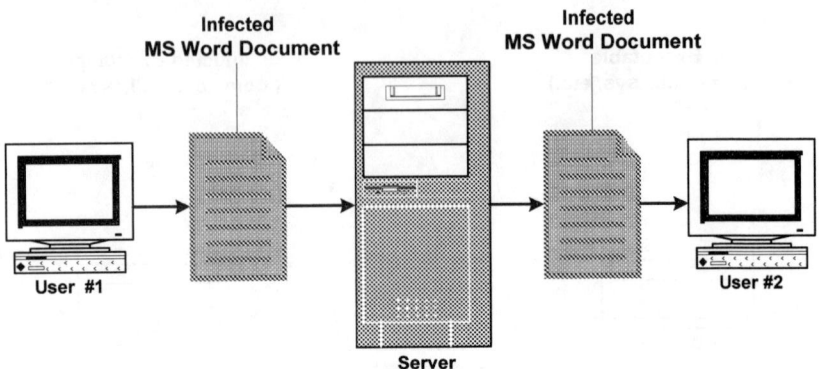

Figure 13.2   How a macrovirus is transported

displaying messages such as "South Park: Why Animals Eat Their Young." However, some macroviruses can be harmful and destructive because they propagate at an alarming rate.

Figure 13.2 shows how macroviruses can spread. The macrovirus is embedded in a document or spreadsheet and sent from one computer to another when documents and files are shared. Most macroviruses are designed to attack when the user first opens the file. It makes no difference how the file is opened: Once the file is opened, the virus is executed and does its damage. Sometimes the damage is not immediately apparent. In such cases, by the time the user realizes he or she has been attacked, the damage has spread to other documents on the user's computer or to other computers.

Infected E-Mail Attachments

As a general rule, the basic text of an e-mail message will not contain a virus. That's because the text of an e-mail message does not have any executable software. It is a *read only* document, so it is safe for recipients. E-mail attachments, however, may be executable programs that can include viruses. These viruses can transport the user to a pornographic web site, send mass mailings to individuals listed in the user's address book, or perform other malicious activities.

There are many ways e-mail attachments can be exploited by attackers. Often virus writers use social engineering to entice victims into opening e-mail attachments that include the virus. For example, the recipient may receive a message that appears to be from someone

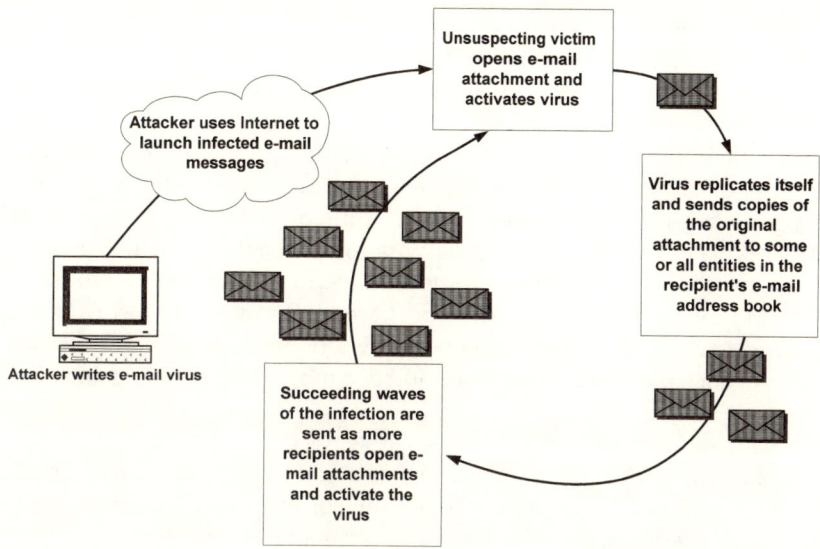

Figure 13.3 How an e-mail virus is transported

in the company and contains the following message: "Hi! Please check the attached invoice." The unsuspecting recipient opens the attachment, and the virus is immediately executed.

Figure 13.3 shows the anatomy of an e-mail attachment virus attack. The virus attacker writes an infected macrovirus attachment and launches it via the Internet. The unsuspecting user opens the attachment, and the virus immediately replicates itself and sends out copies to a certain number of entities in the address book or to everyone in the address book. Next, the recipients of the tainted e-mail messages open the attachments, and the process starts all over again. Each new user is immediately infected (unless antivirus software inoculates the user's computer). For more about antivirus solutions, see the section on Antivirus Technologies and Your Web-based Business in this chapter.

➤ Worms: Self-Directed Viruses

A worm is designed to copy itself as it moves from one computer to another, often over a network (or via e-mail). The worm spreads itself to many computers on the network without the help of humans. Therefore, computer worms can spread more quickly than pure viruses. Worms often slowly consume all the resources on your PC. For example, one type of worm gets into the computer's memory and starts filling it with gibberish data. With less memory, the computer processes more slowly than usual. Other worms may consume bandwidth by talking with one another. This can slow customer traffic. Like viruses, worms have two tasks. First, the worm attaches itself to existing programs and does what it was designed to do. The second task is to propagate itself. The method by which a worm propagates is different from that of a pure virus. Worms have self-contained programs for propagation, which can exploit loopholes in Internet protocols. Once released, they essentially act on their own. Thus, when Robert Morris Jr. released a worm as an experiment in 1988, it eventually brought down approximately 10 percent of the Internet in a short period of time after compromising each computer's security.

Network worms use network gateways to spread from system to system. Once inside a system, the worm can implant a virus or Trojan horse program with which to attack the software and hardware of the web-based enterprise. The network connections that worms use include the following:

➤ Network mail facilities (the worm mails a copy of itself to other systems)
➤ A remote execution capability (the worm can log on to remote systems as a user and execute a copy of itself on another system)
➤ Remote log-in capability (the worm can log into a remote system as a user and execute a copy of itself from one system to another)

➤ Trojan Horses: Older than Viruses

Trojan horses are often considered to be the most basic of the virus mischief-makers. Many professionals rank Trojan horses somewhere between a virus and a hack attack. A hack attack usually targets one individual, network, or enterprise. A virus attack is somewhat less focused. That is, once the virus is released, the attacker has little or no control over how quickly the attack is spread and who gets infected. The threat of a Trojan horse falls somewhere between these two types of attacks. However, if a Trojan horse is specifically designed for your web-based business, it could be devastating.

Trojan horses are not viruses but programs that can carry viruses or worms. Trojan horse programs (or routines) are concealed in software and installed on computers without the knowledge of the user. A Trojan horse looks like a program that appears to perform a useful service. For example, the Trojan horse program could be concealed in a downloadable calculator or game program. The calculator program may look like it is completing its one primary function when it is actually (and secretly) performing another. The malicious program could be attempting to reformat your hard disk drive or send your personal passwords to the hacker.

Internet users can receive Trojan horses from a wide variety of sources. Examples include Usenet News Groups, AOL password-stealing Trojans, and Word Macro Trojans. In the 1990s, attackers created a Trojan horse program that posed as a new version of PKZIP, a file compression application program. According to PKZIP officials, the bogus program will attempt to erase all directories in the user's hard drive if run. PKWARE, the makers of PKZIP, asked for assistance in locating the origins of the rogue program and noted that users that downloaded the program from legitimate web sites would receive an uninfected copy of the PKZIP program.

➤ Using a Back Door to Install a Trojan Horse

Sometimes programmers use so-called back doors for debugging and monitoring software programs. Back doors are problematic if unscrupulous programmers gain unauthorized access to them or if the programmer forgets to remove them when the program is released as a commercial product. When this happens, attackers do not have to reinvent the wheel and can easily infect a legitimate program with a Trojan horse.

One back door program for Microsoft Windows programs is called "Back Orifice." Sarah Gordon and David M. Chess of the IBM T.J. Watson Research Center (1998) point out that the program allows the attack organization to communicate with the user's system over the Internet to issue commands, install or alter files, delete data, and monitor the data of the user. In other words, the attackers can take complete control of the user's system without the latter's knowledge. Luckily, many firewalls and Trojan detecting programs can discover and block this threat.

Some Trojan horse programs include a root kit. A root kit is designed to compromise the user's ID and password combinations, e-mail, and credit card and personal information. Other Trojan horse programs may include sniffer programs, which are used to obtain user IDs and passwords for users that access remotely or access a network. Gordon and Chess (1998) conducted an informal survey with a sample size that was statistically too small to provide hard facts. However, the trends identified by the survey indicate that Internet users who downloaded documents, programs, and other materials and used their computers for both recreation and work were more likely to receive a Trojan horse than users who only used their computers for work. Additionally, for those companies whose computers were used only for work but who received viral infections or Trojan horses, the existence of a security policy was critical. These victims were able to log the event that posed possible security concerns. A survey respondent company that did not have a security policy and received a Trojan horse subsequently disconnected all the company's computers from the Internet after spending many man-hours and dollars in a futile effort to correct the problem.

➤ Symptoms of Virus Attacks

With the proliferation of viruses, it is difficult for antiviral technology to keep current. Therefore, it is the responsibility of the savvy manager to make certain that employees are aware of the symptoms of a viral infection. Table 13.1 provides a quick overview of the symptoms of the most common viruses. Industry experts suggest that about five percent of all viruses actually damage hardware and system contents. Although your firm may have a one in twenty chance of being seriously affected, the likelihood of being a victim is increasing. According to the ICSA, a research and security product certification firm, in 1996 the average infection rate among PC computers was 10 in 1,000, and in 1999 this rate escalated to 80 in 1,000.

Sometimes viruses are not the source of a computer's problems. Some legitimate computer problems may look like viruses but be due to nonviral problems, such as a fragmented hard disk, reboot corruption, or simply someone else's misuse. Occasionally incompatibilities, such as attempting to use a software application on the wrong operating system or the inability of one device to work with another, or software defects (bugs) cause viruslike problems. When analyzing the troubled computer, keep in mind that viruses replicate themselves. If the problem exists in only one computer out of the entire system, then it is probably not a virus.

■ HOAXES AND URBAN LEGENDS ABOUT COMPUTER VIRUSES

Just as viruses prey on user trust, virus hoaxes prey on user fear and ignorance. Viruses and virus hoaxes can waste valuable user time and re-

Table 13.1 Symptoms of Various Viruses

Malicious Activity	Symptoms
Network-aware infection	Infected files are discovered on file servers or systems. Virus indicates capacity to spread rapidly through the network.
Mass mailing	E-mail servers slow down or crash.
File destruction	General system instability. Programs may not launch. Files may not be available.
Data export	There may be no outward signs of this attack. Higher-than-usual Internet access charges may indicate the virus.
System interception	Additional e-mail messages may accompany normal traffic. Internet browser functionality may be limited or slower than usual.
Hardware damage	Power-on self-test may not begin, hard drives may not be properly identified.
Visual payload	Different messages and visual images may appear.
Backdoor/remote control	Excess network traffic, unusual activity on IP/UDP ports.
Social engineering	Users may receive an e-mail message for which either an enticing subject or a deceiving message encourages users to open the e-mail attachment, which launches the virus.

Source: Adapted from Symantec Security Reference Chart, copyright April 2001.

sources. Virus hoaxes are convincing and are often well written: Internet users will frequently send these mass e-mailings to others in an effort to be good netizens. This can create panic and waste time as others debunk the allegations of the bogus warnings. The following are a few of the features to examine as you determine whether the e-mail warning you received is a hoax.

➤ The Hook: A dire warning, such as "Danger" or "Virus Alert," which is geared to create an emotional response. The warning message may be in all capital letters with an accompanying statement like "This is not a hoax," when, of course, it is.

➤ The Threat: The e-mail message appears believable because it is sent from an ostensibly credible association and includes technical language. Note whether the e-mail message is geared for an emotional response. Check the web site of the so-called expert source to substantiate the warning.

➤ The Request: The first line of the warning suggests that the recipients send a copy of the warning to everyone they know.

If the virus warning message states that this information was never released before, be suspicious. Did a genuine computer security expert send the alert? Does the e-mail message suggest that you look for outside references? Does the message provide links to Web sites like Trend Micro's Virus Tech Center (antivirus.com/pc-cillin/vinfo), which lists the latest virus threats? Does the message provide links to web sites corroborating the information? Look for logical inconsistencies, violations of common sense, and obvious false claims. Check to see if the e-message has been debunked by web sites such as Hoaxbusters (hoaxbusters.com) or Vmyths (vmyths.com).

■ DEVELOPING A USER ANTIVIRUS POLICY

Developing an effective user antivirus policy can go a long way in ensuring that your organization remains virus free. There are tens of thousands of different types of viruses, but your organization does not need that many user antivirus policies. The following are a few user guidelines that can assist you in developing an effective user antivirus policy:

1. Document and share the standards your firm employs in its user antivirus checklist.
2. Provide user awareness materials and train users to consistently follow safety standards.
3. Train users to consistently follow safety standards. Schedule periodic antivirus scans and provide users with the latest updates of antivirus software. (Use different antivirus technologies for different parts of the company that require different levels of security.)

4. Keep users informed of the latest virus threats via voice mail, e-mail, or hard copy memorandums.
5. Tell users not to use programs on diskettes from noncommercial sources—that is, pirated, hacked, or other illegally copied programs.
6. Remind users not to open unknown e-mail attachments or to download and run programs from unfamiliar databases without first screening for a potential virus.
7. Tell users not to leave diskettes in floppy drives when they leave the office or when computers are turned off.
8. Require users to log in and log out of local and remote computers used by more than one person.
9. Require users to follow a predetermined schedule for virus checking in backup data.
10. Require users to make frequent backups of critical data and to maintain two or three copies.
11. Require users to check backup copies for viruses before restoring the system after a virus attack.

■ ANTIVIRUS TECHNOLOGIES AND YOUR WEB-BASED BUSINESS

Many industry professionals believe that antivirus software is a key component of the security market. The market leaders in antivirus software are Computer Associates, IBM/Tivoli, Network Associates, and Symantec. Some antivirus products are wrapped in security suites, while some are purchased as stand-alone products or are outsourced services. Different types of antivirus software can be designed for mainframe to desktop computers. According to Carolyn DiCenzo of the Gartner Group (2001), the antiviral technology market had revenues of about $968 million in the year 2000, of which 80 percent was for machines using the Microsoft Windows platform. The following are a few examples of antiviral solutions:

➤ Computer Associates International's InoculateIT (ca.com) provides a management console, virus scanning, documentation, and notification options. InoculateIT is a part of Computer Associate's eTrust Defense Solution Set and is one of 17 security software products within the eTrust family.

➤ Network Associates' Virus Scan (mcafee.com) works with many other McAfee security modules. The program can detect and repair virus-infected files. Additionally, it has the ability to send doubtful files into quarantine and sniffs out viruses before they are downloaded to the user's machine. The program includes a firewall and encryption to protect users against hack attacks.

➤ Symantec's Norton AntiVirus 2001 Pro (symantec.com) checks many possible entry points of virus infection. Many consider this product an all-in-one tool that can protect PC computers and personal digital assistants against file-borne viruses, Trojan horses, active content viruses, memory resident infections, and the like. The program is also known for its easy installation. Norton AntiVirus 2001 Pro runs automatically on start-up and offers many utilities that you might otherwise have to purchase separately. Advanced tools include an unerase program, Palm Pilot operating system protection, and Live Update to download protection for the latest viruses.

➤ Sophos (www.sophos.com) is an antivirus technological solution designed for businesses with networks that use a variety of operating system platforms. The Sophos antivirus solution monitors virus entry points such as disks, programs, documents, network drives, and CD-ROMs in addition to Internet downloads, e-mail messages, and archived files.

➤ TrendMicro's PC-cillin 2000 (trendmicro.com) has an excellent user interface, good reporting features, and a quarantine feature, and performs quick virus scans. However, the program only scans for viruses for Eudora and Outlook Express e-mail programs.

■ ESTABLISHING POSTVIRUS ATTACK PROCEDURES

If a virus, worm, or Trojan horse attacks your web-based business, corporate secrets and your customers' personal information may be copied, stolen, or tampered with by the attackers. Virus writers may launder their true identities and places of origin. For example, the attack may come from a slave machine that is under the control of a master machine. Law enforcement or IT professionals need to trace back the attack to the point of origin. In this situation, even incomplete or approximate information, such as the type or date of the attack, is helpful.

The scope of the virus attack will determine if the enterprise should use a full court press of web, broadcast, and radio media to launch the crisis communication plan (see Chapter 9). As you attempt to identify the scope and impact of the event, the following list of questions may be helpful.

1. Is this a multisite incident?
2. How many computers in your system are infected?
3. Is sensitive customer or corporate information involved?
4. What are the entry points of the virus infection? (server, network, local terminal, etc.)
5. Is the press already involved?
6. What is the potential damage (in reputation, downtime, and cost) of the virus infection?
7. What is the estimated time to close out the virus infection incident?
8. What resources could have prevented the virus infection?
9. What resources are required to handle the virus infection?
10. Is law enforcement already involved? (Are you required to inform law enforcement?)

➤ Investigating a Virus Attacker

In most organizations, system administrators are the first individuals to notice or receive automated alerts regarding computer, network, and system anomalies. If system administrators take action in the first few moments of a virus infection, they can often save mission-critical data and assist investigators in tracking cyber-criminals.

In a perfect world, at the first sign of trouble the system administrator would isolate the suspect computer. This might protect the information system and preserve vital evidence. In some situations, system administrators' haste to get the web site and system up and running prevents them from taking time to preserve evidence that can be used to prosecute attackers. Therefore, it is important for the organization to have a predetermined plan. The following are a few procedures you may want to follow as you formulate your virus security response plan:

1. Designate an employee to secure evidence. This employee should trap and trace the viral infection with the upstream provider in an effort to locate the source of the infection.
2. Identify the intrusion method, date, and time. Have the IT de-

partment gather as much information about the virus attackers as possible. List all the files that were infected by the virus.

3. As you determine the method and extent of the intrusion, focus on these specific questions: Did the virus attacker install a packet sniffer file? What files are connected to it? Did the intruders manage to install a root kit using a Trojan horse? Were any operating system programs replaced? What programs were written in-house? What is the history of the source code? Could source code possibly include a back door?
4. Make certain that old backup files are not infected.
5. Retain evidence and compare it to previous virus attacks.
6. Install or update antiviral software. Make every effort to prevent new attacks.

Once the infected files, machines, or networks have been isolated, no one should attempt to recover or view files. Industry professionals suggest that all handwritten notes, storage media, and documents should be collected and isolated. Computer disks, CD-ROMs, tape storage media, and additional hard drives found in the area should also be protected. These items may be important to the investigation and, if left unattended, could physically disappear or be destroyed with a few well-chosen keystrokes from a skilled attack organization that wants to avoid detection.

■ LAW ENFORCEMENT'S ROLE IN YOUR CYBER-CRIME INVESTIGATION

Overall, you will have to decide when to prosecute and when not to prosecute virus attackers. Calling in the authorities is a course of action with many benefits but also disadvantages. First among these is the possible loss of control over the investigation. Additionally, the resources and manpower available for the investigation of cyber-crime vary according to the type of cyber-crime and by geography. In many situations, the FBI does not have the resources to take on cases that do not have significant losses or that lie outside their jurisdiction. Moreover, the FBI will not take cases that are unlikely to be solved. Local, state, and county law enforcement may be able to help your investigation if your cyber-crime does not fit within the FBI guidelines. However, local law enforcement agencies often cannot solve cyber-crimes because they lack adequate manpower, training, and resources. Reporting a cyber-crime to law enforcement has other disadvantages:

➤ Media attention to the cyber-crime often causes public relations problems, such as a loss of customer confidence, and may allow competitors to exploit your enterprise's misfortune.
➤ The facts about cyber-crimes are often distorted, causing additional problems.
➤ Law enforcement may require your organization to keep the facts of the cyber-crime under wraps until the investigation is complete. This means that you may be prevented from releasing critical information that could affect the reputation of your firm and its future profitability.

Recently, the FBI completed the outfitting of its field offices with Regional Computer Crime Intrusion squads. The Department of Justice has established a special Computer Crime & Intellectual Property division to handle gaps in copyright and trademark laws. The multi-agency New York Electronic Crimes Task Force, which is coordinated by the U.S. Secret Service, also tackles cyber-crimes. Moreover, law enforcement is beginning to assign undercover agents to investigate ongoing computer crimes to seek out attackers in the act of perpetrating cyber-crimes and individuals who are responsible for ongoing criminal acts. This approach helps investigators bypass the typical problems of a cyber-crime investigation (anonymity of perpetrators, a lack of records, and so on). It also allows law enforcement to intercept and record actual hacking activities on a victim computer.

Enterprises such as regulated financial institutions, nuclear power plants, air traffic control centers, and health care facilities are required by law to report security breaches, data loss, or cyber-crimes. Thus, sometimes law enforcement should be called because it is the right thing to do. Keep in mind that it is unethical to hide threats to human life, and withholding this information may make the web-based enterprise liable for the results of the criminal activity that was not reported. The advantages of calling law enforcement include

➤ The availability of sophisticated technical capabilities (expensive equipment, sophisticated software, and access to large databases)
➤ Access to the FBI's criminal laboratory for forensic computer analysis

➤ Assistance in dealing with countries or individuals who speak languages other than English
➤ The ability to recover deleted or lost data (such as data that were overwritten due to the virus), the recovery of which could lead investigators to the attack organization

Savvy managers need to decide in advance what the organization's policy will be before an event occurs. In-house experts can visit local law enforcement facilities and determine the amount of support they can expect in case the web-based business experiences a cyber-crime. Moreover, the organization should uncover exactly what kinds of cyber-crimes the FBI investigates. This knowledge allows the enterprise to take an immediate stance in regard to protecting customers and ensures that managers will not lose time in a crisis by arguing about the merits of different courses of action.

■ HIRING CONSULTANTS TO INVESTIGATE A VIRUS ATTACK

It is unlikely that there are highly skilled cyber-crime investigators in your IT department. Most IT departments are geared toward keeping the system running and spotting potential problems. Your organization may have purchased antivirus software and other security technological solutions with which to start this process. However, an in-depth technical investigation may require a different set of skills than those of the individuals on staff. For example, collecting a large amount of data and assembling them into reports often exceeds the capabilities of a normal IT department. Other advantages of consultants include

➤ The ability to track cyber-criminals by sorting through mountains of diverse evidence (web site codes, server log files, paper documents, public records, personnel records, etc.)
➤ Skills in the use of visualization tools and sophisticated software programs with which to perceive the case as a whole
➤ The ability to provide quick status reports on the impact of the virus attack on the web-based business. This can assist management in avoiding delays for needed upgrades, security patches, new software, and additional personnel.

There are some disadvantages to hiring consultants to investigate a cyber-crime. Many supposedly reformed hackers and other computer consultants offer immediate results, but it is often difficult for managers to determine if they are getting what they pay for. Additionally, management must determine what role this consultant will play within the organization. For example, will consultants be allowed to interrogate all personnel?

■ ANTIVIRUS TECHNOLOGY AND YOUR ONLINE BUSINESS CHECKLIST

The economic impact of viruses and worm attacks on web-based businesses has dramatically increased over the last few years. Not only is the economic impact greater than before, but the frequency of attacks is also increasing. Antivirus technologies are helpful, but 10 to 20 new viruses are released each week. There are easily downloaded virus construction kits that can spawn a virus outbreak by virus writers without programming skills. Web-based businesses can protect themselves from many of these threats by using the following checklist.

- ✓ Select the right level of antivirus technology protection for the assets you are protecting. Use antiviral scanners on all data and applications before they reach your PCs, network, or servers.
- ✓ Recognize that protecting your web-based business against virus attacks requires persistence. This means implementing the latest security patches on computers and servers. Contact your antivirus technology vendor, and check for any security holes that may not be self-evident.
- ✓ Designate an individual in the IT department to be responsible for subscribing to antivirus mailing lists and checking web sites for new information. Subscribe to the mailing lists of antivirus vendors to discover the latest viruses.
- ✓ Install content-filtering technology, such as instruction detection software, where appropriate. Intrusion detection software can assist you in archiving and analyzing log data if you are subject to a virus attack.
- ✓ Train and educate users in enterprise safety standards. Encourage the prevention of problems instead of emphasizing the prospect of after-the-fact punishments.

✓ Encourage users to report potential viruses to a central database.
✓ Evaluate existing antivirus applications. Verify that you are using the right antivirus software for the type of computer.
✓ Develop a schedule individuals should follow for updating the antivirus software on their machines.
✓ Establish predetermined management and reporting procedures to warn employees of a virus infection before it spreads throughout the network.

■ REFERENCES

Computer security incident handling. 1997. Chap. 12 in *An introduction to computer security: The NIST handbook.* Washington, D.C.: National Institute of Standards and Technology.

Connolly, P. J. 2001. Beef up your defense against e-mail viruses. *InfoWorld Test Center,* 13 February. Available at [http://www.infoworld.com/articles/tc/xml/01/02/26/010226tctcap.xml]. 10 December 2001.

DiCenzo, Carolyn. 2000. Internet and e-commerce drive security software growth. *Gartner Group Research Brief,* 25 September. Available at [http://www.siventures.com]. 10 December 2001.

First responders manual. 2001. Computer Forensics Laboratory, U.S. Department of Energy, Washington, D.C. Available at [http://downloads.securityfocus.com/library/firstres.pdf]. 10 December 2001.

Gordon, Sarah, and David M. Chess. 1998. Where there's smoke, there's mirrors: The truth about Trojan horses on the Internet. Paper presented at the Virus Bulletin Conference, October, in Munich, Germany. Available at [http://www.research.ibm.com/antivirus/SciPapers/Chess/Threat/Threat.html]. 10 December 2001.

Haney, Kevin. 1995. Computer viruses: Background safe computing practices, and recommended anti-viral software. Advanced Laboratory Workstation System, 1 February. Available at [http://csb.dcrt.nih.gov/security/viruses/virinfo/viruses.txt]. 10 December 2001.

Hosmer, Chet, John Feldman, and Joe Giordano. 2001. Advancing Crime Scene Computer Forensic Techniques. A corporate publication of Wetstone Technologies, Inc., 28 June. Available at [http://www.wetstonetech.com/crime.htm].

Larson, Eric, and Brian Stephens. 2000. *Administrating web servers, security and maintenance.* Upper Saddle River: Prentice Hall.

Lee, Chris. 2001. Virus attacks pick up pace. *ZDNet (UK),* 19 March. Available at [http://techupdate.zdnet.com/techupdate/stories/main/0,14179,2698615,00.html]. 10 December 2001.

Lucas, Julie. 2001. Winning the malicious logic battle: Understanding the enemy. Global Network Technology Services white paper, 1 January. Available at [http://www.enterasys.com/security/information_assurance/battle.pdf]. 10 December 2001.

Moran, Douglas B. 2000. Trapping and tracking hackers: Collective Security for Survival in the Internet Age. Proceedings of the Third Information Survivability Workshop. Boston: Institutions of Electrical Engineers, 24–26 October.

Parker, Donn B. 1998. *Fighting computer crime.* New York: Wiley.

Power, Richard. 2001. *2001* CSI/FBI computer crime and security survey. *Computer Security Issues and Trends* 7(1).

Schwartau, Winn. 2000. *Cybershock.* New York: Thunder's Mouth Press.

Stephenson, Peter. 1999. *Investigating computer-related crime: A handbook for corporate investigators.* New York: CRC Press.

Chapter
14

Developing an Effective Security Policy

In this chapter:

➤ How a Good Security Policy Supports Organizational Goals and Objectives
➤ Developing an Effective Security Policy
➤ Defining Your Security Policy
➤ Selecting the Team to Create the Security Policy
➤ The Continuous Life Cycle of the Security Policy
➤ Distribution and Education of the Security Policy
➤ Developing a Security Policy Checklist

Any firm with an online presence should have a security policy. Traditional brick-and-mortar businesses would not consider operating without some type of security, such as security guards, an alarm system, video cameras, and the like. In contrast, many web-based businesses view security as an unnecessary expense. However, the cost of a security breach is often much greater than the financial expense of a security system in terms of downtime expense and loss of reputation and customer good will.

Large web-based businesses are more likely to suffer a hack attack, but small online enterprises are not exempt. Attack organizations are constantly seeking companies that are easy targets. The more visible and vulnerable an online organization is, the greater the reward it offers the attack organization. Consequently, business enterprises, not-for-profit organizations, and government agencies are all candidates for intruders. Each of these entities needs an effective security policy to protect it from the unexpected. Keep in mind that you do not want to start writing your security policy while you are under attack.

Focusing on the right issues can assist you in developing an effective policy. Security concerns for web-based enterprises include both inside and outside threats. Disgruntled or temporary employees may perpetrate insider attacks. Attacks by outsiders may be due to anything from thrill seeking to industrial espionage. In either case, a hack attack can result in (among other things) the loss of data, access to unauthorized services, or the introduction of viruses to the network. Trying to write a document that identifies all the risks that threaten your web-based business, while simultaneously showing an understanding of what employees and users expect from the system and company resources, may seem like an insurmountable task. Breaking this chore down into smaller bites is one way to achieve the desired results. Accordingly, Table 14.1 shows the eight key points of an effective security policy.

> ➤ Identify critical resources. Different types of enterprises have different security needs. The information security needs of a military organization will differ from those of a retail organization. For example, whereas a military organization will be concerned with the information security of outgoing traffic, a retail organization will be more concerned with the security of incoming traffic. The assets within each type of organization are also different. A retail organization may use two servers, the first for the company's brochureware, and the second for online catalog sales. The second server is mission-critical to the business and requires a higher level of security.

> ➤ Evaluate the likelihood of an attack. Attacks on mission-critical resources (such as servers, applications, proxies, etc.) must be identified and documented. This provides the web-based enterprise with a baseline. The results of this evaluation should include a listing of the assets that require protection and their value. Business-critical systems, applications, and communications devices are then ranked for vulnerability.

> ➤ Determine if the security policy is working. The main body of the security policy spells out exactly what users can and cannot do with the enterprise's computers and information assets.

Table 14.1 Key Points in Developing an Effective Security Policy

Key Point	Description
Identify the assets that need protection	Answer as specifically as possible, and prioritize your assets. This will help you tailor your policy to your business needs.
Assess the risk	Consider the types and levels of protection your enterprise requires. What assets are likely to be attacked? Who are likely attackers, "script kiddies" or sophisticated industrial spies?
Define the acceptable use of assets	The likelihood of attack can help you determine acceptable use of assets. Is your web site frequently attacked?
Determine the effectiveness of the security policy	Ensure that the right metrics are in place to determine the success of the security policy.
Educate and communicate to users	Ask yourself how your organization makes users aware of security. What types of training or education do you offer?
Deal with policy violations	Determine the possible result of an attack by intruders. Will an attack put your enterprise "out of business"?
Safeguard and proceed	Decide how much security you can afford. What security measures are "must-haves" for your organization?
Track and prosecute	Find out whether you are required to report cyber-crimes. How will you preserve evidence and track cyber-criminals?
Foil the next attacker	Determine how you can contain lessons learned and fend of another attack.

Knowing the likelihood and frequency of attacks can help you tailor a policy to protect the organization and focus on where the toughest security is needed. Measuring the number of attempted attacks on the organization can assist you in quantifying the success of the security policy.
➤ Communicate with users. Education and training of IT personnel, management, and users is an ongoing process. Use of the firm's Intranet for communicating within the organization

can assist you in distributing the new security policy and can provide users with the latest updates and modifications to the security policy.

➤ Deal with violations. The punishments for security policy infractions need to be clear. Provide users with contact information so that reports of suspicious activities can be made anonymously.

➤ Safeguard and proceed. Provide users with step-by-step instructions on what to do if a virus, Trojan horse, or other type of attack is suspected.

➤ Track and prosecute. Designate an employee to track an intruder upstream to the ISP or host. Make certain IT personnel have predetermined procedures for preserving evidence. Know in advance if you are required to report the attack. Have a predetermined plan of action as to whether you will seek help from law enforcement agencies.

➤ Foil the next attacker. Collect as much data about the attack as possible. Archive the information and compare it to trends within the company and industry. Determine how you can stop a similar attack before it happens.

■ HOW A GOOD SECURITY POLICY SUPPORTS ORGANIZATIONAL GOALS AND OBJECTIVES

To make an effective security policy, management must first determine what the enterprise's security goals are. If management skips this planning step, the security tools employed by the organization will not be well coordinated, services can be redundant, and technology misconfigurations can turn newly purchased security tools into open doors for attackers. In other words, poor policy decisions or a lack of good operational standards can undermine reliable technology. The following list includes some of the advantages of a security policy.

➤ A security policy can create a security-aware culture, which may be even more effective than the purchase of security tools.

➤ Better security frequently equals less liability and fewer losses due to hack attacks, fraud, and theft.

➤ Planning ahead allows management to assign roles and responsibilities before an incident occurs.

➤ Performing advance background checks on personnel lowers

the chances that employees will be unjustly suspected of an insider attack.

➤ A security policy can assist management in achieving the enterprise's most important business goal — survival.

➤ A security policy assures the security and trust of online customers and their private information.

➤ A security policy limits the organization's liability of compromising customer information.

A security policy also has its limitations. A few of which are as follows.

➤ The business must spend vital resources (money and manpower) on security improvements rather than the achievement of new business objectives.

➤ Education is required to teach users how to follow security policy procedures.

➤ Obsolete security policies may force employees to waste time and effort by working against the system.

➤ Retooling an existing system can cause employee anxiety, fear, and resentment.

➤ Excellent communication with the security policy team is needed.

➤ Management, staff, and suppliers must wholeheartedly buy into the protective measures in the organization's security policy in order for it to be successful.

➤ The Security Policy Functionality Trade-Offs

All users want greater availability, faster response times, and access to more information. The following is a list of security versus functionality trade-offs that you can expect to address when creating a security policy.

1. Offering a variety of services versus high security. Each type of online offering presents its own type of risk. Some services are so risky that it is cost-prohibitive to secure them. Consequently, your organization may want to consider not offering the service. For example, your web-based business may import data from a third party source and present them on a web page to customers. If you have no control over what is imported, you may not want to offer the service.

2. Ease of use versus security. The extreme solution in this category is to allow all users access without any security devices (password and user ID combinations, etc.) However, requiring free or one-time passwords can greatly increase security and reduce the likelihood of an attack.

3. Cost of security versus loss if attacked. Losses can take many forms, from the obvious—monetary losses, performance losses, and ease-of-use losses—to the more insidious, such as losses of privacy, data, and service. Knowing the value of an asset, the cost to protect that asset, and the priority of the asset can assist you in writing an effective security policy that weights the relative value of the different kinds of losses you wish to avoid.

■ DEVELOPING AN EFFECTIVE SECURITY POLICY

An effective security policy must address the needs of the entire web-based business. There are many off-the-shelf templates and models for developing a security policy from scratch. In some situations, companies must take an existing policy and adapt it to the e-commerce environment—a task that is much harder than starting at ground zero. Whether you have to create a security policy from the start or rework an existing security policy, the goal is the same—to create a security policy that meets your business objectives and requirements.

Becoming aware of the need for a security policy and of the elements to consider in creating a security policy is important. There are many books, software programs, and online resources to assist managers in getting started on developing a security policy. The following are a few examples of online resources:

➤ "Does Your Organization Need Information Security Policies?" This article is available online at *Pentasafe Publications* [http://www.baselinesoft.com/doyouneed.html]. Pentasoft also provides helpful security policy books and software.

➤ "How to Develop a Network Security Policy: An Overview of Internetworking Site Security." This Sun Microsystems white paper is available online at [http://www.sun.com/software/white-papers/wp-security-devsecpolicy].

➤ "What Do I Put in a Security Policy?" by William Farnsworth. This SANS Institute white paper is available online at [http://www.sans.org/infosecFAQ/policy/policy.htm].

➤ "The Value of Documentation: A Useful System Security Plan Template," by Falan Memmott. This SANS Institute white paper is available online at [http://www.sans.org/infosecFAQ/policy/document.htm].

➤ "A System Security Policy for You," by David Milford. This SANS Institute white paper is available at [http://www.sans.org/infosecFAQ/policy/sys_sec.htm].

➤ Other online resources include the National Security Assurance Group (www.information-security.net/news.htm) and the Center for Internet Security (www.cisecurity.org), which include news and links to helpful information about setting up a security policy.

Remember there are no perfect ready-made templates or models, and no one can tell you exactly what your security policy should be. Business security is subjective. Each web-based business has a different culture, threshold of comfort, and technological infrastructure. Therefore each web-based business requires its own unique security policy.

■ DEFINING YOUR SECURITY POLICY

The term *security policy* has a different meaning for different people. Your organization's security policy should be a carefully written statement of the rules that each employee agrees to abide by in return for access to the organization's technology and information assets. Many security professionals believe that the most important step for an online business to take in increasing security is to develop a written security policy. *It is too late to develop a security policy during an attack.* Table 14.2 illustrates the major elements of a security policy for a web-based business.

I. The Purpose of the Security Policy
The security policy is a baseline from which the organization's computers, servers, network, and other assets are assessed to determine whether they meet the company's security policy. The purpose of

Table 14.2 Eight Important Topics That Should be Included in the Security Policy

Topic	Description
Purpose of the security policy	Defines the purpose and goals of the security policy
Related documents	Provides specific instructions for the IT department, management, and users about security procedures
Cancellation	Details how new policies, and modifications or deletions to the existing policy, will be handled
Background of the security policy	States the need for a security policy
Scope of the security policy	Illustrates the issues the security policy will cover
Policy statement	Defines computer and network user actions that are acceptable to the best interests of the organization.
Responsibility	Identifies which people to contact in case of incidents or violations of the security policy
Action	Specifies how and when users and the IT department will respond to certain events

the web-based business's security policy is to define and inform all users (management, staff, partners, suppliers, etc.) of the requirements for using the organization's technology and information assets.

II. Related Documents about Security Procedures

This section of the security policy details the assets to be protected and the threats from which they will be protected. This section of the security policy is helpful in illustrating the underlying logic of the rules that apply to the use of the organization's computers and informational assets.

    A. Availability statement.
        1. Sets users' expectations for availability of resources (operating hours and maintenance downtimes)

2. Covers redundancy and data recovery
3. Provides contact information for reporting system and network failures

B. Information about technology purchase guidelines and security maintenance policy.
1. Defines how internal and external maintenance people are allowed to handle and access technology assets
2. Details whether remote maintenance is allowed and how it is controlled
3. Explains how the outsourcing of maintenance and security is managed
4. Provides the IT department with information about preferred security features (a supplement to existing purchasing standards)

C. Details regarding the impact of an attack or loss of service of the asset. This part of the policy should include the type of vulnerability, the extent of the vulnerability if it is realized, the impact of the vulnerability on the organization, and the potential causes and likely solutions to the problem.
1. Denial of service
2. Destruction of assets
3. Disclosure of information
4. Theft of sensitive customer information
5. Theft of corporate secrets
6. Unauthorized assess to the system

III. Cancellation and Changes in the Security Policy
This section details how to handle changes in the security policy. The mechanisms for updating the policy should be clearly stated, as should the names of those who are to be involved and those who can approve the changes.

IV. Background of the Security Policy
A risk that is often overlooked in web-based businesses is the insertion of technology managers between business managers and staff. Thus, any change in a business unit is often dependent upon the responsiveness of the technology group. However, the technology division is usually more concerned about infrastructure and access rules than business requirements. This creates tension within the organiza-

tion as the company faces the contradictory demands of rapidly changing technology and the need to share knowledge and customer information. The security policy reduces this tension and provides a way to manage information security standards and procedures in a structured and thorough way.

V. Scope of the Security Policy

The security policy spells out the firm's stance on privacy, copyright, intellectual issues, and the like.

VI. Policy or Acceptable Use Statement

The acceptable use part of the security policy makes it clear what users can and cannot do on the various components of the organization's system. While acceptable use of the enterprise's information resources may seem apparent to management, acceptable use may have a different meaning for users, employees, suppliers, partners, and others. The following are a few examples of the different policies that should be included in the acceptable use statement and the functions these policies should perform:

    A. Privacy policy
        1. Explains management's stance on monitoring electronic mail, logging keystrokes, and accessing users' files
        2. Details circumstances when the firm or access provider can intrude or monitor usage
        3. Explains copyrights and digital rights management policies

    B. Access and changing default passwords policy
        1. Defines the rights and privileges of different users
        2. Identifies password use and format
        3. Provides guidelines for remote access and connecting devices to the network
        4. Provides guidelines for adding new software to the system

    C. Accountability policy
        1. Defines the responsibility of users, operations staff, and management
        2. Specifies audit capacity
        3. Provides incident handling guidelines for intrusion detection

D. User authentication (a critical policy for the security of the organization)
　　1. Establishes trust with an effective password policy
　　2. Sets guidelines for remote access login
　　3. Defines how remote logins are managed and authenticated

E. Software and access to databases
　　1. Identifies who has authorization to grant privileges to processes
　　2. Defines what acts are permissible
　　3. Sets guidelines regarding who has physical access to databases (owners, groups, or users)

F. Disclosure of information
　　1. Defines who has access to sensitive information
　　2. Identifies permissible acts
　　3. Sets guidelines as to who has physical access to confidential information (to read, write, or execute)

G. Use of other network technologies
　　1. Explains how modem lines are managed
　　2. Details how dial-in and dial-out users are authenticated

H. Security backup copies of data
　　1. Defines user responsibilities for creating backup files
　　2. Sets guidelines and schedules for testing backups to determine if they are uncorrupted
　　3. Identifies what data need to be stored off-site

I. Etiquette
　　1. Acceptable (nonoffensive) forms of expression for e-mail
　　2. Unacceptable practices (such as forging press releases or e-mail messages)

VII. Roles and Responsibilities
Define the organization's violations reporting policy. The policy may encourage anonymous reporting of security policy violations to help foster a nonthreatening atmosphere.

A. What types of security policy violations (privacy, security, internal, and external) must be reported

B. Who is responsible for receiving the security policy violation reports

VIII. Incident Response Plans

Computer incidents may be real or false alarms. It is often difficult to determine the exact type of an attack and its extent. An effective security policy can help the enterprise avoid any early mistakes and can assist the organization in preserving evidence that may be helpful in tracking the attack organization.

A. Before the incident
    1. Have a predetermined plan.
    2. Test the plan before the firm is attacked.
    3. Ensure that your system cannot be used to launch attacks against other organizations.
    4. Minimize the likelihood of negative exposure.

B. During the incident, provide
    1. Contact information provided for each type of security policy violation.
    2. Timing and requirements of any backups and logging.
    3. Computer system quarantine policies.
    4. Statement of how to preserve evidence.
    5. Instructions on how to handle outside queries about a security incident.
    6. Instructions on how to handle information that may be considered confidential or proprietary.

C. After the incident
    1. What happened?
    2. How can it be stopped?
    3. How can the organization avoid the same vulnerability?
    4. Assess the impact and damage of the incident.
    5. Update security policies as needed.
    6. Track the attack organization and discover the cyber-criminals.

■ SELECTING THE TEAM TO CREATE THE SECURITY POLICY

All levels of the organization, especially upper management, must understand and support the security policy. Many organizations appear to be working against their own security policies because the security policies are not designed to be applied by humans. In other words, it is better *not to have a security policy* if employees are forced to work around the policy in order to complete some aspect of their jobs. Once employees acquire the mindset that they are exceptions to the policy, the culture of the organization changes. Workers feel they do not have to follow the rules in other areas, and this can cause mischief, misbehavior, and more severe problems.

When creating the security policy team, it is important to remember that all levels of employees in all departments must accept the security policy. Therefore, the authors must be influential in the organization and have the authority to enforce the policy. A security policy without the full support of high-level management quickly becomes a meaningless document with little impact on the organization. The following are a few examples of individuals who should be on the team:

➤ Site security administrator
➤ IT technical staff (from the IT department, or staff from the computing center)
➤ Administrators of large user groups within the organization
➤ Security incident response team
➤ Representatives of the user groups affected by the security policy (branch offices, etc.)
➤ Responsible management
➤ Legal counsel (if appropriate)

If your web-based business is small, one person may cover several of the jobs listed. For large organizations, additional individuals, such as audit personnel, should be included. Policy creation must be the joint effort of a representative level of personnel. Decision makers must have the authority to enforce the policy at different levels within the organization. IT personnel must have the expertise to advise the team on the ramifications of the security policy. Day-to-day users must have an equal vote about the usability of the policy. Overall, team members should be key stakeholders who have budgetary and policy authority, technical staff who are familiar with what can be supported, and legal counsel who are familiar with the ramifications of various policy choices (for example, changing the privacy statement).

Thomas Wadlow (2000) points out that a good security policy can assist the IT department in determining what to do when. The following are a few insights about potential problems your organization may encounter when addressing the issue of creating a security policy:

➤ A good policy written today is better than terrific security policy written next year.

➤ A weak but well-distributed policy is better than a strong but complex policy that no one is familiar with.

➤ More employees will accept an easy-to-understand policy than a complicated security policy that no one takes the time to read.

➤ The security policy must be a living document, constantly changing.

■ THE CONTINUOUS LIFE CYCLE OF THE SECURITY POLICY

An effective security policy is consistent with the business goals of the organization. In other words, successful security policies support the business objectives and assist the enterprise in monitoring for vulnerabilities, attacks, and misbehaviors. Figure 14.1 shows the interrelationship of the elements of a good security policy. According to Internet Security Systems (2001) and other professionals how these elements interact form a continuous life cycle that ensures a high level of security for a web-based enterprise. The following expands this concept.

➤ Evaluate

Gain a good understanding of what you are protecting. The security policy must determine the scope of the problem or, in other words, identify what assets are being protected and why they are being threatened. The risk analysis stage of the security policy life system involves the following steps:

➤ Describing what assets are being protected and why. This includes examining all of the risks to data (backups, audit logs),

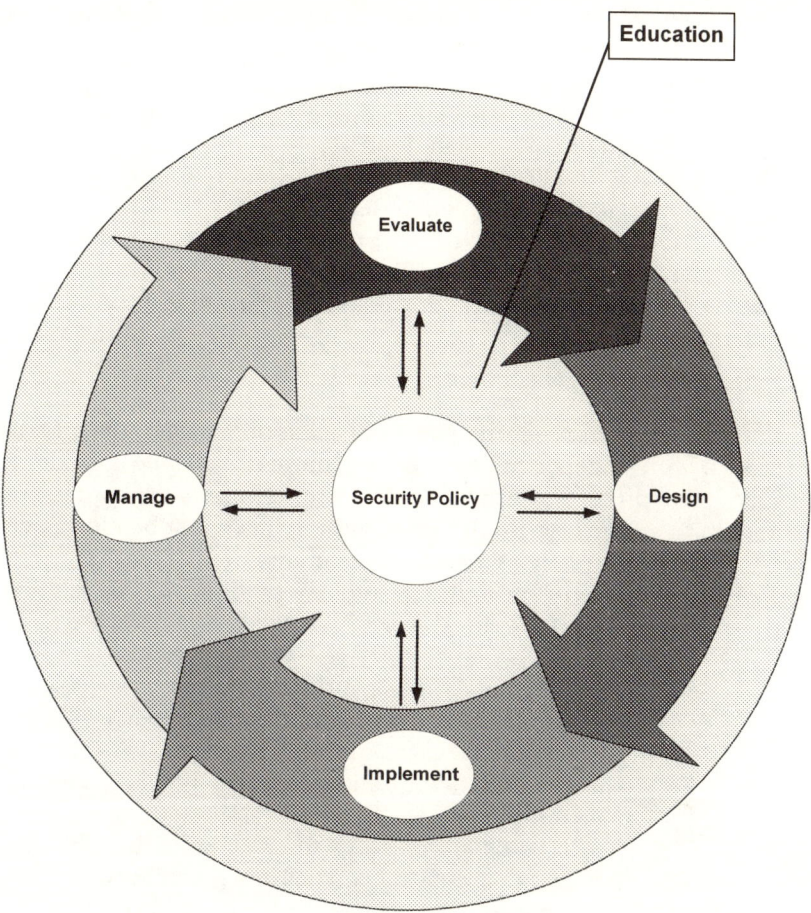

Figure 14.1 The life cycle of the security policy process
Source: Adapted from "Creating, Implementing, and Managing the Information Security Lifecycle." Internet Security Systems white paper, 2000. Available at [http://documents.iss.net/whitepapers/securityCycle.pdf]. Retrieved 10 December 2001.

corporate secrets, intellectual property, software (source programs, diagnostic programs, operating systems), hardware (computers, servers, routers), documentation (on programs, hardware systems, local administrator procedures), and people (users, customers, partners).

➤ Determining the cost to protect each asset.

➤ Prioritizing the order in which information assets are to be protected.

➤ Prioritizing what level of security is required for certain assets.

➤ Allowing for policy exceptions for specific parts of the organization under certain conditions.

➤ Providing the IT department with a valid reason to accept or decline requests from other departments.

➤ Requiring the IT department to coordinate its activities with management.

➤ Identifying and prioritizing risks according to level of severity.

➤ Design

To design an effective security policy, all levels of management and the policies within all departments of the organization must be considered and agreed upon by the security policy team. This means that the system and procedures for implementing the policy must be clearly defined and understood by all users. At the completion of this stage, the security policy is written and the implementation plan developed. These are some steps to follow during this stage:

➤ Select a security policy management team that is representative of users and that has the authority and expertise to execute the security policy.

➤ Verify that all of the organization's security needs are clearly defined and enforceable.

➤ Specify required or preferred security features that will supplement existing purchasing policies and guidelines.

➤ Consult legal counsel regarding the specific requirements for the organization. Many web-based enterprises have regulatory requirements that affect the security policy.

➤ Consider the strategic goals of the organization. Remember that different departments within the enterprise may have different requirements.

➤ Implement

Each web-based enterprise has specific needs and peculiarities. All of these elements should be taken into consideration when implementing the organization's security policy. Additionally, the security policy must be enforceable through the following measures:

➤ Purchasing the appropriate security tools
➤ Deploying security sanctions when action prevention is technically not feasible
➤ Educating users, administrators, and management about their security policy roles and responsibilities

➤ Manage

A successful security policy provides a baseline that management can use to determine the effectiveness of the firm's security measures. Once the security policy is implemented, management can measure the effectiveness of the program by, for example, tracking the number of attempted attacks. Other useful metrics include tracking the number of attempted and successful security violations.

A failed security policy is one that users or management believe to be stupid. Security policies usually fail because they are implemented before users accept them, do not accommodate the unique peculiarities of the web-based business, or interrupt normal workflow.

Some users reject a policy because they are not aware of how their actions will affect the security of the online business. Other reasons for security policy failure may include the following:

➤ Users do not understand why certain security precautions are needed. (A security awareness and education program can assist in this area.)
➤ Security policies are not enforced. (Management may want to consider assessing adherence to security policies as part of each worker's performance evaluation.)
➤ Security policies are too high for the criticality of the function. (Policies may not be enforced because they are out of date or not applicable to a certain job function.)

➤ Start All Over Again

Security for an online business is a continuous process. Keep in mind that what was safe yesterday and today may not be protected tomorrow. A good example of this is the World Trade Center catastrophe. During the height of the event, all telecommunications on the east coast were disrupted. For weeks after the event, many networks and servers (that were in top condition, having been beefed up because of Y2K fears) were not working. This points out the need for backup servers and databases to be placed in underground cement bunkers or stored in different geographic locations.

Industry professionals agree that the security of your web-based business is not a product but a *goal.* However, reaching the goal of security awareness is difficult. Therefore, the first step in building a secure e-commerce environment is to create a security-aware culture. The second step is to provide training and education to all users (including management, staff, and IT personnel). The third step is to create an environment where it is everyone's responsibility to be constantly vigilant in fending off the faceless security threats the enterprise encounters each day.

■ DISTRIBUTION AND EDUCATION OF THE SECURITY POLICY

The greatest security policy in the world is useless if it is hidden in a three-ring binder on someone's shelf. Once the security policy is complete, it should be distributed throughout the organization. User education is a necessary part of developing an effective security policy. Keep in mind that many of the web-based enterprise's users are unaware of computer and information threats and proper usage.

All users should be responsible for keeping confidential business data from leaking outside the company. For current employees, it is often wise to have all personnel sign a statement indicating they have read, understood, and agreed to follow the security policies detailed in the statement. The human resources department may be responsible for briefing new employees on the organization's security policy and for debriefing departing employees as to their continued responsibility not to discuss confidential customer or enterprise information.

Promoting and campaigning for user awareness is often the weakest link in implementing an effective security policy. Providing users with ongoing security awareness training is essential for user buy-in. In addition, users need to understand the importance of the security policy and organization-wide compliance. Keep in mind that it is essential for each employee to know and provide information on virus prevention, e-mail security, password management, privacy, and more.

■ DEVELOPING A SECURITY POLICY CHECKLIST

Many individuals consider the enterprise's security policy another meaningless act of management interference with getting the real job done. In some sense this is true, as even the most basic security measures will reduce productivity. Therefore, educating individuals in your web-based business about the value of security is a top priority. Practicing information security is not intuitive: It is a learned behavior that needs constant reinforcement by management. Keep in mind that your security policy may never be perfect. Moreover, it will never be finished. There will always be new threats to your web-based business, and your security policy must be a living, constantly changing document in order to effectively assist your organization to fend off those threats. The following is a checklist to help you get started in the right direction.

- ✓ Become aware of the likely threats to your web-based business. Some web-based businesses are prone to certain types of attacks. Other online enterprises may not be frequently attacked, but if attacked may be at a high risk due to public perception of the firm's safety.
- ✓ Make your security policy simple. An effective policy is easy to remember and use.
- ✓ Make the security policy a living document. Provide clear guidelines for updating and modifying the document. An obsolete security policy cannot help your organization fend off attackers.
- ✓ Build your security policy in such a way as to make it hard for people to complete activities you do not want them to do. Making it easy for users to do the right thing helps create a culture based on security awareness.
- ✓ Craft the firm's security policy in such a way that it will be easy for management and staff to detect problems. Make certain the security policy provides guidelines regarding security tools that provide false positives.
- ✓ Create a security policy from which it is difficult for outsiders and insiders to hide. Deploy security tools that detect attempts to violate security and successful security violations. Keep track of security violations.
- ✓ Perform regular health checkups. Test to make certain everything is working the way it is supposed to. Consider breaking into your system to test for vulnerabilities.

■ REFERENCES

Butler, Philip, and Greg Collins. 1998. Securing your computerized business data against internet hackers. Digital Innovations, Inc., and DQI Systems white paper. Available at [http://www.globeserver.com/misc/intsecwp.pdf]. 10 December 2001.

Creating, implementing and managing the information security life cycle: Security policy, e-business and you. 2000. Internet Security Systems white paper. Available at [http://documents.iss.net/whitepapers/securityCycle.pdf]. 10 December 2001.

Connolly, P. J. 2000. Test center: Security starts from within. *InfoWorld,* 10 July. Available at [http://www.infoworld.com/articles/es/xml/00/07/10/000710essecurity.xml]. 10 December 2001.

Does your organization need information security policies? 2001. Pentasafe Publications Online. Available at [http://www.baselinesoft.com]. 6 September 2001. No longer available online.

Fraser, B., ed. 1997. Site security handbook. Network Working Group Memorandum. September. Available at [http://www.cis.ohio-state.edu/cgi-bin/rfc/rfc2196.html]. 10 December 2001.

How to develop a network security policy: An overview of internetworking site security. 2001. Sun Microsystems white paper. Available at [http://www.sun.com/software/white-papers/wp-security-devsecpolicy]. 10 December 2001.

An introduction to computer security. 1997. *The NIST Handbook,* 20 November. Available at [http://documents.iss.net/whitepapers/securityCycle.pdf]. 10 December 2001.

Kessler, Gary C. 2000. Web of worries. *Information Security Magazine,* April. Available at [http://www.infosecuritymag.com/articles/april00/cover.shtml]. 10 December 2001.

McMillian, Rob. 2001. Site security policy development. Information Technology Services white paper, 11 September. Available at [http://secinf.net/info/policy/AusCERT.html]. 10 December 2001.

Parmar, S. K., ed. 1999. *An introduction to security* [security manual]. *Security Focus,* 4 May. Available at [http://www.sans.org/infosecFAQ/policy/creating.htm]. 10 December 2001.

Powell, Deron. 2000. Enterprise security management (ESM) centralizing management on your security policy. SANS Institute white paper, 20 December. Available at [http://www.sans.org/infosecFAQ/policy/ESM.htm]. 10 December 2001.

Wadlow, Thomas A. 2000. *The process of network security: Designing and managing a safe network.* Reading, Mass.: Addison-Wesley.

Walters, Irene. 2001. When a security policy matures into a security solution. SANS Institute white paper, 2 April. Available at [http://www.sans.org/infosecFAQ/policy/matures.htm]. 10 December 2001.

Why security policies fail. 1999. Security Focus Control Data white paper. Available at [http://downloads.securityfocus.com/library/Why_Security_Policies_Fail.pdf]. 10 December 2001.

Worthington, Mark. 2001. Creating security policies: Lessons learned. SANS Institute white paper, 4 May. Available at [http://www.sans.org/infosecFAQ/policy/creating.htm]. 10 December 2001.

Glossary

A

Abuse of privilege. The performance of an action that, according to organizational policy or law, the user should not have taken.

Access. The ability to enter a secured area or the process of interacting
with an information system.

Access authorization. Permission granted to use programs or workstations.

Access control. A set of procedures performed by hardware, software,
and administrators to monitor access, identify users requesting access, record access attempts, and grant or deny access.

Access sharing. Permitting two or more users to have simultaneous access to file servers or devices.

ACK. Acknowledgement code; communicates that a system is ready to
receive data from a remote transmitting station, or acknowledges
the error-free transmission of data.

Active content. Web pages that contain programs that are automatically
downloaded and executed by Internet browsers.

Anonymous FTP. A guest account that allows anyone to log in to an
FTP server. It can be a point of access to the host server.

Antivirus software. A tool that examines a system or network for
viruses and removes any that is found.

Antivirus software definitions. The latest virus protection updates, developed by research teams shortly after a virus is discovered. These
updates are available for immediate download as soon as a remedy
for the virus has been created.

Applets. Small software programs that are often written in the Java programming language.

Application gateway. A firewall that inspects and filters data at the application level.

Asymmetric encryption. Encryption using pairs of public and private keys.

Attachment. Any file linked to an e-mail message.

Audit. The review of records to access their veracity and completeness.

Audit trail. In computer security systems, a chronological record of when users log in, how long they are engaged in various activities, what they were doing, and whether any actual or attempted security violations occurred.

Authenticate. In networking, to establish the validity of a legitimate user or an object (e.g., a communications server).

Authentication. Identity verification often required to gain access to computer systems or networks (e.g., the providing of a username and password to log in to an ISP).

Authorization. The process of determining which activities are permitted, usually in the context of authentication; once authenticated, the user may be authorized for different levels of access or activity.

Availability. The portion of time that a system can be used for productive work, expressed as a percentage.

B

Back door. A loophole in the security of a computer system; sometimes deliberately coded by programmers, but more often an unforeseen entry point to abuse the system. Also known as a *trap door.*

Bandwidth. Information-carrying capacity of telephone or network wiring as well as system buses, radio frequency signals, and monitors. Measured in cycles per second, hertz (Hz, which is the difference between the lowest and highest frequencies transmitted), or in bits or bytes per second.

Bastion host. Often a component of a firewall, but may also exist outside web servers or public access systems.

Browser. The user's interface to the World Wide Web; interprets hypertext links and lets the user view sites and navigate from one Internet node to another.

Browser sniffing. The process by which a web site detects which versions of various browsers are being run by users, in order to determine whether the users can access certain web site features.

Business-critical applications. The vital software needed to run a business, whether custom-written or commercially packaged (e.g., accounting/finance, enterprise resource planning (ERP), manufacturing, human resources, sales databases, etc.).

C

CA. See Certificate authority (CA).

CERT. The Computer Emergency Response Team, established at Carnegie-Mellon University in 1988.

Certificate authority (CA). An internal entity or trusted third party that issues, signs, revokes, and manages digital certificates.

CGI (Common Gateway Interface) standard. Lays down the rules for running external programs in a web HTTP server; external programs are called *gateways* because they open an outside world of information to the server.

Client. The customer side of a client/server setup. With client/server architecture, the client is the software that runs on the users machine and relays to the server.

Client/device. Hardware that retrieves information from a server.

Computer security. Technological and managerial procedures applied to computer systems to ensure the availability, integrity, and confidentiality of information managed by the computer system.

Computer security audit. An independent evaluation of the controls employed to ensure appropriate protection of an organization's information assets.

Content filtering. The blocking of undesirable Internet content (e.g., businesses can block content based on traffic type).

Cookie. Small data files written to the user's hard drive by some web sites when the sites are viewed via the user's browser. Typical data stored include the user's surfing habits, preferences, and demographic data. Also used to identify users and customize web pages, or to track user activity within a web site.

Cryptography. The science of transforming readable text into cipher text and back again.

Cyberspace. Virtual reality, the Internet, the World Wide Web, and many other kinds of computer systems within which users become immersed.

D

Data packet. Large blocks of information that a computer and modem send when the user is surfing the Internet, downloading files, or sending e-mail; more efficient than sending data one character at a time.

Decoding. Conversion of encoded text to plain text through the use of a code.

Decryption. The conversion of either encoded or enciphered text into plain (i.e., readable) text.

Denial of service (DoS) attack. An action that prevents any part of a system or network from functioning properly. Can result when a system (e.g., a web server) has been flooded with illegitimate requests, making it impossible for the system to respond to real requests or tasks.

Distributed denial of service attack (DDoS). A denial of service attack that is coordinated by a single host managed by the attacker and launched by using several infiltrated computers that act as agents to carry out the attack.

Digital certificate. An electronic "document" that uses high-security encryption keys to verify identities for the purpose of executing secure transactions online; also, an electronic document that verifies the owner of a public key. May be called a *public-key certificate, digital ID,* or *digital passport,* and is issued by a certificate authority.

Digital signature. Any type of text or message encrypted with a private key, thereby identifying the source. The functional equivalent of a paper signature; can be legally binding. Usually verified in a manner similar to digital certificates.

DNS (domain name system; domain name server). A look-up system that translates the domain name of a computer that is connected to the Internet into an IP address.

DNS spoofing. Assuming the DNS name of another system by either corrupting the name service cache of a victim system, or by compromising a domain name server for a valid domain.

Domain name. In an e-mail address, the part of the address to the right of the "@" sign; in a URL, about the first ten characters—CNET's domain name, for example, is cnet.com. Will have different endings based on the nature of the owner (e.g., ".com" for a commercial enterprise, ".edu" for an educational establishment, ".gov" for a governmental body, ".mil" for a division of the military, ".net" for a network, or ".org" for a nonprofit organization). May also use a geographical notation.

DoS. See Denial of service (DoS) attack.

E

E-mail (electronic mail). A message sent via computer in any of several ways (across a local area network, via the Internet, or through an online service), which the recipient may read later. May be sent to a single recipient or to multiple recipients.

E-mail bombs. Code that sends many messages to the same address(es) for the purpose of using up disk space or overloading the e-mail or web server.

Encryption. The process of changing data into a form that can be read only by the intended receiver. To decipher the message, the receiver of the encrypted data must have the proper decryption key.

Encryption algorithm. A mathematical formula used to encrypt or decrypt a string of text.

Enterprise resource planning (ERP). One of many software applications that can assist business managers in overseeing the resources of all facets (strategic planning, marketing, sales, manufacturing, etc.) of organization.

Extranet. A web site that provides nonpublic information to a select group of people, such as business partners or customers; may look like an ordinary web site, but requires a password or the use of digital encryption to access it (e.g., Federal Express's customers can track packages on the company's extranet by simply entering a tracking number).

F

FAQs (frequently asked questions). Text files intended to answer all the questions a newcomer to a web site might have. Designed to cut down on basic tech-support queries, FAQs can be organized in virtually any structure, and often cover a far wider range of subjects than basic site orientation.

Finger. A program allowing the user to place the mouse pointer on the username of someone on a networked system and uncover that user's full name, most recent login time, and other information. Also used as a verb meaning to apply the program to a username.

Firewall. A system or combination of systems that enforce borders between two or more networks, regulating access between networks according to a specific security policy (almost like an invisible barrier that protects a network or computer).

Flooding programs. Code that, when executed, will bombard the selected system with requests in an effort to slow or shut down the system.

FTP (File Transfer Protocol). The transfer of files across a network.

G

Gateway. A bridge between two networks (i.e., a program or piece of hardware that passes data between networks).

Gopher. Developed before the World Wide Web at the University of Minnesota to search global indexes of resources stored in Gopher databases. Today, most gopher databases have been converted to web sites that can be searched by web search engines.

H

Hack. Any software in which a significant portion of the code was originally another program.

Hacker. A person who attempts to gain access to computer systems that he or she is not authorized to access. This individual explores the details of computers, including security holes, and may exploit them for whatever purpose (entertainment, profit, theft, prank, etc.). The meaning of the term *hacker* has changed over time. It was previously used to describe a dedicated programmer or devoted programming hobbyist.

Host-based security. The technique of securing an individual system from attack. Is dependent on a specific operating system and version.

HTML (Hypertext Markup Language). A mechanism used to create web pages. When the mouse is pointed to a URL, the browser interprets the HTML commands embedded in the page and uses them to format the page's text and graphic elements.

HTTP (Hypertext Transfer Protocol). The native protocol of the Internet used to transmit and receive all data over the World Wide Web.

Hyperlinks. The easy-to-spot underlined words or phrases on which the user clicks in World Wide Web documents to jump to another screen or page. Contain HTML-coded references that point to other web pages, to which the browser then jumps. Also called *anchors.*

I

ICMP (Internet Control and Message Protocol). Used to communicate problems or availability information on the Internet (the PING program uses ICMP to determine whether a remote computer system is powered on and is available on the Internet). Also used to communicate when a system cannot be found.

Insider attack. An attack originating from inside a protected network.

Internet. Originated in 1969, in the midst of the cold war, as a "nuke-proof" communications network. Received most of its early financing from the U.S. Department of Defense; now consists of countless networks and computers across the world, allowing millions of people to share information.

IP (Internet Protocol). The communications standard that defines how the Internet works: both how data are formatted and the particular information they contain to allow information to be exchanged on computer systems existing on a variety of different networks using different hardware.

IP address. A unique string of numbers that identifies a computer on the Internet. The numbers are usually shown in groups separated by periods, e.g., 123.123.23.2. All resources on the Internet must have an IP address—or else they are not on the Internet at all.

IP datagram. A piece of a message transmitted over a packet-switching network. In addition to the data being sent, a packet also contains the destination address. In IP networks, datagrams are often called packets.

IP fragment. A fragment of an IP packet or datagram. Packets are sometimes broken into fragments to be transported.

IP sniffing. Stealing network addresses by reading the packets. Harmful data are then sent stamped with internal trusted addresses.

IP spoofing. Any of several methods for changing an IP address to one acceptable to a firewall, so as to trespass on an internal network.

IRC (Internet relay chat). A means of hooking up with other Internet users to exchange written comments, both live and in real time.

ISDN (Integrated Services Digital Network). Wide-bandwidth digital transmission using the public, switched telephone network. Under ISDN, a phone call can transfer 64 kilobits of digital data per second.

ISP (Internet service provider). The individual's doorway to all that the Internet offers. Most ISPs have a network of servers (mail, news, web, and the like), routers, and modems attached to a permanent, high-speed Internet "backbone" connection. Subscribers can then dial into the local network to gain Internet access.

K

Kbps (kilobytes per second). A measurement of speed indicating the number of bits of data transferred in a second.

Key. In encryption, a sequence of characters used to encode and decode a file. May be small, hand-held hardware devices similar to pocket calculators or credit cards, or may be loaded onto a personal computer as copy-protected software.

L

LAN (local area network). A computer network that covers a relatively small area. Most are kept to a single building or group of buildings. Users share data stored on hard disks and can share printers connected to the network.

Least privilege. Designing operational aspects of a system to operate with a minimum amount of system privilege. Reduces the authorization level at which various actions are performed and decreases the chance that a process or user with high privileges may be caused to perform unauthorized activity, resulting in a security breach.

Logging. The process of storing information about events that occurred on the firewall or network.

Log-on or log-in. A way for a computer system or network to recognize legitimate users. In an effort to recognize authorized users, workers often have to enter the correct combination of a user name and password before being allowed to execute programs or access the network.

Log processing. How audit logs are processed, searched for key events, or summarized.

Log retention. How long audit logs are retained and maintained.

M

Mail bomb. An e-mail that is sent, often multiple times, to an enormous number of recipients, urging them to respond to a single system or person. The result can often overload and crash a system.

Malicious code. Hardware, software, or firmware that is intentionally introduced to a system for an unauthorized or malicious purpose.

O

Operating system. System software that controls a computer and its peripherals.

P

Packet. A block of data that transmits the identities of sending and receiving stations, error-control information, and data.

Packet filter. A firewall or router that allows or forbids packets to enter or exit a network based on IP address and origin or destination port.

Packet sniffer. A device or program that monitors packets traveling between computers on a network. Can be used to compromise computer security by intercepting data (such as confidential financial information or passwords) in transit between two machines.

Password. A secret code assigned to a user. Knowledge of the password associated with the user ID is considered proof of authorization.

Performance. A major factor in determining the overall productivity of a system; primarily tied to availability, throughput, and response time.

Perimeter-based security. The technique of securing a network by controlling access to all points of entry and exit on the network.

PGP (Pretty Good Privacy). A set of programs for exchanging encrypted and authenticated e-mail messages, designed for a variety of platforms.

PIN (personal identification number). A personal identification number used during the authentication process; known only to the user.

PING (Packet Internet Groper). A program that "bounces" a request off of another computer over a network to determine whether the remote computer is still responding. If the PING comes back, the remote computer is still alive.

Policy. Organizational-level rules governing acceptable use of computing resources, security practices, and operational procedures.

POP (Post Office Protocol). The current access standard for Internet e-mail mailboxes.

PPP (Point-to-Point Protocol). A method of connecting a computer to the Internet. This methodology is considered more reliable than the earlier SLIP method. Although most Internet service providers (ISPs) use either PPP or SLIP methodologies, some offer both approaches.

Port scanning. An attempt by a hacker to find the weaknesses of a computer or network by scanning or probing system ports via requests for information. Internet technology professionals can also use it as a legitimate tool to discover and correct security holes.

Private key. In asymmetric encryption, the key that a user keeps secret. Can encrypt or decrypt data for a single transaction but cannot do both.

Protocol. Communications rules for computers. The Internet is a heterogeneous collection of networked computers with numerous different protocols, including PPP, TCP/IP, SLIP, and FTP.

Proxy. Acts as an intermediary. Can be a method of replacing the code for service applications with an improved version that is more security aware. Can also be a software agent that acts on behalf of a user.

Proxy server. A system that caches items from other servers to speed up access. On the web, a proxy first attempts to find data locally, and if they are not available, fetches them from the remote server where the data reside permanently.

Public domain. Having no copyright restrictions whatsoever. Also called downloads in the public domain.

Public key. In asymmetric encryption, the key that a user allows the world to know. Can encrypt or decrypt data for a single transaction but cannot do both.

R

Remote access. The hookup of a remote computing device via communications lines, such as ordinary phone lines or wide area networks, to access network applications and information.

Risk analysis. The analysis of an organization's information resources, existing controls, and computer system vulnerabilities. Establishes a potential level of damage in dollars or other assets.

Router. Hardware that sends data from a local area network (LAN) to a long-distance telephone line. Also allows only authorized machines to transmit data into the local area network so that private information can remain secure. Handles errors, keeps network usage statistics, and handles security issues.

RSA (Rivest-Shamir-Adelman). A popular encryption and authentication standard that uses asymmetric keys, named for its inventors, Rivest, Shamir, and Adelman.

S

SATAN (Security Administrator Tool for Analyzing Networks). A tool that permits network administrators to seek and identify the vulnerabilities of systems on IP networks from a remote location to find system security weaknesses.

Screening router. A router configured to permit or deny traffic using filtering techniques; based on a set of permission rules installed by the administrator. A component of many firewalls usually used to block traffic between the network and specific hosts on an IP port level.

Secret key encryption. A method in which a single key known only to the participants encrypts and decrypts data.

Server. The control computer on a local area network that controls software access to workstations, printers, and other parts of the network.

Server-based computing. An innovative, server-based approach to delivering business-critical applications to end-user devices, whereby an application's logic executes on the server and only the user interface is transmitted across a network to the client.

SET (Secure Electronic Transactions). A standard sponsored by Visa and MasterCard that provides secure communications across the Internet among the card provider, the card holder, the card holder's financial institution, and merchants' financial institutions.

SHTTP (Secure Hypertext Transfer Protocol). A protocol developed for secure commercial transactions on the Internet.

SLIP (Serial Line Internet Protocol). An older method of connecting to the Internet that does not include error-checking features.

Smart card. A credit-card-sized device with embedded microelectronics circuitry for storing information about an individual. Not a key or token, as used in the remote access authentication process.

SMTP (Simple Mail Transfer Protocol). A protocol for sending e-mail messages between servers, and for regulating mail servers.

Smurfing. A denial of service (DoS) attack in which an automated program attacks a network by exploiting IP broadcast addressing. An attacker will spoof (impersonate) the source address of an ICMP echo request (PING) and send it to many systems on a network at once, causing a flood of echo replies. This causes clogging of the network and prevents normal network communication.

Social engineering. An attack based on deceiving users or administrators at the target site. Social engineering is way of subverting information system security using nontechnical methods (i.e., social means).

Spam. The functional equivalent to unsolicited, electronic junk mail. Spam floods a user's inbox with irrelevant, unwanted messages. Spam can also be a mass mailing to bulletin boards, newsgroups, or lists of people.

Spider. Also known as a web spider, this software explores the World Wide Web by retrieving a document and following all the hyperlinks in it. After following the links, spiders generate catalogs that can be accessed by search engines.

Spoofing. Faking the sending address or otherwise masquerading as an authorized user in an attempt to gain illegal entry into a secure system.

Spyware. Any software or program that employs a user's Internet connection in the background without his or her knowledge or explicit permission. If permission is not obtained, the act is considered to be information theft.

SSL (Secure Sockets Layer). A transport-layer technology that allows secure transactions among compliant browsers and servers. Provides authentication and confidentiality on top of existing applications such as web browsers. Digital certificates and digital signatures use this protocol layer to enhance security during online transactions.

Swap file. An area on a hard disk used as virtual memory. Virtual memory management software swaps data between it and the main memory (RAM).

Symmetric encryption. A method involving a single secret key for both encryption and decryption.

SYN. The mnemonic for ASCII character 22, representing Synchronous idle, often used to control display monitors, printers, and other modem devices.

SYN flood. A flooding of the SYN queue making it impossible to open a new connection.

T

TCP (Transmission Control Protocol). One of the main protocols in TCP/IP networks. Enables two hosts to establish a connection and exchange streams of data; guarantees that data will be delivered and that packets will be delivered in the same order in which they were sent.

TCP/IP (Transmission Control Protocol/Internet Protocol). Two protocols developed by the U.S. military to allow computers to talk to each other over long-distance networks. TCP is responsible for verifying delivery from client to server; IP is responsible for moving packets of data between nodes. TCP/IP forms the basis of the Internet and is built into every common modern operating system.

Telnet. A terminal emulation program for TCP/IP networks; runs on the computer and it connects to a server on the network. When the user enters commands through the Telnet program, each direction given is executed as if it were entered directly on the server console, enabling the user to control the server and communicate with other servers on the network.

Thin client. A low-cost computing device that works in a server-centric computing model. Typically does not require powerful processors and large amounts of RAM and ROM because it accesses applications from a central server or network. Can operate in a server-based computing environment.

Trin00. A Trojan program that is run from a remote host and that can be used to control a system or cause it to attack another network. Classified as a distributed DoS attack tool.

Trojan horse. (1) Any program designed to do things that the user of the program did not intend to do, or that disguises a program's harmful intent. (2) A seemingly useful and innocent program that contains hidden code allowing the unauthorized modification, exploitation, or destruction of data. Generally distributed via the Internet; games, freeware, and screen savers are common vehicles.

Tunneling router. A router or system capable of routing traffic by encrypting it and encapsulating it for transmission across an untrusted network, for eventual de-encapsulation and decryption.

U

UDP (User Datagram Protocol). Protocol used for applications that transmit short bursts of data. Offers a limited amount of service and is therefore the mechanism of data communication for applications that do not require verification of delivery at the destination.

UNIX. A multi-user, multi-tasking operating system that is mainly used as the master control program in workstations, particularly servers.

URL (uniform resource locator; universal resource locator). The Internet equivalent of an address.

User. Any person who interacts directly with a computer system.

User ID. A unique character string that identifies the individual user.

User identification. The process by which a user identifies himself or herself to the system as a valid user. (As opposed to *authentication,* which is the process of establishing that the user is indeed who he or she purports to be and that he or she has a right to use the system.)

User interface. The part of an application with which the user actually works. Can be text-driven (e.g., DOS) or graphical (e.g., Windows).

V

Virtual network perimeter. A network that appears to be a single protected network behind firewalls, but which actually encompasses encrypted virtual links over untrusted networks.

Virus. A self-replicating code segment, program, or piece of a program that can "infect" or "contaminate" other programs by modifying them to include a copy of itself. Viral code is typically malicious and detrimental to data or system integrity. Viruses may or may not contain attack programs or trapdoors.

VPN (virtual private network). A network in which, although some of the parts are connected using the public Internet, the data sent across the Internet is encrypted so that the entire network is "virtually" private. A typical example would be a network for a company having offices in two different cities. Using the Internet, the two offices merge their networks into one, but encrypt traffic that uses the Internet link.

W

WAN *(wide area network)*. A communications network that covers a wide geographic area, such as a state or country. It usually consists of several LANs.

Webmaster. Name for anyone in charge of managing the hardware and software that make up a company's web site; Internet systems administrator.

World Wide Web. A client/server hypertext system for retrieving information across the Internet; also known as the WWW, the W3, or most often simply as the web. On the web, everything is represented as hypertext (in HTML format) and is linked to other documents via URLs. The web encompasses its native HTTP protocol, as well as FTP, Gopher, and Telnet.

Worm. An independent program that replicates itself, crawling from machine to machine across network connections. Can clog networks as it spreads, often via e-mail.

Z

ZIP. An open standard for compression and decompression used widely for personal computer download archives. The file extension given to ZIP files is ".zip."

Resource Center

The Internet provides a wide variety of resources for managers. This resource center provides a sampling of some of the information you will find. Note, however, that this Internet information security resource center is not comprehensive. With the constant growth and change that characterize the World Wide Web, it is almost impossible for anyone to create an all-inclusive directory that lives up to such a claim.

Some of the sites listed in this information security resource center (and elsewhere in this book) may have changed or simply vanished due to mergers with larger sites. Some web sites provide links to new locations. If you cannot find what you are seeking, try the search engine of a security-specific web site, such as Security Focus (securityfocus.com) or the Center for Internet Security (www.cisecurity.org). If you still cannot find what you are looking for, a search engine like Google (google.com) or Alta Vista (altavista.com) may help you locate the resource you need.

■ ACCESS AND CONTENT FILTERING

Default Login/PW Database [http://www.mksecure.com/defpw] provides a central resource for verified default log-in and password pairs from common network devices. The log-ins and passwords contained in the database are either set by default when the machine is first installed or may be hard coded into the device.

Palisade [http://www.palisadesys.com] provides hardware and software products for blocking web sites and for using certain applications, managing Internet usage policies, and analyzing employee computer activities.

Pearl Software [http://www.pearlsw.com/work/index.html] provides stand-alone or network products that block objectionable web sites and control and monitor communications. Pearl software products are designed to increase productivity by providing tools that manage inappropriate use of the Internet.

■ ADVISORIES

Advanced Laboratory Workstation System, Center for Information Technology, National Institute of Health [http://www.nih.gov/security/security-advisories.html] compose a listing of groups that provide online information about security vulnerabilities and methods for removing or reducing the danger of certain vulnerabilities for different information systems.

CIAC (Computer Incident Advisory Center) [http://www.ciac.org/ciac/] features computer incident bulletin releases from the Department of Energy.

Microsoft Security Advisor [http://www.Microsoft.com/security/] provides news, security bulletins, best practices, tools, checklists, products, and technologies.

■ ANONYMITY

The Anonymizer [http://www.anonymizer.com/affiliate/landing.shtml] offers many services, including web browsing, e-mail accounts, and news reading.

Electronic Frontiers Georgia [http://anon.efga.org] provides tools for privacy, anonymous remailers, and anonymizing web proxies, as well as a listing of similar web sites.

Ultimate Anonymity [http://ultimate-anonymity.com/] provides innovative tools and techniques to those seeking complete online anonymity, from anonymous web surfing, newsgroups, and e-mail to web-based chat rooms.

■ AUTHENTICATION

ASP Authentication [http://www.aspforums.com/ASPAuthentication/] features software that allows users to password-protect Active Server Pages (ASP) so that no unauthorized person can view them.

Authentify, Inc. [http://www.authentify.com] enables the user to easily and readily identify anyone on the Internet. The product is embedded into the company's existing network and automatically runs whenever a user is logged on. The product is valuable to firms that want to avoid fraud by authenticating customers and users.

Entrust TruePass [http://www.entrust.com/truepass/index.htm] is a web security and privacy solution that enables trusted relationships between online businesses and their customers, suppliers, and partners.

Mosaic User Authentication Tutorial [http://hoohoo.ncsa.uiuc.edu/docs/tutorials/user.html] surveys the current methods of restricting access to documents.

RSA SecurID [http://www.rsasecurity.com/products/securid/] is a two-factor authentication application that is based on a password (or PIN) and an authenticator.

■ COMPUTER SECURITY NEWS AND INFORMATION

CNet Networks, Inc. [http://www.cnet.com] is a global source of information and commerce services for the technology industry.

Computer Security News Daily [http://www.mountainwave.com] is sponsored by Cyberwolf and provides breaking security news divided into several topic areas.

NIST Computer Security Resource Center [http://www.csrc.ncsl.nist.gov/] is a popular security web site that includes research, test results, and news about emerging technologies. In addition, it fea-

tures information about security management, guidelines, awareness, and education.

Security Portal [http://www.securityportal.com] is a source of security research and information.

■ CONFERENCES

Annual Computer Security Applications Conference [http://
www.acsac.org], a resource for the security community, is sponsored by Applied Computer Security Associates.

RSA Conference [http://www.rsa.com/conference/] is an annual en-
cryption-oriented conference sponsored by the security firm RSA
(Rivest, Shamir, Adleman). The conference is geared toward cryp-
tographers, developers, analysts, and businesspeople.

■ COOKIES

Cookie Central [http://www.cookiecentral.com] is a comprehensive
resource on Internet cookies, including what they are and how to
block or stop them.

CookiePal [http://www.kburra.com] features Kookaburra Software,
which assists users in maintaining their privacy by keeping track
of their cookies.

■ CYBER-CRIME NEWS

CNet Networks, Inc. [http://www.cnet.com] is a global source of information and commerce services for the technology industry.

MSNBC [http://www.msnbc.com] provides full coverage of the day's
events, updates on breaking stories, and in-depth reports on the issues that shape our world.

■ DENIAL-OF-SERVICE INFORMATION

Help Defeat Denial of Service Attacks: Step-by-Step [http://www.sans.org/dosstep/index.htm] reduces the chances that your network could be used to damage other networks if you implement its two steps.

IBM Global Services Denial-of-Service Attacks [http://www-1.ibm.com/services/continuity/recover1.nsf/news/fs-Denial + of + Service + Attacks] is a paper written to help those concerned about denial-of-service attacks.

"Take Down: Massive Denial of Service Attacks Take Down Yahoo!" [http://www.thesynthesis.com/tech/takedown/index.html] is an article by Bronc Buster for Synthesis Magazine.

■ DIGITAL SIGNATURES

National Institute of Standards and Technology [http://csrc.nist.gov] features a computer security division, which raises awareness of IT risks, vulnerabilities, and protection requirements, particularly for new and emerging technologies.

■ ELECTRONIC MAGAZINES AND NEWSLETTERS

Advanced Laboratory Workstation System, Center for Information Technology, National Institute of Health [http://www.nih.gov/security/security-ezines.html] provides a listing of a few electronic magazines and newsletters that provide timely information about information security.

Coast News and Newsletter [http://www.cerias.purdue.edu/coast/coast-news.html] provides news and information about information security.

Cipher [http://www.ieee-security.org/cipher.html] is the electronic newsletter of the technical committee on security and privacy.

Infowar [http://www.infowar.com] offers up-to-the-minute news on information security, hacking, and attacks as well as related news, reviews, and opinion.

SC Info Security Magazine [http://www.infosecnews.com] is an on-line news service backed by *SC (Security Council) Magazine,* an information security magazine with a large circulation.

Security Magazine [http://www.securitymagazine.com] offers daily news, an events database, a new product database, and more.

■ EMPLOYEE INTERNET MANAGEMENT

Advanced Productivity Software [http://www.aps-soft.com] is an employee productivity tool that tracks Internet online services access.

SafeNet Corp.com [http://www.safenetcorp.com] provides employee Internet management software that can increase productivity by enforcing time-of-day policies, remotely monitoring workstations, and displaying a quick slide show of recently visited web pages.

Sequel Technology [http://www.sequaltech.com] provides network solutions that allow management to monitor, manage, and report employee usage of the Internet and corporate networks.

■ ENCRYPTION INFORMATION

The Center for Democracy and Technology [http://www.cdt.org/crypto/] works to promote democratic values and constitutional liberties in the digital age.

"Digital John Hancocks" [http://www.wired.com/news/politics/0,1283,19937,00.html] is a *WIRED News* article about the Digital Signature Act of 1999.

Federal Information on Encryption [http://csrc.nist.gov/encryption] is available from the Computer Security Division's (CSD) Security Technology Group, which is involved in the development, maintenance, and promotion of standards and guidelines that cover a wide range of cryptographic technology.

RSA (Rivest, Shamir, Adleman) Data Security [http://www.rsa.com] provides encryption products and standards, job postings, and software downloads.

■ ENCRYPTION SYSTEMS

Pretty Good Privacy (PGP) Encryption [http://www.pgp.com] offers products and services that focus on solving privacy and data confidentiality issues.

■ FREQUENTLY ASKED QUESTIONS (FAQS)

Advanced Laboratory Workstation System, Center for Information Technology, National Institute of Health [http://www.nih.gov/security/security-faqs.html] contains links to information about information security topics.

■ GROUPS AND ORGANIZATIONS

Advanced Laboratory Workstation System, Center for Information Technology, National Institute of Health [http://www.nih.gov/security/security-groups.html] features a web page that is divided into computer security organizations and organizations with computer security subgroups. These organizations provide information to their members or to the public about information security issues and trends.

■ FIREWALL INFORMATION

Coast Archive, CERIAS (The Center for Education and Research in Information Assurance and Security) [http://www.cerias.purdue.edu/coast/firewalls/fw-index.html] is a listing of books, papers, products, tests, and firewall tools.

Harrier Zeuros Firewall [http://www.harrierzeuros.co.uk/technologies/Networks/firewall.html] provides a way to secure and protect business-critical data without other additional costs.

Network Associates, Inc. (NAI) [http://www.nai.com] is conducting research in the areas of network security, cryptographic technologies, security infrastructure components, secure execution environments, adaptive network defense, distributed systems security, and information assurance architecture, modeling, and management.

Secure Computing [http://www.sctc.com] offers technical and product information about firewalls.

■ HARDWARE-BASED SECURITY SYSTEMS

Cisco Systems Private Internet Exchange (PIX) [http://www.cisco.com] provides firewall protection that is designed to protect the system from the external world. PIX allows secure access to the Internet from within existing private networks.

Livingston IRX Router Portmaster [http://www.Livingston.com] features routers that use state-of-the-art technical standards for security, thus ensuring that remote LAN users secure interconnectivity to critical enterprise resources.

Lucent Technologies [http://www.lucent.com] provides customers with innovative communications systems, products, technologies, and customer support.

■ INTERNET USAGE AND MANAGEMENT

Elron Software [http://www.wlfonsoftware.com] provides e-mail monitoring to lower the risk of confidential data loss. Other products include usage policy management, spam protection, and anti-virus and firewall software.

Softex [http://www.soft-ex.net/html/main.htm] provides server based monitoring of e-mail and Internet activity that provides data with which management can determine whether certain activities meet the guidelines of the firm's usage policy.

Telemate.Net Employee Internet Usage [http://www.telemate.net/product/internet/stopwatch.asp] provides an Internet management solution that integrates blocking and reporting to give businesses control of web site access, bandwidth consumption, and e-mail usage.

Websense [http://www.websense.com] provides Internet management software that filters, manages, monitors, and reports on employee use of the Internet.

■ INTRUSION DETECTION

Cisco Secure IDS [http://www.cisco.com/univercd/cc/td/doc/pcat/
nerg.htm] is an enterprise-scale, real-time intrusion detection system designed to detect, report, and terminate unauthorized activity throughout a network.

EnGarde Systems: IP Watcher [http://www.engarde.com/software/
ipwatcher/] is a network security and administration tool that can
control any log-in session on the organization's network.

NFR Security [http://www.nfr.net] offers a threat detection portfolio
that monitors for intrusions and suspicious activity anywhere
within the IT infrastructure.

Symantec Intruder Alert(tm) [http://enterprisesecurity.syman-
tec.com/products/products.cfm?ProductID=48] detects unauthorized and malicious activity and assists in keeping systems, applications, and data secure from misuse and abuse.

■ IP SPOOFING INFORMATION

IP Spoofing Definition [http://webopedia.internet.com/TERM/
I/IP_spoofing.html] offers the Webopedia definition of IP spoofing
and includes links to terms used in the definition.

IP Spoofing: Hide Your True Identity [http://www.ryanspc.com/ip-
spoof.html] provides programs that will hide your identity online,
making it appear that you are someone else.

"Web Spoofing: An Internet Con Game" [http://www.cs.prince-
ton.edu/sip/pub/spoofing.html] is a paper that describes an Internet security attack that could endanger the privacy of World Wide
Web users and the integrity of their data.

■ MAILING LISTS

Internet Security Systems [http://xforce.iss.net/maillists/otherlists.
php] provides a listing of information security mailing lists that are
divided into three sections: general security lists, security products, and vendors and organizations.

■ NEWSGROUPS

Advanced Laboratory Workstation System, Center for Information Technology, National Institute of Health [http://www.nih.gov/security/security-newsgroups.html] is a listing of Usenet newsgroups that can be useful for obtaining the latest information about a specific information security topic. The quality of newsgroups varies, making some newsgroups better than others.

■ PACKET SNIFFING

AntiSniff [http://www.securitysoftwaretech.com/antisniff/] is a proactive security monitoring tool with the ability to scan a network and detect whether or not any computers are in promiscuous mode (an indication that they have been compromised).

■ ONLINE EDUCATION AND GUIDES

The Center for Education and Research in Information Assurance and Security (CERIAS) [http://www.cerias.purdue.edu] is a large collection of online security resources.

Computer Research and Technology, National Institutes of Health Security Web Sites [http://www.alw.nih.gov/Security/ALW/ALW-security.html] is a well-organized guide to computer security for web sites.

Computer Security Institute [http://www.gocsi.com] provides testimony, surveys, guidebooks, and other educational literature on computer security from an international information security information organization.

Department of Energy (DOE) Information Security [http://doe-is.llnl.gov] is an advanced web server whose goal is to enhance information security data sharing within the United States DOE community.

Electronic Frontier Foundation Archive [http://www.eff.org/pub/privacy] is a large list of security information about privacy, cryptography, and surveillance.

Hacker Whacker [http://www.hackerwhacker.com/prevent.dyn] takes some commercial security scanners and also uses hacker tools to scan your system for holes.

Network Computing, The Technology Solution Center [http://www.networkcomputing.com/core/core7.html] presents business, technology, and management issues related to network and system security.

TruSecure [http://www.trusecure.com/] is an independent organization that offers opinions on computer security issues in addition to links to antivirus and firewall products.

■ PRETTY GOOD PRIVACY (PGP)

NCSA [http://hoohoo.ncsa.uiuc.edu/docs/PEMPGP.html] offers a resource similar to this one on using PGP encryption.

PGP User's Guide [http://www.gildea.com/pgp/] provides a user guide and public key server via the web.

Where to Get PGP? [http://cryptography.org/getpgp.htm] is a FAQ page about how and where to get an appropriate copy of PGP and documentation.

■ PRIVACY

Center for Democracy and Technology [http://www.cdt.org] is a watchdog organization lobbying to protect Internet security.

Cookie Central [http://www.cookiecentral.com] offers online information about how to take control of cookies.

Electronic Frontier Foundation [http://www.eff.org/privnow] is a not-for-profit organization working to protect the civil rights of Internet users.

Hushmail [http://www.hushmail.com] encrypts notes within its network.

Junkbusters [http://www.junkbusters.com] offers tips and tools for getting rid of junk e-mail messages.

Pop3now [http://www.pop3now.com] is a free e-mail encryption service.

SecurityPortal [http://www.securityportal.com/about/privacy.html] is a high quality web site with a variety of online resources.

■ PUBLIC KEY INFRASTRUCTURE (PKI)

Baltimore Technologies [http://www.baltimore.com] offers PKI-Plus, a developer toolkit that provides a rich feature set containing all the necessary functionality to request and process digital certificates, communicate with directories, generate and store cryptographic keys.

Entrust Authority [http://www. entrust.com/authority/index.htm] offers interoperable and standards-based PKI solutions that allow enterprises to open up channels to employees, suppliers, partners, and customers with confidence, thus achieving a foundation of trust for your e-business.

Novell Public Key Infrastructure Services [http://www.novell.com/info/security/public_key.html] enables the use of public key cryptography and digital certificates in an NDS environment.

RSA Security [http://www.rsasecurity.com/products/keon/] offers Keon PKI products, which enable, manage, and simplify the use of digital certificates.

Verisign OnSite [http://www.verisign.com/enterprise/index.html] is a fully integrated PKI-managed service designed to secure intranet, extranet, virtual private network (VPN), and e-commerce applications.

■ SECURE SOCKETS LAYER (SSL)

Introduction to SSL [http://developer.netscape.com/docs/manuals/security/sslin/index.htm] introduces the SSL protocol.

RSA Security [http://www.rsasecurity.com/standards/protocols/ssl_tls.html] explains SSL technology.

■ SECURITY RESOURCES

Beginner's Guide to the Internet [http://nml.ru.ac.za/carr/~krisanne/begin.html] contains the research completed as part of a computer-aided research course (CARR) in the Rhodes University Journalism Department, South Africa.

Center for Education and Research in Information Assurance

and Security [http://www.cerias.purdue.edu/] is a university center for multidisciplinary research and education in areas of information.

CERT® Coordination Center [http://www.cert.org/] studies Internet security vulnerabilities, handles computer security incidents, publishes security alerts, researches long-term changes in networked systems, and develops information and training to help improve security.

Computer Security Information [http://www.alw.nih.gov/Security/security.html] features general information about computer security. Information is organized by source, and each section is organized by topic.

Computer Security Information Resource Portal [http://www.infosyssec.com/] is a comprehensive computer and network security resource for information system security professionals.

Computer Security Institute [http://www.gocsi.com/] is an international membership organization offering training specifically targeted to information security professionals.

Security Related Net-pointers [http://www-cse.ucsd.edu/users/bsy/sec.html] is a list of pointers to security-related information, such as books, papers, and other sources.

■ SECURITY SOFTWARE

Advanced Laboratory Workstation System, Center for Information Technology, National Institute of Health [http://www.nih.gov/security/security-prog.html] is a listing of noncommercial security software products for authentications, encryption, firewalls, networks, system enhancement, and system monitoring.

Antivirus Products certified by ICSAlabs [http://www.icsalabs.com/html/communities/antivirus/index.shtml] identifies for the user community a set of products that effectively use antivirus technology to provide desired security services.

Cryptography Products certified by ICSAlabs [http://www.icsalabs.com/html/communities/cryptography/index.shtml] identifies for the user community a set of products that effectively use cryptography to provide desired security services. ICSA Labs' interaction with the cryptography industry is focused in the Cryptography Product Certification Program.

The Encyclopedia of Computer Security (TECS) Security Products Database [http://www.itsecurity.com] offers news, links, and more on security issues and products.

Firewall Products certified by ICSAlabs [http://www.icsalabs.com/html/communities/firewalls/index.shtml] identifies for the user community a set of firewall products that provide the desired security services.

ITtoolbox Security [http://security.ittoolbox.com] is an IT community web site with a listing of security technology solutions.

Software Products by ZDNET [http://techupdate.zdnet.com/techupdate/] is an online newsletter with the listing of security products and reviews.

■ SURVEILLANCE

007 Stealth Activity Monitor [http://www.iopus.com/sam.htm] is a new, easy-to-use tool for monitoring the use and abuse of PCs.

Omniquad Desktop Surveillance [http://www.omniquad.com/omniquad_desktop_surveillance.htm] features Omniquad Desktop Surveillance Personal, which allows you to supervise web surfing, e-mail, and chat rooms and monitor other activities taking place on your computer in your absence.

Stealth Activity Recorder and Reporter [http://www.iopus.com/starr.htm] combines PC and Internet surveillance tools to monitor the use and abuse of PCs.

■ SECURITY ALERTS AND NEWSLETTERS

Advisor Articles [http://www.advisor.com/articles.nsf] presents magazines, journals, newsletters, CDs, conferences, seminars, and web sites to advise on e-business strategies, IT management, software development, and business technology solutions.

AntiOnline [http://www.antionline.com/index.html] discusses computer security, hacking and hackers, and the latest security-related news.

CERT [http://www.cert.com]. The CERT® Coordination Center

(CERT/CC) is a center of Internet security expertise at the Software Engineering Institute, a federally funded research and development center operated by Carnegie Mellon University. Among other things, this organization provides timely security alerts for industry professionals.

Dartmouth College Institute for Security Technology Studies [http://www.ists.Dartmouth.edu] and its core program on cybersecurity and information infrastructure protection research serve as a principal national center for counter-terrorism technology research, development, and assessment.

Hoaxbusters [http://hoaxbusters.ciac.org] describes some of the warnings, offers, and pleas for help that are filling our mailboxes and clogging our mail servers and that generally have no basis in fact.

Microsoft Security Advisor [http://www.Microsoft.com/security] provides practical guides, information on security technologies, and ways to ensure that your system is protected against all known attacks.

SecureAgentSoftware's Secure Newsletter [http://www.securenotes. com] provides useful security solutions for any size business in any industry, from comprehensive enterprise management software to secure e-mail.

TruSecure [http://www.trusecure.com] provides security alerts, the latest information on viruses, and computer security help lines and forums.

■ SECURITY ORGANIZATIONS

Computer Emergency Response Team (CERT) [http://www. cert.org] is a center of Internet security and expertise, located at the Software Engineering Institute, a federally funded research and development center operated by Carnegie Mellon University. The web site provides research on information security vulnerabilities, incidents, security alerts, and more.

Computer Security Institute (www.gocsi.gov) provides practical, cost-efficient ways to protect an organization's electronic information.

DOE-CIAC (Department of Energy Computer Incident Advisory

Center) [http://doe-is.llnl.gov/] is an advanced web server on the Internet whose goal is to enhance information security data sharing within the United States DOE community, which includes all DOE sites and contractors. The server contains tools and documents related to information security that have been made available by many sources both within and outside the DOE.

■ SECURITY INFORMATION FOR MANAGERS

Beginner's Guide to the Internet [http://nml.ru.ac.za/carr/ ~krisanne/begin.html] contains the research completed as part of a computer-aided research course (CARR) in the Rhodes University Journalism Department, South Africa.

Center for Education and Research in Information Assurance and Security [http://www.cerias.purdue.edu/] is a university center for multidisciplinary research and education in areas of information.

CERT® Coordination Center [http://www.cert.org/] studies Internet security vulnerabilities, handles computer security incidents, publishes security alerts, researches long-term changes in networked systems, and develops information and training to help improve security.

Computer Incident Advisory Center (CIAC) [http://www.ciac.org/ ciac/] is a computer incident bulletin from the Department of Energy.

Computer Security Information [http://www.alw.nih.gov/Security/security.html] features general information about computer security. Information is organized by source, and each section is organized by topic.

Computer Security Information Resource Portal [http://www.infosyssec.com/] is a comprehensive computer and network security resource for information system security professionals.

Computer Security Institute [http://www.gocsi.com/] is an international membership organization offering training specifically targeted to information security professionals.

Security-Related Net-Pointers [http://www-cse.ucsd.edu/users/bsy/ sec.html] is a list of pointers to security-related information, such as books, papers, and other sources.

■ SECURITY POLICY MANAGEMENT

Conquest [http://www.conqwewt.com/policy] is a developer of Internet security and policy management products for companies seeking to leverage the effectiveness of their security and network policies.

Languard [http://www.languard.com/languard/languard.htm] provides security and network policy enforcement and monitoring software for improved employee productivity.

■ SURVEILLANCE

Omniquad Desktop Surveillance [http://www.omniquad.com/omniquad_desktop_surveillance.htm] features Omniquad Desktop Surveillance Personal, which allows management to supervise web surfing, e-mail, and chat rooms and monitor other activities.

Stealth Activity Recorder and Reporter [http://www.iopus.com/starr.htm] combines PC and Internet surveillance tools to monitor the use and abuse of company computers.

■ SECURITY ALERTS AND NEWSLETTERS

Advisor Articles [http://www.advisor.com/articles.nsf] presents magazines, journals, newsletters, CDs, conferences, seminars, and web sites to advise on e-business strategies, IT management, software development, and business technology solutions.

AntiOnline [http://www.antionline.com/index.html] discusses computer security, hacking and hackers, and the latest security-related news.

CERT® Coordination Center [http://www.cert.org/] studies Internet security vulnerabilities, handles computer security incidents, publishes security alerts, researches long-term changes in networked systems, and develops information and training to help improve security.

Dartmouth College Institute for Security Technology Studies [http://www.ists.Dartmouth.edu] and its core program on cybersecurity and information infrastructure protection research serve as a principal national center for counter-terrorism technology research, development and assessment.

Hoaxbusters [http://hoaxbusters.ciac.org] describes some of the warnings, offers, and pleas for help that are filling our mailboxes and clogging our mailservers and that generally have no basis in fact.

Microsoft Security Advisor [http://www.Microsoft.com/security] provides practice guides, information on security technologies, and ways to ensure that your system is protected against all known attacks.

SecureAgent Software's Secure Newsletter [http://www.securenotes.com] provides useful security solutions for any size business in any industry, from comprehensive enterprise management software to secure e-mail.

TruSecure [http://www.trusecure.com] provides security alerts, the latest information on viruses, and computer security help lines and forums.

■ SECURITY RESOURCES

The NT Toolbox [http://www.nttoolbox.com/] contains suggested methods, from various sources, for securing your Windows NT 4.0 installation. While no method is completely foolproof, the guidelines listed here should be at the very least adequate for general consumption.

Windows NT Security Resources [http://home.pacific.net.au/ ~huth/] shows how the security aspects of Windows NT have been built.

■ SECURITY WHITE PAPERS AND RESEARCH

CERT® Coordination Center [http://www.cert.org/] studies Internet security vulnerabilities, handles computer security incidents, publishes security alerts, researches long-term changes in networked systems, and develops information and training to help improve security.

Forum of Incident Response and Security Teams [http://www.

first.org] has a large collection of white papers about various computer issues.

ICAT Metabase [http://icat.nist.gov] is a searchable index of information on computer vulnerabilities. It provides search capabilities at a fine granularity in addition to statistics and a list of the top ten vulnerabilities.

Insecure.org [http://www.insecure.org] shares the free information available regarding the Internet and the culture of sharing that pervades the hacker community, including several papers, pages, and code projects.

Linux Security [http://www.linuxsecurity.com] is designed to serve as the primary Internet-based source of information, insight, and news relating to Linux and Open Source security issues.

SANS (System Administration, Networking, and Security) Institute [http://www.sans.org] contains many free SANS resources, such as news digests, research summaries, security alerts, and award-winning papers.

Security Focus [http://www.securityfocus.com] provides contact, company, and advertising information, press releases, and partner information.

■ SECURITY TOOLS AND UTILITIES

CERIAS (The Center for Education and Research in Information Assurance and Security) [http://www.cerias.purdue.edu/coast] offers multidisciplinary research and education in areas of information security. This includes computer, network, and communications security as well as information assurance.

ICSALabs Virus Hoax Information [http://www.icsalabs.com/html/communities/antivirus/index.shtml] provides up-to-date information on computer viruses, worms, and the newest forms of malicious code.

Security Profile Inspector for Networks [http://ciac.llnl.gov/cstc/spi/spinet.html] is freely available to all U.S. government agencies and to contractors directly supporting the U.S. Departments of Defense and Energy.

■ VIRUS HOAXES

Symantec Antivirus Research Center [http://www.sarc.com] provides information on recent viruses, including how to detect and defeat them.

The Truth About Computer Virus Myths and Hoaxes [http://www.vmyths.com] helps you learn about computer virus myths, hoaxes, urban legends, hysteria, and the implications if you believe in them. You can also search a list of computer virus hoaxes and episodes of virus hysteria from A to Z.

■ VIRTUAL PRIVATE NETWORKS

PC Magazine [http://www.zdnet.com/products/stories/reviews/0,4161,2404675,00.html] provides *PC Magazine* Labs' tests on VPN solutions.

"Push is on for Virtual-Private-Network Solutions" [http://www.eetimes.com/story/OEG19990312S0005] is an eetimes.com article on VPN solutions.

"Take A Hard Look At Virtual Private Networks" [http://www.networkcomputing.com/817/817colmoskowitz.html] recommends that before you spend your organization's hard-earned profits (or your scarce product evaluation resources) take some time to find the VPN technology that will meet your networking needs.

"Virtual Private Networking (VPN) Security" [http://www.microsoft.com/ntserver/techresources/commnet/VPN/VPNSecurity.asp] is a white paper on VPN from Microsoft.

The VPN Source Page [http://www.internetwk.com/VPN/default.html] is TechWeb's list of articles and papers about VPNs.

VPN Tutorial [http://www.iec.org/online/tutorials/vpn/] was created by the International Engineering Consortium to address the basic architecture and enabling technologies of a VPN.

■ VIRUS PROTECTION PRODUCTS

Antiviral Toolkit Pro Distributor [http://www.avp.ch] includes frequent updates (usually weekly)and provides the identifies of and cures for a very large number of viruses. It also includes a code analyzer to detect many new or unknown viruses, offers scanning of packed executables and archive files, and features powerful utilities, virus effects demonstrations, and much more.

Leprechaun Software [http://www.leprechaun.com.au/] offers a fast antivirus solution that detects known and unknown viruses and protects your system from all virus types, including program, macro, boot sector, and script viruses.

McAfee Associates [http://www.mcafee.com] provides a variety of antivirus software, including VirusScan, NetShield, WebScan, WebShield, and Companion Solution.

Norton AntiVirus [http://enterprisesecurity.symantec.com/Content/ProductLink.cfm?PID=8008630] wants to be considered the best-of-breed antivirus protection for even the largest wide area network.

Sophos Anti-Virus [http://www.sophos.com] was designed specifically for organizations that use different applications and operating systems on their networks. The technological solution aims to offer an easily updated, flexible business solution for managing the complexity of networks ranging from small LANs to large multiserver, multiplatform WANs.

Trend Micro [http://www.antivirus.com] solutions are designed to protect the flow of information on PCs, file servers, and e-mail servers and at the Internet gateway, providing a complete, centrally controlled virus wall for enterprise networks.

■ WEB SERVER SECURITY

Center for Democracy and Technology Security and Freedom through Encryption (SAFE) Forum [http://www.crypto.com/safe] is sponsored by the computer industry in order to raise awareness of encryption technology's importance and to discuss U.S. cryptography policy.

■ VIRUS INFORMATION

Chalk Talk [http://www.chalktalk.com] deals with the risk of viruses and intruders.

Symantec Antivirus Research Center [http://www.sarc.com] offers valuable information on recent viruses, including how to detect and defeat them.

■ VULNERABILITIES DATABASES

Common Vulnerabilities and Exposures [http://www.cve.mitre.org] is a high- quality web site that includes, among other things, news, security product comparisons, and a free newsletter.

Security Bugware [http://oliver.efri.hr/ ~ crv/security/] is a source for UNIX and NT vulnerabilities, with information about and descriptions of exploits, bugs, patches, and more.

Shake Communications [http://www.shake.net] provides information and Internet security solutions to organizations, as well as offering the subscription-based vulnerabilities database and Shake Security Journal.

Index

About the Author

Kathleen Sindell is the author of four previous books, *Loyalty Marketing for the Internet Age* (2000), *Investing Online for Dummies* (2000, 1998, 1997), the *Unofficial Guide to Buying a Home Online* (2000), and the *Handbook of Real Estate Lending* (1996). Additionally, Dr. Sindell has written numerous popular, academic, and professional articles and web sites. Dr. Sindell is an adjunct faculty member in the Johns Hopkins University MBA Program and the former associate director of the financial management and commercial real estate programs for the University of Maryland, University College Graduate School of Management and Technology.

Dr. Sindell provides consulting and publications about management, marketing, finance, and real estate in the e-commerce environment. Her goal is to improve the quality of life and economic well-being of people and business organizations by providing information that they might not otherwise have or understand.

She received a B.A. in Business from Antioch University, an MBA from the California State University at San Jose, and a Ph.D. in Administration and Management from Walden University's Institute for Advanced Studies.

Dr. Sindell lives and writes in Alexandria, Virginia. She is interested in your comments about this book and can be contacted through her web sites, located at [http://www.kathleensindell.com], [http://www.loyaltymarketingfortheinternetage.com], and [http://www.safetynetonline.com].